Brecht on F....

Brecht on Film and Radio

Original work entitled:
Bertolt Brecht Werke. Grosse Berliner und Frankfurter Ausgabe
(vols. 19, 21, 23, 24)

translated and edited by

MARC SILBERMAN

Bloomsbury Methuen Drama
An imprint of Bloomsbury Publishing Plc

B L O O M S B U R Y
LONDON · NEW DELHI · NEW YORK · SYDNEY

Bloomsbury Methuen Drama

An imprint of Bloomsbury Publishing Plc

Imprint previously known as Methuen Drama

50 Bedford Square	1385 Broadway
London	New York
WC1B 3DP	NY 10018
UK	USA

www.bloomsbury.com

First published in the United Kingdom in 2000 by Methuen Publishing Limited

Methuen Drama series editor for Bertolt Brecht: Tom Kuhn

Original work entitled
*Bertolt Brecht Werke. Grosse Berliner und
Frankfurter Ausgabe* (vols. 19, 21, 23, 24)

British Library Cataloguing-in-Publication Data
A catalogue record for this book is available from the British Library.

ISBN: PB:	978-0-4137-2760-2
ePDF:	978-1-4081-7128-8
ePub:	978-1-4081-6987-2

Library of Congress Cataloging-in-Publication Data
A catalog record for this book is available from the Library of Congress.

Series: Diaries, Letters and Essays

Typeset by SX Composing DTP, Rayleigh, Essex

CONTENTS

List of Illustrations

1. Charlie Chaplin in *The Gold Rush*. Courtesy of the Wisconsin Center for Film and Theater Research, Madison (United Artists Collection).
2. Lotte Reiniger's *Abenteuer des Prinzen Achmed*. Courtesy of Stiftung Deutsche Kinemathek, Berlin.
3. Still from *Youth of Maxim* by Kosintzev and Trauberg. Courtesy of Kristin Thompson, Madison.
4. 'Rotting meat' sequence from Eisenstein's *Battleship Potemkin*. Courtesy of Kristin Thompson, Madison.
5. Lars Hanson in Mauritz Stiller's *Saga of Gösta Berling*. Courtesy of Kristin Thompson, Madison.
6. Alfred Kerr, Bertolt Brecht and Ernst Wiechert broadcasting 'The Crisis in the Theatres', April 1928. Courtesy of the Bertolt Brecht Archive (Stiftung Archiv der Akademie der Künste, Berlin).
7. Erik Wirl, Bertolt Brecht and Hanns Eisler, 1931. Courtesy of the Hanns Eisler Archive (Stiftung Archiv der Akademie der Künste, Berlin).
8. Cover page of *Illustrierter Film-Kurier*. Courtesy of Stiftung Deutsche Kinemathek, Berlin.
9. First page of the contract between Bloch-Erben and Nero-Film for the *Threepenny Opera* film. Courtesy of the Bertolt Brecht Archive (Stiftung Archiv der Akademie der Künste, Berlin).
10. Production still from *Kuhle Wampe* with Adolf Fischer, Bertolt Brecht and Martha Wolter. Courtesy of the Bertolt Brecht Archive (Stiftung Archiv der Akademie der Künste, Berlin).
11. *Kuhle Wampe* publicity poster. Courtesy of the Bertolt Brecht Archive (Stiftung Archiv der Akademie der Künste, Berlin).
12. First page of the score for 'Solidarity Song' by Hanns Eisler for *Kuhle Wampe*. Courtesy of the Hanns Eisler Archive (Stiftung Archiv der Akademie der Künste, Berlin).
13. Outdoor location shot of *Kuhle Wampe*. Courtesy of the Bertolt Brecht Archive (Stiftung Archiv der Akademie der Künste, Berlin).
14. Bertolt Brecht and Sergei Eisenstein in 1932. Courtesy of the Bertolt Brecht Archive (Stiftung Archiv der Akademie der Künste, Berlin).
15. Fritz Lang. Courtesy of the Wisconsin Center for Film and Theater Research, Madison (United Artists Collection).

Introduction

Few readers of Bertolt Brecht (1898–1956) are familiar with his writings about and for the cinema or radio broadcasting. Even in Germany, where he is one of the most produced dramatists on the contemporary stage and his poems and stories are regularly anthologized in school readers, his work on these media is perceived to have been scattered and intermittent. Similarly, in the English-speaking world Brecht's reputation is based on his contributions as a great dramatist and notable theorist of the theatre. This volume gathers together for the first time in English translation the pertinent writings of a creative artist and trenchant thinker who also turned his attention to new technologies that marked the first half of this century.

Brecht's engagement with the movies and radio constitutes only one dimension of his work in various other media, including theatre, opera, music recording, photography, fine arts, ballet and book printing. One might best understand his entire artistic career as an ongoing and explicit experiment in how to reach an audience by using the specific advantages of different presentational modes. The fact that his 'experiments' often did not succeed led him to reflect time and again on the possibilities and limitations of such endeavours. Similarly, the boundaries between his experimental projects should not be drawn too starkly, since they all belong to a larger learning process and often were undertaken in parallel with each other. Brecht never produced a theory or systematic critique of the media, but both his practical work and his commentaries on it were devoted to articulating media-specific modes of representation and reception. As an experimenter, then, he was more interested in the challenges presented by the changing demands of technology and history, making the familiar strange – as he did in his plays too – so that the audience perceives the principles governing reality and learns how to manipulate them.

Although it is generally known that some of Brecht's early *Lehrstücke* (literally 'didactic plays', but it has become common to refer to them as 'learning plays') were conceived for radio broadcast, or that he co-authored and co-directed a major film project, *Kuhle Wampe* (1932), or that he struggled to break into the Hollywood movie industry during his exile years in the United

States, the overall picture of his activities in this area is muddled. For example, Brecht participated directly in several live radio broadcasts and tapings of radio play adaptations in the second half of the 1920s. He then went on to develop a critique of public radio institutions based on this experience. In addition, he worked collaboratively on screenplays for major movie productions, including the early sound-film adaptation of *The Threepenny Opera* (Georg Wilhelm Pabst, 1930) and the Hollywood feature *Hangmen Also Die* (Fritz Lang, 1943). Yet, in his own eyes these works in their final form compromised his artistic integrity, so much so that in both cases he sought, unsuccessfully, to protect his contribution. Numerous other scenarios – some elaborately worked out and others only short exposés – were never realized as motion pictures during his lifetime. Moreover, the many essays and notes on the cinema and radio have appeared, even in the German editions of his works, scattered among his other voluminous writings on theatre, literature and politics. Hence the need for a volume that aims to present the reader with a clearer view of Brecht's varied attempts to engage with the popular media.

There is no question about Brecht's enthusiasm for new modes of communicating with the mass public. His diary and journal entries, as well as reminiscences by friends and acquaintances, testify to frequent excursions to the movies and his enjoyment of film entertainment. In fact, Brecht's scenarios, film notes and plans for the movie industry or radio broadcasting accompanied his entire career, and though neither their quality nor their frequency remained constant throughout his life, his work on such projects typically sought unconventional solutions.

In his earliest writings on the cinema after the First World War, Brecht criticized the practice of marketing a false ideology to earn profits, but he also recognized that the sensationalism, suspense, grotesque humour and the documentary quality of showing events and objects were cinematic effects that appealed to a broad public. Moreover, the movie industry represented an outright challenge to prevailing forms of high-culture production and reception, a development that the young iconoclast appreciated. These became the themes that dominated his commentaries on the cinema during and after the Weimar Republic (see Part I).

While his diaries of the early 1920s indicate that Brecht was thinking about numerous possible movie projects, he completed only three scripts (see Part III), probably motivated more strongly by financial need than commitment to the medium. The scripts adapt genre conventions of the silent cinema – eccentric characters, mysterious events, intense suspense – but transform the metaphysical soul-searching and melodrama of the Expressionist period with humour and irony. The depiction of narrative events is sometimes visually striking, including descriptions of visual structures and details about image composition and editing. Of course, the scripts are only preliminary sketches of films that never materialized, but they do reflect a real fascination with questions of the medium and film genre that would continue to interest Brecht.

With the introduction in Germany of the broadcast medium in 1923, and the establishment of public radio in 1926, Brecht recognized another new technology for introducing his plays and adaptations to a broader public. His practice of cutting and sharpening the dialogue for his radio plays undoubtedly influenced the development of his 'epic theatre' form: characterizing the figures by means of language and tonal quality, revealing attitudes among the figures through language and sharpening awareness about the different possibilities of one-dimensional (radio), two-dimensional (cinema) and three-dimensional spatial relations. In his sporadic commentaries he began by using the new medium as a point of departure for criticizing the status quo in the theatre that was unreceptive to new plays. Brecht also did not hesitate to criticize middle-brow programming tendencies and to call for innovations that would use the new technology to document topical issues and to create original forms of public accountability. Soon the tension between the two media led him to experiment with new forms of staging, especially for the radio broadcasts of the early *Lehrstücke*, which could alter the collective process of audience reception (see Part II). Brecht's insistence on the disparity between new technology and old content – that is, on the inappropriate use of the broadcast institution to reproduce or imitate other arts (theatre, concerts, opera, etc.) rather than producing its own media-specific programming – is symptomatic of his approach. For Brecht, radio broadcasting offered a potential model for transforming the listener from a consumer into a producer by making maximum use of the communicative function inherent in the technology.

Among the cultural critics of the Weimar Republic, Brecht was unusual in that he did not fear the entertainment industry. On the contrary, he sought out opportunities to use its mechanisms against conservative and progressive intellectuals alike who held on to the elitism of traditional art forms. Nothing illustrates this practice better than the fate of *The Threepenny Opera* in its metamorphosis from the most successful stage production of the Weimar Republic

(1928), to the screenplay, 'The Bruise' ('Die Beule', 1930), that was commissioned for a commercial film adaptation, to the actual film by Georg Wilhelm Pabst (1930), to the fragmentary *Threepenny Novel* (1934). Accompanying these were the lawsuits initiated by Brecht and the composer Kurt Weill against the film production company for copyright infringement (1930) and the book-length essay 'The *Threepenny* Lawsuit' ('Der Dreigroschenprozess', 1932), Brecht's most incisive and sustained reflection on the conditions of cultural production under capitalism (see Part IV).

If the 'Lawsuit' essay is Brecht's most sophisticated contribution to media theory, then the contemporaneous film project *Kuhle Wampe* is his most important legacy to film history, the only example of his practical work that came close to realizing the idea of de-individualizing (aesthetic) production in the cinema (see Part V). Not only the film's planning and shooting, but also its themes and structure integrate the collective experience with new ways of representing reality. In a self-conscious attempt to counteract the hierarchical studio arrangements in the commercial industry, Brecht brought together a production team consisting of the Bulgarian émigré Slatan Dudow, novelist Ernst Ottwald and composer Hanns Eisler, as well as well-known actors from the workers' theatre movement and thousands of enthusiasts organized in workers' sports clubs for the film's finale. For Brecht the successful completion of the shooting was a significant public event because it had engaged leading Leftist intellectuals with workers' organizations in a creative process. The entire project was also an exceptional example of how to link questions of representation, social change and the subject who will effect that change – issues that preoccupied Brecht during the early 1930s.

Brecht was among the first writers to leave Germany in 1933 under the threat of Hitler's accession to power. Yet he continued to pursue cinema projects, undoubtedly both for financial and political reasons. During the exile years in Scandinavia he sought, through fellow émigrés such as Erwin Piscator in Moscow and Leo Lania in London, opportunities to place original exposés, to negotiate contracts for film adaptations of his plays or to obtain commissions for film scripts. Despite promising leads with directors such as Alexander Korda, Joris Ivens and Hans Richter, nothing materialized, other than the lame project for a British film adaptation of Leoncavallo's opera *I Pagliacci* in 1936, for which the exile actor Fritz Kortner secured Brecht a contract to help write the dialogues. He was paid for the contributions, but his texts were not used. Generally the film plans receded behind more intensive work on projects in other media (plays, novels, stories, poems and political and literary essays).

Brecht arrived with his family at the port of Los Angeles in July 1941. He decided to settle on the West Coast rather than in New York, where he also had an invitation, because of its large community of German émigré artists and because of his potential contacts with the movie industry in Hollywood. He was encouraged by reports that German screenwriters actually enjoyed a good reputation in the industry and during his six years in Hollywood he rubbed shoulders with many of the most important studio personalities. Yet obviously Brecht in no way conformed to the pattern of Hollywood movie-making. He held its formula writing in contempt, criticized its immense waste and shared none of its sensitivity to serious criticism. While Brecht still considered the script to be a literary text, Hollywood practice had already broken it into a series of separate responsibilities (idea, treatment, scenario, script, shooting script). And his notion of collective production did not fit the studio model of industry specialization and rationalization. At the same time, Brecht's reputation in the United States was not established, so he was dependent on friends and acquaintances to open doors for him. Brecht never lost his fascination for American movies, however, as the many entries about screenings in his journals from these years indicate. That he mentioned or actually brought to paper at least fifty film projects evidences his determination to break into the industry, especially in view of the fact that his hopes were hardly fulfilled. Not one of the projects actually became the film he envisioned, few found their way into more than fragmentary textual form and they occupied Brecht's time as much to earn income as to reach the mass audience with an anti-fascist message.

Brecht did have two qualified 'successes' in Hollywood. The script collaboration with John Wexley for Fritz Lang's *Hangmen Also Die* about the assassination of Hitler's henchman Heydrich was ultimately taken out of his hands (working titles were 'Never Surrender' and 'Trust the People'). In an appeal Brecht brought before the Screen Writers Guild contesting the movie's credits, Wexley was ruled to have been the sole scriptwriter, based on Brecht's and Lang's original story. Brecht was paid well by United Artists for his intense work on the script during 1942 (see his many journal entries during the second half of 1942), but the final cut reflects few of the distinctive qualities associated with his name. Although it counts among Hollywood's best anti-fascist features, the sensationalist gangster and action effects mark it as a Fritz Lang classic.

Brecht was also able to sell indirectly the idea of his play *The Visions of Simone Machard*. His fellow exile author Lion Feuchtwanger had written a novel based on Brecht's 1942 play about a modern-day Jeanne d'Arc in the French Resistance for which MGM purchased the story rights in 1943. Feuchtwanger split the sizeable sum with Brecht, but the film was never made because the lead actress became pregnant and by the time shooting was again possible France had been liberated by the Allies.

Brecht's many other film projects during these years disclose a curious mixture of willingness to adapt to the demands of the movie industry and refusal to compromise on its terms. His plans for cinematic adaptations of classical as well as modern literary texts emphasized the contemporary, everyday familiarity of the conflicts rather than literary 'quality'. The exposés for bio-pics avoided heroism and sentimentality in favour of portraying the social conditions behind historical figures. The ideas for topical films conformed to established genre conventions while seeking every opportunity to sharpen the social contrasts. Towards the end of the war, Brecht became active in the 'Council for a Democratic Germany', an émigré organization formed to prepare for the post-war transformation of the country. However, his plans to produce agitational and didactic films for re-educating Germans did not gain the support of the American government. Quite to the contrary, on 30 October 1947 Brecht was called with other motion picture personalities before the congressional House Un-American Activities Committee (HUAC) where he could state with a clear conscience, but not without irony: 'I am not a film writer and I am not aware of any influence I have had on the film industry, either politically or artistically.'

Brecht left the United States for Europe following his HUAC hearing and, after almost a year's wait in Switzerland for the necessary visa papers, arrived in East Berlin prepared to form a theatre ensemble. This meant the opportunity at last to produce plays under congenial conditions, to continue the theatre experiments broken off in 1933 and to see his own plays come to life in the context for which they were written. It is all the more surprising, then, that he found any time for the film projects that continued to preoccupy him until he died, including supervision of screenplay rewrites for the *Mother Courage* and *Puntila* plays (see Part I). Ironically, though, under the socialist regime in East Germany, Brecht found himself once again confronted with the limitations of an industrially and ideologically conservative production apparatus at the newly established East German DEFA film studios.

Brecht's practical and critical interventions in the cinema and broadcast media spanned his entire artistic career. The selection here is intended to provide English-language readers with an overview of his writing in these areas from 1919 through to the mid-1950s as well as with a sense of the textual diversity it encompasses. Except for the scene segmentation of the film *Kuhle Wampe*, the material is drawn exclusively from the thirty-volume edition of Brecht's works published by Aufbau Verlag and Suhrkamp Verlag (*Werke*, Grosse kommentierte Berliner und Frankfurter Ausgabe, 1988–1998). The volume and page numbers are indicated (GBFA volume/pages) at the beginning of each commentary (in square brackets after each text). Some of the commentaries have also been adapted from this same edition. Entries in the *Diaries 1920–1922* (edited by Herta Ramthun and translated by John Willett and Ralph Manheim, Methuen, 1979) and *Journals 1934–1955* (edited by John Willett and Ralph Manheim and translated by Hugh Rorrison, Methuen, 1993) concerning the cinema in general and specific film projects have not been included, since they are readily available in English translation. Similarly, the film exposés Brecht wrote in English during his American exile are available in the original version in the edition mentioned above. These include:

'On the Eve of Their Marriage' (1941, GBFA 20/17–20), co-author Ruth Berlau, in an earlier version under the title 'Safety First'.

'The King's Bread' (1941, GBFA 20/30–9), co-author Ferdinand Reyher.

'The Senator's Conscience' (1942, GBFA 20/88-9).

'Henry Dunant: The Founder of the Red Cross' (1942, GBFA 20/527–32).

'Silent Witness' (1944, GBFA 20/97–120), co-authors Vladimir Pozner and Salka Viertel.

'The Goddess of Victory' (1944, GBFA 20/120–40).

'Lady Macbeth of the Yards' (1945, GBFA 20/143–62), co-authors Peter Lorre and Ferdinand Reyher.

Since no textual evidence for Brecht's own version of, or his contributions to, the screenplay of *Hangmen Also Die* ('Never Surrender') is extant, it is not included here. Archival copies can be found at the Wisconsin State Historical Society at the University of Wisconsin (Madison, John Wexley's copy) and at the Rare Books Library of the University of California (Los Angeles, Fritz Lang's copy).

Marc Silberman
Madison, March 1999

Acknowledgements

I wish to thank John Willett in London, who was an enthusiastic supporter of this project from the very start. His own volume of translations, *Brecht on Theatre* (Methuen, 1964), was my model. In fact, short excerpts from three selections that I present here in fresh translation appeared previously in that anthology: 'An Example of Paedagogics', taken from the Notes to *The Flight of the Lindberghs*; 'The Film, the Novel and Epic Theatre', taken from sections III.1 and III.6 of 'The *Threepenny* Lawsuit'; and 'The Radio as an Apparatus of Communication'. Similarly, I wish to thank Tom Kuhn at Oxford University – who now co-edits the Methuen Brecht edition with Willett – for his unusually collegial encouragement and his truly selfless suggestions for improving the translations. I also wish to acknowledge the help of Jerold Couture in New York City, who at the outset facilitated communication with Stefan Brecht regarding the English-language rights to Brecht's works, and of Helene Ritzerfeld at Suhrkamp Verlag, Frankfurt, who advised me on questions of copyright. Dr Erdmut Wizisla, director of the Bertolt Brecht Archive at the Academy of Arts in Berlin, and his staff were especially helpful for bibliographical references and in locating visual material. Finally, without the financial support of the Wisconsin Alumni Research Foundation (WARF) and the College of Letters and Science at the University of Wisconsin, which granted me a sabbatical leave, I would not have been able to complete these translations in a timely fashion.

Part I

Texts and Fragments on the Cinema

(1919–1955)

On Life in the Theatre

If the cinemas continue to be permitted to show the smut they do now, soon there will be no one going to the theatres any more. As soon as republican freedoms blossomed for the cinema people, they discovered their sympathy for poor girls and their obligation to open the eyes of the Republic: they made sex education films. The goods were not new because they had to be profitable. Yet the police, who were not particularly well disposed toward the whorehouses, had previously prohibited this kind of sex education. Now, however, it earned a lot of money and everyone learned that the destiny of the fallen is certainly pitiable, but therefore all the more splendid. The career of a lost soul leads in the cinema from the narrow, sparsely furnished back room to glittering nightclubs, where the poor fallen angels, exhausted by the dancing, guzzle champagne and rock back and forth on the knees of intoxicated, paying and corrupt cavaliers, right on into pompous houses of joy furnished like the sets in the film *The Jewels of the Duchess*.[1] There is no turning back on this path. The poor victims of male desire are thrust down by their fellow human beings and the police into the merry mirrored rooms. The young girls sitting in the cinema, usually next to the young man who has paid for the ticket, learn that all resistance on the part of the fallen only leads further downward and even the most desperate struggle to return to the high road is useless and only leads to deeper misery. All bosses are afflicted with male desire and offer wine to their secretaries; there *can be* no refusal. If the wanton girl has a baby, then the poor worm starves, and the baby is not saved by placing it in an orphanage, but rather the unhappy mother sacrifices herself and proceeds to the whorehouse, accompanied by organ chords, although the sentimental sobbing in the cinema, thank God, almost masks the organ. The young girls are tickled by the fantastic pleasures the world offers and imagine with horror the mirrored rooms from *The Jewels of the Duchess* behind the walls of the houses of ill repute. The young men watch with pleasure how 'easy it is', how even distinguished gentlemen do it, how small the risk is, if you are as devilishly clever as the cavalier on screen. Thus, they all get their money's worth, the business flourishes, the film *Prostitution* is extended often 'by popular demand',[2] and freedom is the best of all conditions.

[GBFA 21/40–1. Printed in the newspaper *Der Volkswille* (Augsburg), 7 November 1919. This is Brecht's first published commentary on the cinema, written for his home town's newspaper. After Germany's defeat in the Great War, there was a loosening of censorship regulations, which led in turn to a flood of prurient films, marketed under the guise of moral education.]

On Film

Here are the obstacles that in my opinion stand in the way of working on a screenplay:

1. The screenplay is a kind of improvised play. The writer stands outside and does not know the needs and means of the various studios. No engineer draws up plans in advance for a complicated water treatment plant in the hope that someday a company will come along that urgently needs just this design.

2. The fellows who sit at the source have a deep aversion towards the fellows who want to sit at the source. This aversion is shared by the fellows who sit near the fellows, etc.

3. Competition among the films themselves resembles horse-carriage races, where most attention is focused on the purple caparisons and the horses' ornamentation. Writers cannot maintain this tempo.

4. If the film industry believes that kitsch tastes better than good work, it is an excusable error, called forth by the public's infinite capacity to consume kitsch (in this case the devil bites the dust) as well as by the writers who consider higher art to mean boredom, by those 'misunderstood writers' who exclude the public from their readings. The error of those writers, however, who consider films to be kitsch and yet write them, is inexcusable. There are accomplished films that have an impact even on people who consider them to be kitsch; but there are no accomplished films produced by people who consider them to be kitsch.

5. We would have achieved a lot if at least the distribution of artistically acceptable film stories were to be organized.

[GBFA 21/100. *Berliner Börsen-Courier*, 5 September 1922. This Berlin daily newspaper began a series under the title 'German Writers on the Cinema' with this contribution by Brecht, who was introduced as an important writer of the younger generation.]

The German Chamber Film

In order to interest the export market, one must produce different films from those made in foreign countries. What constitutes the really effective qualities of a film is what all Nordic countries share. The timing of the good American films can be had anywhere on the Continent where the screenplays are inspired by natural and modern life and where the directors and actors are matter-of-fact and honest in their work. The truthfulness of the most effective Swedes derives from their ability to relate to people and to understand something about psychology.[3] What we do not have, though, are, for example, grotesque actors like Chaplin or the natural talents like Hanson.[4] We must try to exploit in the cinema the qualities of German actors. We must use internal motivation, be oriented to strongly visual effects, compose every millimetre of the screen and give the screenplay an individual tone. We must recognize that film needs its own truthfulness, that just as in all other successful enterprises, there must be in the cinema people who count for something. And the most important thing: film may be anything as long as it is not boring.

[GBFA 21/105. Unpublished typescript written in 1924. *Kammerfilm* or chamber film mentioned in the title is a genre derived from the chamber play, characterized by restricted space and a small number of characters. *Hintertreppe* (Backstairs, directed by Paul Leni and Leopold Jessner, based on a screenplay by Carl Mayer) is a good example from the German Expressionist cinema.]

Less Certainty!!!

I saw Chaplin's film *The Gold Rush* only quite recently because the music being played in the cinema where it now screens is so awful and unartistic. But then the deep discouragement that seems to grip all my acquaintances from the theatre prompted me to go. I find their discouragement to be justified.

I do not hold the view that what this film achieves cannot be done today in the theatre because it is incapable of it. Rather I believe that it cannot be done anywhere – in the theatre, in vaudeville, in the cinema – without Charlie Chaplin. This artist is a document that today already works by means of the power of historical events. But from the point of view of content, what the film *The Gold Rush* achieves would be insufficient for any stage and for any theatre audience. There is, of course, a certain charm when in such young arts as the cinema the joy in particular personal experiences has not yet been displaced by a dramaturgy that has the experience of an old whore. When Big Jim can no longer find his gold mine because of his amnesia and meets Charlie, the only man who could show him the way and they cross paths without noticing each other, something happens that on the stage would irreparably destroy any audience's confidence in the author's ability to resolve a plot with vigour.

Film has no responsibility, it does not need to exert itself. If its dramaturgy has remained so simple, it is because the film consists of nothing more than a few miles of celluloid in a metal can. You don't expect a fugue from a saw that someone bends between his knees.

Naturally the cinema today no longer poses any technical problems. Its technology is advanced enough not to notice them. Today the theatre is much more of a technical question.

The cinema's potential is to be found in its capacity to collect documents. To present some philosophy or another, or the images of life, by means of the sad fate of a once interesting actor of the fantastic who has fallen victim today to that noble, measured existence with which little Johnny imagines that Julius Caesar crossed the Tiber, a noteworthy singer who inspires us through his acting to meet him live on the theatre stage.

[GBFA 21/135-6. Unpublished text written in 1926. Charles Chaplin's *The Gold Rush* was produced by United Artists and opened in the USA in August 1925. According to a note by Brecht's secretary Elisabeth Hauptmann, he saw the film in March 1926. The last sentence is fragmentary in the original typescript. For Brecht, Chaplin's non-psychological acting style contrasted with the introspective habits of German actors in the 1920s and became a major factor in the economy of expression that he later developed with the notion of gestic acting in the epic theatre.]

From the ABCs of the Epic Theatre

¶17 *Film*

Film can be of great importance in the epic theatre. Yet it must be used in a way that is appropriate to its artistic or scientific nature, precisely as if it stood on its own. Film obeys the same laws as graphic art. It is essentially static and must be treated like a series of tableaux. Its effect must arise from the clear interruptions, which would otherwise just be common errors. The tableaux must be so composed that they can be taken in at a single glance like a sheet of paper, but yet they must withstand separation into details so that every detail corresponds in the larger scheme with the centre. This fundamentally static aspect of film gives rise to the following basic rule: film is limited to a vision which itself stands motionless but into which each individual phase leads for greater effect. Thus, the structuring of the individual sequences must exactly reproduce on a large scale the structure of the smaller, discrete shots. Any kind of imprecision is unartistic. This basic rule of the cinema, as strict as any in the other domains of art, thus makes film resistant to the logic of plot. Also the non-three-dimensional nature of film, which creates this spiritual effect, defies plot in the dramatic sense. Not to account for this rule seriously limits a film's life-span. Since film has no capacity to emphasize one thing over another, it relies entirely on this sort of selection of all the points in a plot which are needed for its own time period, being utterly dependent on this time. Moreover, fashionable taste is so important for its realization that film quickly becomes laughable. And a final point: it cannot simplify. What could it eliminate without becoming unnatural?

Film in its own right can be used in the epic theatre as a kind of optical chorus. In this case it is a good idea to maintain realism – that is, not to construct, let alone design something. For film in any event already lacks substance vis-à-vis the word and therefore needs the common stuff of reality. Obviously numbers, statistical formulations, maps, etc., are pure objects of reality and suitable for choruses.

In connection with the set or an acoustical chorus the sharpest dialectic possible must be created and exploited. Since film can represent reality in such an abstract way, it lends itself to confrontations with reality. It can confirm or dispute. It can recall or prophesy. It can assume the role of those spectral phenomena without which for a long time – even at the best times – there were no great dramas. And yet here it plays a really revolutionary role, for as spectre it causes naked reality to appear, the good deity of the revolution.

If film is used only as decoration to create an environment, then it must be artistically formed, that is, simplified. It must present what is typical. In this case one can even design or construct. Most importantly, however, the film – if it presents a real environment – must not be allowed to destroy once and for all the pleasure in the dialectic between the three-dimensional and the non-three-dimensional.

(These rules are aimed less at the artists, who precisely in their rejection of such pearls of wisdom perhaps produce something, than at the viewers, who are perhaps preparing themselves for these more progressive works of art precisely by accepting them.)

[GBFA 21/210–12. Unpublished typescript written in 1927. There exist no other 'paragraphs' as would be indicated by '¶17' at the top and probably no others were written. Possibly this is one of several fragments, most of which were written later, meant to describe the epic theatre. Brecht is remarking here, of course, on the silent cinema, before sound film was introduced in Germany. In a review of Robert Louis Stevenson's complete works in a German edition, Brecht had already articulated briefly his position on the cinematic nature of literature:

> It is interesting to note that, as we can see quite clearly in Stevenson's stories, the filmic perspective existed on this continent before the cinema itself. Not only for this reason is it ridiculous to claim that cinematic technology introduced a new visual perspective into literature. *On a purely verbal level the regrouping according to the optical perspective began long ago in Europe.* Rimbaud, for example, is already oriented in a purely optical way. But for Stevenson all events are organized now visually.

(See Brecht, 'Glossen zu Stevenson', GBFA 21/107, originally published in *Berliner Börsen-Courier*, 19 May 1925.)]

Mutilated Films

Recently Lotte Reiniger's film *The Adventures of Prince Ahmed* was screened in the cinema 'Die Kamera' (Unter den Linden) in a completely massacred version made silly by the ridiculous cuts.[5] This important film, produced with a lot of talent and an almost Asiatic diligence by people who can by no means be counted as belonging to the film industry, was screened in such a bizarre form even at its opening in a UFA cinema that one can hardly escape the feeling that it is being shown so that it can be canned. Whether the cinema has not *succeeded* in making it a commercial run or whether it has succeeded in not *making* it a commercial run, they have now made cuts that were either very stupid or – an even more interesting possibility – very clever, so that it has become a complete *artistic* fiasco! Instigating a small investigation of such incidents would possibly look foolish, since it is only a mere artistic matter, that is, something extremely rare, unusual and not really of concern to anybody.

[GBFA 21/248. *Berliner Börsen-Courier*, 30 August 1928; an editorial note at the head of the article states: ' "Die Kamera", which deserves credit as the first Berlin cinema to show a regular programme of outstanding older German and foreign productions, unfortunately shows these films sometimes distorted by cuts. We print here a letter from Bert Brecht that will perhaps open the necessary discussion about the rights of film makers.']

The World is Yours

A stranger who sets foot in one of this continent's huge cities, let's say New York, to attend to his business, perhaps not such promising business, for example, the business of theatre, such a man would undoubtedly speak of good fortune if one day – in the circumstances in which he will inevitably find himself – he discovers the importance of certain small and sometimes also larger stores that are spread out over the entire city and sell 120 minutes of entertainment, the cinemas. Together with a remarkable number of other people, who apparently find themselves in similar circumstances, probably because their business is equally unpromising, he will be able, to his joy, to find some relief there.

[GBFA 22/168. Typescript written in November/December 1935. According to a note written by Brecht about a year later ('Begrenzung der Illusion', GBFA 22/262), the title – in English in the original – refers to a neon sign seen outside a window in an unidentified American gangster play.]

Intoxicating Effect

It is an error that the 'boredom' of the villages and towns drives the people into the cinema; they need it more in the large cities and most in the largest cities. The hunger for substitute experience is greatest where the gap between work and recreation is widest, where the contradiction between the acceleration and retardation of the pressure to perform is intensified. The atomization of life is unbearable and demands integrative actions. It is the actions of others which cause our powerlessness; our defence is to empathize with these actions.

[GBFA 22/173. Typescript, 1935 (dating uncertain).]

V-Effects of Chaplin

Eating the boot (with proper table manners, removing the nail like a chicken bone, the index finger pointing outward).

The film's mechanical aids:

Chaplin appears to his starving friend as a chicken.

Chaplin destroying his rival and at the same time courting him.

[GBFA 22/223. Typescript about 1936 (dating uncertain). The scene is from Charles Chaplin's film *The Gold Rush* (1925). *Verfremdungseffekt* or *V-Effekt* refers to Brecht's notion of distancing or rendering the familiar strange. It is variously translated into English as alienation, distanciation or estrangement.]

The *Verfremdungseffekt* in the Other Arts

Joyce uses the *Verfremdungseffekt* in *Ulysses*.[6] He alienates both the way of representing (mainly through the frequent and rapid changes) and the events.

The integration of documentary film material into theatre productions also brings forth the *Verfremdungseffekt*. The on-stage actions are alienated by juxtaposition with the more general actions on the screen.[7]

Painting alienates when it (Cézanne) exaggerates the hollow form of a vase.

Dadaism and Surrealism use the most extreme kinds of *Verfremdungseffekt*. Their objects never return from the alienation.

The classical *Verfremdungseffekt* produces heightened understanding.

[GBFA 22/223–4. Typescript, 1936 (dating uncertain).]

On Film Music

¶1 *Theatre's experience useful for the cinema?*

The special nature of the experiments undertaken by the German theatre during the time before Hitler enables us to use some of its experiences for the cinema as well – assuming that this is done with great care. This theatre owes not a little to the cinema. It made use of epic, gestic and montage elements that appeared in films. It even made use of film itself by exploiting documentary material.[8] Some aesthetes protested against this use of film material in theatre productions, unjustly in my view. One need not ban film in order to preserve theatre as theatre; you only have to employ it theatrically. – The cinema too can learn from the theatre and use theatrical elements. This does not mean that theatre is simply filmed. In fact the cinema constantly employs theatrical elements. The less consciously it does so, the worse the effects. It is actually quite depressing how much bad theatre the cinema produces! – The turn to discretion and the use of familiar types, the rejection of enhanced expression (anti-hamming), which grew out of the transition from silent to sound cinema, cost the cinema much of its expressiveness without liberating it from the claws of the theatre. It suffices to listen from the galleries to these anti-hams to notice immediately how operatically and unnaturally they speak.

¶1 *Musical inflation in the cinema*
The *swamping of our films with music* is easily understandable. A sensible practice from the silent film period, when music played the role it had already for a long time in mime, became a dubious habit in the sound cinema, which has no more to do with mime than does stage drama. Dialogue drowns in music. From the musical perspective our actors become silent opera singers. The only thing that one can say in defence of the domination of so much music in films is basically that no one hears it anymore. If, as in the case of the typical film, up to 75 per cent of the playing time has music, inflation sets in and the music is completely devalued.

¶9 *Opportunity*
On the other hand, society constantly develops in that it produces contradictions. If each of its constituent parts is dependent on all other parts, then each has the opportunity to influence all others. The opportunities multiply to the extent that the constituent part considers the entire situation. Cynics forget or sneer at this. To accept a certain dependency is not to surrender but to take up the fight.

¶10 *Prerequisite for collaboration on an unequal basis*
The composer must orient himself to the storyteller film, not only for technical reasons but also because as a popular entertainment

the cinema today has integrated music in a very limited quantity and as a supplement or expedient. But this is no grounds for defeatism. Here, too, changes are possible. The collaboration of unequally strong partners depends fundamentally on the stronger recognizing the weaker as an independent producer. If music's intransigence is not possible, then the cinema as well does not gain what it could by fully dominating music. Its hara-kiri, its total dissolution, does not serve the cinema.

¶10 *Even limited elbow room is elbow room*
On the other hand, society constantly develops in that it produces contradictions. Entertainment might contribute to my livelihood, but at the same time its specific form might threaten that livelihood. I may need drugs to be able to live and at the same time I may endanger my life with the drugs. General conditions might force me to ask art to lend its achievements the character of a drug and at the same time I may ask art to participate in the elimination of these conditions. Thus, artists have a contradictory task and they sense it more or less. Not only they but also the industry senses this task, for its source is the victims, who are also the clients. Here is an opportunity for the artist who deals with film, a small opportunity but the only one. They should not engage in speculation as to how much art the public is prepared to accept. Rather, they must find out how little narcosis the public needs in its entertainment. The lowest limit of the latter is also the highest limit of the former.

¶11 *Collaboration?*
The division of labour in our industry is organized in such a way that it not only guarantees the technical implementation of production but also the system that regulates its commercial exploitation. These two functions, which any team creating a film must respect, contradict one another to a certain extent. Composers, writers and directors sometimes serve the first function better when they ignore the second one. Purely financial calculations force the industry to organize innovations and simultaneously to protect the status quo, to purchase progress and simultaneously to purchase methods that liquidate progress; the teams suffer and can also profit from this state of affairs.

¶11 *Situational music*
The American cinema has not progressed beyond the stage of situational comedy and situational tragedy. The average lover,

villain, hero, mastermind, moves through certain situational settings. The accompanying music is consequently situational music. In other words it expresses the feelings of the dramaturg. His 'Oh, how sad!' and 'Oh, how exciting!' is transformed into music. Since there are no characters, there is an awful void for this dramaturgical music. In contrast to the Americans, who are very proud of their individualism but have no individuals in their films (except possibly for those by Orson Welles, where damaged individuals appear),[9] the Russians have created, on their admittedly collectivist basis, films with real individuals (*Mother*, *The Youth of Maxim*, *Baltic Deputy*, etc., etc.).[10] There the accompanying music also has dramaturgical character but has an easier time of it, so it seems to me.

¶11 *Separation of elements*

Perhaps it would be advisable at this point to mention certain far-reaching experiments which, in the realm of film, have only been attempted in the documentary, that is, in a relatively limited field, but which have gained quite some significance in the theatre. I am speaking of the *separation of elements in the theatrical work of art* tested primarily in pre-Hitler Germany. That is, music and action were treated as completely independent components of the work of art. The musical pieces were recognizably positioned in the action. The actors' performance style changed when songs or the musical underscoring of a dialogue set in. Generally the orchestra was visible and it was drawn into the set design by means of special lighting when it played.[11] The set design itself constituted a third independent element. Thus it was possible to construct scenes in which music and set worked together without action, for example, when in *Man Equals Man* a short serenade was played and images were projected.[12] In the opera *The Rise and Fall of the City of Mahagonny* the principle was implemented in another form. The three elements, action, music and image, appeared together but yet separated: in one scene – which shows how a man eats himself to death – in front of a huge screen, on which could be seen a larger-than-life glutton, the actor (who did not resemble the projected glutton) mimed the suicidal gluttony, accompanied by a chorus who chanted a description of the act. Music, image and actor performed the same act independently.[13] These examples are relatively extreme and I do not believe that they can be realized in today's narrative films. I mention them mainly to show how *the separation of elements* is to be understood. In any case the principle made it possible to use music for its own value to heighten the full impact. Three of the best German composers, Eisler, Hindemith and Weill, contributed to it.[14]

¶12 *Separation of elements in the narrative film*
Used carefully, this principle of separating the elements of music and action could provide the narrative film with some new effects. This presupposes, however, that the composer would not be drawn in only after the event, as generally has been the case up till now. He would have to be integrated into the planning of the film's effects from the start. For music can assume certain functions from the start, but they must be reserved for the music. If, for example, music is to be and can be used to express emotional states in people, then many actions are no longer needed whose only purpose is to express these emotional states. Making a decision to do something, say, can then be performed by mime, that is, a man can be shown by himself, walking back and forth, while the music can take over the performance of his emotional curve. The less miming on the part of the actor, the stronger the impact, presumably. In this kind of a scene the music is completely independent and represents a true dramatic complement. Let's consider another possibility. A young man rows his girlfriend out on a lake, overturns the boat and lets the girl drown.[15] The composer has two choices. He can anticipate the audience's feelings in his accompanying music, developing the tension, amplifying the evil of the deed, etc. Or instead he can express in the music the lake's serenity, nature's indifference, the event's everyday quality insofar as it is a simple excursion. If he chooses this latter possibility, allowing the murder to appear even more horrendous and unnatural, he gives to the music a far more independent function.

¶12 *Prerequisite for collaboration on an unequal basis*
Within a team creating a progressive film the status of the composer is weak precisely because he can most easily be exploited 'to render unto the industry that which is the industry's'.

¶13 *Question of quantity*
If music can indeed say so much, it must be permitted to speak relatively infrequently so that it is heard. Music can become more important to the extent that it is used in smaller quantities. And it will serve its functions better, the fewer those functions are. Most importantly, those functions must be distinguished carefully. For example, it would be wrong in the two scenes mentioned in ¶12 to apply the music in the suggested way if these scenes followed one

another. The music's function would be too different. The listener would not be able to follow the divergence. Moreover, it is necessary to realize that the potential advantage of invigorating with music a weakly conceived dialogue scene entails the disadvantage that the music in a subsequent scene may fail. Music shares this characteristic with other drugs.

¶14 *Can the emotional effects of music be standardized?*
Composers know little about the effects of music. Generally they leave their study to the barkeepers. One of the few research results I have seen in the past decade was the notice of a restaurant proprietor in Paris about the different drinks his guests ordered under the influence of different music. He claimed to have found that certain beverages were always consumed with music of certain composers. Undoubtedly the cinema would benefit much if composers were in a position to deliver music that could influence the audience with more or less precisely determined effects. Then we could have musical backdrops, emotional platforms and if they were sufficiently atonal, they could even be standardized. Their constant usage would probably not diminish the effect, but rather strengthen it. Associated time and again with exciting actions, these backdrops would probably also transfer the special excitement to the new actions with which they were connected. The Chinese theatre produces these types of effects with masks.

¶15 *Tempo*
For the invention of patterns as well as original forms the composer should free himself from all conventions because our conventions do not favour patterns. For a chase scene, for instance, in general simply a fast piece of music is written. Various considerations suggest that the music should represent obstacles rather than movement. Isolated note clusters every ten seconds produce a good enhancement of the sense of tempo. In this way music works like a clock.

¶16 *Natural moods*
For natural moods naturalistic descriptions are not always the most effective.

¶ *Enhancing the pleasure of art through music*
The total deactivation of the concert public reveals itself in the glorification of the orchestra conductor. Here the public can still consume the way in which music is produced. The act of pro-

duction becomes consumable. Moreover, this magician models the effect he intends, he pretends to be shocked, enthusiastic, sentimental, sensitive, expectant, cheerful, filled with doubt, spiritually cleansed, etc., etc. Music serves the cinema in a similar way. When the ballet's rat king, known as the conductor, expresses with gestures his sweet sadness, which in his opinion the score is supposed to bring forth, he seems to be preoccupied with infecting the musicians with his own sadness. In reality he is trying to infect the public with it, directly, above and beyond the music. Similarly film music anticipates what the actions on the screen are supposed to bring forth. It pre-savours. It tries on its own to express the storm of emotions which are supposed to be brought forth by the filmed action (and are perhaps not being brought forth).

¶ *Art as 'phenomenon'*
It is essential for hypnosis that the necessary manipulations are made as unobtrusively as possible, at least after the hypnosis has begun. The hypnotist avoids anything that might draw attention to himself. In its attempts to produce a mood the Stanislavsky Method makes the actor into a 'vessel for the word', an unobtrusive 'servant of art', etc. Sources of light and sound are hidden. The theatre does not wish to be identified as theatre. It appears anonymously. Under these conditions the set has no interest in appearing as the set. It presents itself as nature, possibly as enhanced nature. – It is apparent why the best film music is that praised for not being heard.

¶ *Feeling of logic*
As mentioned, music is often used to 'drown out' a plot's arbitrariness, breaks and absurdities. It is easy for the composer to construct musically a kind of artificial logic, that is, to produce the feeling of fatalism, inescapability, etc. The composer serves up logic like certain cooks serve up vitamin tablets with their meals. In fact the capacity of composers to bring out with a few artistic flourishes, so to speak, the logic of the material's construction, which is inherent in their musical pieces and thereby produce an independent sense of logic, used properly, could be significant for the cinema. This kind of music can be used to connect disparate events, to point contradictory events in a particular direction. Expressed differently, the film scriptwriter can portray the course of events much more dialectically, i.e., in their real contradictoriness and disjointedness, if the music places the public in the constructive attitude of 'collecting details'. An example: a man is

shown to be influenced by (a) the death of his father, (b) share increases at the stock market, (c) the onset of war. If the music is responsible for drawing together these events, then the montage can be richer, more complicated and also simply longer. – Eisler and Ivens used such music in a documentary feature when they combined two large processes in one film: land reclamation by the construction of the Zuider Zee dike and the burning of Canadian wheat for the purpose of fixing the price.[16]

¶ *Art as event*
An example of 'art as event': in the parable *Man Equals Man* the hero is a petty-bourgeois man who is enticed into a military camp under the pretence of making a deal there. He spends the night sitting on a chair. At this point the production showed him sitting on his wooden chair while a short serenade was played. Three elements came together here without really combining: set, story and music. The set provided far more of a pure image effect than an illusion, the story as experience receded and permitted meditation, the music came forth not 'from the atmosphere' but from the wings and retained its concert quality. Poetry, music and architecture appeared as independent arts within a clearly demarcated event.

¶ *Function of innovations*
It has to be admitted that the attempts of the German theatre were directed mainly against the narcotic function of art. It was not so much an issue of making 'strong', 'lively', 'gripping' theatre, but rather of making reproductions of reality so that the reproduced reality became 'manageable'. Excitement – without which theatre today can hardly be imagined – was also part of this. Yet it resembled more the excitement of people who discover oil (or a really reliable person) than that of children riding a carousel. And music had the task of protecting the audience from a state of 'trance'. It did not serve the enhancement of existing or anticipated effects but rather interrupted or manipulated them. So if there were songs in a play, it was not as if the story 'dissolved into song'. The people in the play did not break into song. On the contrary, they openly interrupted the story. They assumed a pose for singing and presented the song in a way that did not fully correspond to the situation. They also conveyed in their musical performance only a few, chosen aspects of the characters they were playing. In melodramatic sections the music allowed the public to discover the emptiness and conventionalism of certain events which the actors

had played with unshakeable seriousness. The music was also able to generalize certain sections of consistently played realistic scenes, to present them as typical or historically significant. These examples are mentioned here in order to make clear that it was not the function of the innovations to promote the sale of trance to the public.

¶ *Mixing the functions*

In Dieterle's film *Syncopation*, a presentation of the history of jazz, one sequence, which showed the trip of its heroine, a musician, from New Orleans to Chicago, failed in its effect.[17] Travelling through various cities, she hears certain characteristic songs associated with them. The idea of a journey through various jazz forms was not understood by the audience. The reason was that, at the beginning of the film, scenes were accompanied by music in such a way as to emphasize not the music but the scene. The audience did not comprehend that now the scene (the girl's journey) was meant to be less important than the music. The audience had grown accustomed to hear the accompaniment with only one ear and to consider it to be without meaning.

¶ *Tempo. Music as clock*

Music can be used in many different ways to produce the tempo (just as it can in many ways put the audience in a mood to accept certain necessary, long-winded descriptions). In general, for a chase scene simply a fast piece of music is written. Certain considerations can lead, however, to the music representing obstacles rather than movement. A musical clock or isolated note clusters at least every ten seconds (perhaps this could be varied) produce a good enhancement of the sense of tempo. Naturally music can in some circumstances also have the effect that the behaviour of the people in the film appears to be too slow, perceived as inadequate for the necessary tempo. It will then have to develop the feeling of haste.

[GBFA 23/10–20. Unpublished typescript written in April/May 1942. Hanns Eisler requested of Brecht that he provide him with some notes on film music for the research project he and Theodor W. Adorno were conducting at the New School for Social Research in New York City (beginning in spring 1940). The theoretical evaluation of the research data, completed in 1944, was published under Eisler's name as *Composing for the Films* (New York: Oxford University Press, 1947). Adorno's name was not mentioned, although he co-authored the text. The notes are here presented with the section numbers Brecht used, including some unnumbered and repetitive sections.]

Wilhelm Dieterle's Gallery of Grand-Bourgeois Figures

Wilhelm Dieterle inaugurated a gallery of grand-bourgeois figures with his film biographies *Zola, Pasteur, Juarez* and *Ehrlich*.[18] These features – continued later in a much weaker vein (*Edison, Mme Curie, Mark Twain, Wilson*)[19] – differ as much from the usual film fare as do the Elizabethan history plays about feudal figures from 'action dramas'. The action film shows average people whose exciting experiences can be appreciated without difficulty by the average spectator, so that there is no need for character development on the part of the actor. The actor is the a and b of algebraic equations, for which any arbitrary number can be substituted. Dieterle's gallery of above-average figures allowed the actor (Muni and Robinson) to develop the characters, which meant a great step forward.[20] The representation of average people as characters seems to be impossible in the American cinema. Even Dieterle's interesting attempts in this area met with resistance.

The element of conflict in these bourgeois biographies derives from the opposition in which the hero stands vis-à-vis the dominant opinion, i.e., vis-à-vis the dominant class. This is Ibsen's type of the enemy of the people. Society views the mere growth in productive forces as a cancer. Unforgettable the scene in which Zola is asked to defend Dreyfus against the army's anti-Semitism. He hesitates, refuses, becomes petulant as if confronted with an unfair demand, showing that he is conscious of the penalty placed on the pursuit of truth. Truth *overpowers* him, his sense of justice *brings him round*. A bourgeois himself, he then turns against the bourgeoisie and towards humanity. Pasteur is portrayed as a Galileo of medicine, he too risks jail. If one thinks of the remarkable Soviet film *The Deputy of the Baltic Fleet*, you can see how the series continues. Each film represents a courageous deed on Dieterle's part. Each is the result of constant struggles between the production companies and their employee, who was the director/producer. One example of the difficulties: a company planned a biographical film, *The Life of Madame Curie*, based on a single scene. The Curies, who completed their experiments while living in great poverty, refused industry's offer for the patents for radium, so that the entire world could enjoy unhindered access to the remedy. Several scripts were completed at significant cost but did not satisfy the company, until finally it was realized that precisely this scene ruined everything. Refusing millions of dollars had something unnatural about it. It diminished the plausibility of the entire film. And especially this: if the refusal was glorified for its idealism, then wasn't the offer itself being somewhat defamed? The companies' sensitivity makes the portrayal of grand-bourgeois figures itself into a heroic undertaking of sorts.

Dieterle's film biographies, progressive and humanist and intelligent – which alone marks them as a kind of rebellion within the commercial movie industry in America – were also ground-breaking in a dramaturgical sense. Films 'with historical back-ground' had been made up until then with innumerable experts for the details but without a thought about the social workings of the relevant period. In Dieterle's films the historical background moved into the foreground and introduced itself as the protagonist. Even if a comprehensive representation, with full consideration of the class struggle, was not possible under the pertinent circum-stances, nonetheless entirely new emotional fields were opened up. Previously a scientist's passion for his profession was used only as a motive at most for a marriage spat, which then became the film's main theme. Now it became among other things a matter of *dramatizing the microbes*. The hero was a hero in the struggle against them, just as he was a hero in the struggle against people. Yet it was not the integration of science but its poetic and artistic treatment that interested Dieterle.

In a cinema repertoire for a Europe liberated from the Nazis, Dieterle's film biographies could be among the most valuable features that the American movie industry could contribute.

[GBFA 23/42–4. Typescript from about 1944, in the Wilhelm Dieterle Estate Papers, held by the Stiftung Deutsche Kinemathek, Berlin. The German film director Wilhelm (William) Dieterle helped Brecht and his family emigrate to the United States in 1941 and arranged for them their first apartment in Hollywood, which led to a close friendship during the American exile years. Brecht wrote the film script 'Caesar's Last Days' for Dieterle in 1942 and then transformed it into a short story published in *Tales from the Calendar*. In 1945 Dieterle and Brecht wanted to produce a series of short agitational films based on scenes from his anti-fascist plays for use in the American POW camps to re-educate German soldiers. Immediately after Germany's capitulation, they also discussed plans for longer didactic films that could be produced in Germany for the defeated Germans. The American government refused to cooperate.]

Efforts to Save the Film *The Axe of Wandsbek*

The petty-bourgeois public, especially, cannot watch the bank-ruptcy of a small business without deep empathy. Thus – and also because of the love he shows toward his wife – the butcher earns much sympathy. Only brief passages should remain, the wife's confession that she has pawned the linen, the neighbour threatening the laundry, the suicide (but without the religious embellishments, especially the 'as we forgive them that trespass against us'). Perhaps the butcher, while burying the axe, could also be shown looking up and catching sight of the observer above. Then, after the return of the axe, he could draw the Gestapo's attention to the inhabitant in the attic in a brief scene. They could discover leaflets during a surprise visit and arrest the young man. This denunciation would make the butcher into an active Nazi and deprive him of all sympathy. At the end he should only be shown standing at the threshold, looking at the hanged woman. He would be made to walk, drunk, to the Alster and be held back by some workers from clambering over the wall. He would have to tell them his story and his excuses would be met with stony looks. They could leave and suggest to him coldly that he should jump into the river a little further down. (Another version: he could go to a tavern and buy a round of drinks for the workers. Then he tells his story, at which point they reject their beers.)

[GBFA 23/153. Typescript written in late May 1951. Arnold Zweig's novel *Das Beil von Wandsbek* (first published in Hebrew in 1943, first German edition in 1947) was filmed by the East German state film company, DEFA, in 1951 and opened in May 1951 (director: Falk Harnack; scenario: Hans Robert Bortfeld and Harnack; starring Erwin Geschonneck, Käthe Braun, Sefion Helmke and Willy A. Kleinau). There were harsh critiques, leading to the film's withdrawal from distribution. Brecht's suggestions for an alternative ending were an attempt to save the film, but they were not accepted. Arnold Zweig noted in his diary on 31 May 1951:

> Brecht's idea for the end of the axe film is exactly right, but because of DEFA's political position on rendering justice, it is impossible. At the end the 'Führer' must enter in all his pomp and glory, the chief hangman, the axe itself. (Arnold Zweig Archive in the Academy of Arts, Berlin)]

On the Filming of Literary Texts

The Academy of Arts recommends:

The filming of plays like Brecht's *Courage* or *Puntila* and Wolf's *Professor Mamlock* or *Münzer*; of novels like Strittmatter's *Ochsenkutscher* and Renn's *Adel im Untergang* and Bredel's *Störtebecker*. This is not aimed against original films that show the achievements of the GDR and move beyond primitive propaganda. Concerning films with prescribed themes, the Academy of Arts offers to evaluate the artistic quality of the scripts.

[GBFA 23/350–1. Typescript written in 1955. Brecht's play *Puntila and His Man Matti* was filmed by Alberto Cavalcanti for the Austrian producer Wien-Film in 1955. Friedrich Wolf's play *Professor Mamlock* (1935) was filmed by his son Konrad Wolf in 1961 and *Thomas Münzer: Der Mann mit der Regenbogenfahne* (1953) by Martin Hellberg in 1956, both East German DEFA productions. Brecht became Vice-President of the Academy of Arts in East Berlin in June 1954.]

On the *Courage* Film

The irresponsibly sloppy preparations for the film production of *Mother Courage and Her Children* as well as the astonishing miscasting have now caused DEFA to proceed with the film regardless of any considerations of artistic and human demands. Helene Weigel considered it impossible to play the main role under the anticipated working conditions, which were moreover characterized as 'par for the course'. I object to a schedule which endangers the artistic integrity and the health of artists of the German Democratic Republic.

[GBFA 23/351. Typescript dated 15 September 1955. As early as September 1949 the state film production company DEFA in East Germany had contacted Brecht about producing a film of *Mother Courage*. Brecht rejected a first script version by Robert A. Stemmle as well as a second script by Joachim Barckhausen and Graf Alexander Stenbock-Fermor to be directed by Erich Engel. From autumn 1950 until autumn 1952, several versions of a new script were completed by Emil Burri, Wolfgang Staudte and Brecht, but DEFA never signed a contract to obtain the film rights, presumably because of Brecht's financial demands. Brecht continued to push his plan for a film version, offering it through Ruth Berlau to the Danish director couple Astrid and Bjarne Henning-Jensen and later to the Italian director Aldo Vergano (neither Luchino Visconti nor Giuseppe de Santis showed interest in the Italian translation of the script when approached in 1954). In late 1954 a contract with DEFA was signed and a final script version was prepared by Burri and Staudte in consultation with Brecht, to be directed by Staudte and to star Helene Weigel, who had played the role of Mother Courage in Brecht's production at the Deutsches Theater (opened in January 1949). Casting problems (Staudte had engaged Simone Signoret as Yvette and Bernard Blier as the cook from France) and other controversies delayed the production start until mid-August 1955. Then problems with DEFA and differences between Brecht and Staudte led to the cancellation of the entire production in September, after ten days of shooting (see also the next three items). In 1960 DEFA produced a film version of Brecht's own staging at the Berliner Ensemble, directed by his assistants Peter Palitzsch and Manfred Wekwerth.]

Questions [about the *Courage* Film]

1) How many shooting days were scheduled for how many shots in Signoret's contract? Enough? How much margin?

2) How many shooting days were scheduled for how many shots in Blier's contract? Enough? How much margin?

3) Were the shooting days sufficient if both normal and wide-screen versions are to be produced, that is, with an untested technology?

4) Would Signoret's and Blier's engagements have allowed us to include more shooting days with them, or was this the maximum and somehow we had to make do? If Signoret or Blier had been able to begin earlier, could Mr Staudte have done so as well?

5) In case of illness or other indispositions, were opportunities for later shoots anticipated for the French guests? What were they?

6) Why did the production manager, Mr Teichmann, establish a shooting schedule that required Mrs Weigel to be available six days a week, although his representative had been informed on __ June in the office of the Berliner Ensemble that Mrs Weigel could only shoot four and a half days a week because she was on stage two evenings and could not film for the entire day before the *Courage* performance and half a day before the *Chalk Circle* performance!

7) Why were costumes prepared that Brecht, Rodenberg,[21] Kilger[22] and even Staudte (who had seen the figurines) had rejected, because they were operatic in the worst sense, when they saw them a few days before shooting began? Was Staudte willing, despite everything, to continue the shoot with these costumes?

8) Were the figurines shown to the French set designer? Did he accept them? When?

9) Why were locations for intimate and emotionally difficult scenes, which do not allow for post-synchronization, planned for a hall that is well known for its echo effects and therefore necessitates post-synchronization? Was sound sacrificed to the image?

10) Why, contrary to the contract, was the author's consent not sought for the hiring of Blier? Why was a film with this actor, who was unknown to the author, shown to him only after shooting began and the hiring contract had been accepted?

11) Why does Mrs Weigel still have no contract? Why were the working conditions never discussed (number of shooting days each week, length of the shooting days)?

12) Why did Mr Staudte consider colour experiments necessary but then began shooting the film, although he declared the results of the experiments unsatisfactory?

13) Was the initial, well-reasoned decision to shoot practically the entire film in the studio abandoned because 'it's faster outdoors', as Mrs Weigel was told? Important because outdoors the sound is less controllable and frequently post-synchronization is necessary.

[GBFA 23/351–2. Typescript written in 1955.]

File Note [*Courage* Film]

1. It seems to me that the film is not sufficiently prepared. The director, Wolfgang Staudte, was unavailable for the entire summer to prepare the film. Only in late July did he return from Holland. The production manager, Mr Teichmann, was also still involved in June with another film, although the shooting was scheduled to begin on 18 August. For weeks my assistants tried in vain to get Mr Teichmann to show the designs to me for the sets, costumes, etc., and they indicated that I would not allow the use of unrealistic costumes and sets. This discussion did not take place until 5 August, in other words two weeks before the shooting began and after the costumes were already being cut. I was appalled at the set models. The costume sketches were beyond comment (operatic and romantic) and entirely contrary to both the script and the actors in the film.

2. I insisted from the beginning on black-and-white film stock. According to the contract, the decision on colour or black-and-white was to be mine. DEFA or Mr Staudte insisted on colour and I consented only on the condition that the colour film stock tests would satisfy me. The tests that Mr Staudte showed me on 5 August were unsatisfactory. Mr Staudte wished to undertake further tests. Since Mr Rodenberg assured me in writing that I could uphold my right to black-and-white film, we decided finally that the shooting would be with two cameras: one for black-and-white and one for colour.

3. At the last moment it was also decided that the film would be a wide-screen production, so that a third camera was included. This

apparatus was completely unknown in the studio, arrived only one day before the shoot and doubled the shooting time, since the blocking for each camera had to be changed.

4. The scant timing already scheduled for the shoot thus became even more precarious. The number of days scheduled for shooting the French actors was especially limited because they had other obligations in France immediately afterwards. As far as I know, only ten days were allowed for Mr Blier, the actor for the role of the cook, an inadequately calculated time for such a large role. It is easy to establish whether the shooting schedule for the French artists was maintained and whether the wide-screen option was even figured into the schedule.

5. In this situation the film was to be produced no matter what. Hence, Mr Staudte demanded of Mrs Weigel, whose workday in any case lasted twelve hours (eight hours shooting plus putting on and taking off make-up plus travel time), that she be available continuously, including Sundays. I objected to this. Besides being an inhuman demand on any artist, it was in no way artistically defensible. In the cinema it is well known that every moment is a premiere and shooting with exhausted actors is certain to be bad.

6. My objection was also caused by the contemptuous treatment of Helene Weigel during the entire process. Both she and I had the impression that she was being 'tolerated' because she had been written into my contract. For the preliminary discussion about her shooting schedule not the artistic director, not the director, not even the production manager came to her but a completely unknown production assistant. As a result, DEFA argued they were not aware of the agreement that she would have the two afternoons a week free on which she was playing at the Berliner Ensemble in the evenings. Despite her requests she never was shown her costumes. Although she requested to see the takes during the first days so that she could make any necessary adjustments, she was not shown them. There was never any contract at all signed with Mrs Weigel. She was also not paid for the days she was on the set.

7. Three days before shooting was to begin, the actress for the role of Kattrin had still not been chosen.

8. After the shooting began, I learned that extensive post-synchronization would be necessary, since the acoustic conditions on the studio set where the film was being shot were not good. I also learned the news that a major portion of the film was being shot outdoors. Mrs Weigel made clear that she would not be able to post-synchronize the delicate and emotionally demanding

scenes and I suggested that a list of these scenes be prepared so that special attention could be paid to the sound. No one was at all interested. This is an unartistic way to work that is unacceptable.

9. Just as the shooting began too precipitously, so was I suddenly informed on 10 September of the suggestion that the project be abandoned. Although the General Secretary of the SED,[23] Walter Ulbricht, has personally taken an interest in the project and Wolfgang Staudte himself has had the opportunity to explain his views on the matter, I have up until now not had the same opportunity despite my requests.

In the interest of my internationally known play and in the interest of the GDR film production, I consider appropriate working conditions – whether usual or not – to be essential to make possible the production of an artistic film.

[GBFA 23/352–5. Typescript written in 1955.]

The Film *Mother Courage*

In my opinion the film *Mother Courage and Her Children* must unquestionably be produced, if only for the prestige of the German Democratic Republic.

The failure of Staudte's attempt demonstrates what is necessary:

A film for which not only the play but also the stage production is internationally known demands the most careful preparation and a generously measured shooting schedule. If foreign actors are to play roles – which is naturally desirable – then the schedule cannot be too tight and margins for reshooting must be calculated in.

From the beginning I was against colour film at this point. If a colour film is to be produced, however, then extensive and satisfactory tests must be undertaken in order to avoid making a romantic and operatic version of the play. Also, sets and costumes must be designed with special taste and in relation to each other. For example, colour effects must not be allowed to endanger the character of a realistic and poetic chronicle.

For a film like this, which is so dependent on the performers' differentiated acting of intimate and emotionally honest scenes, sound plays a larger role than in many other films. It is necessary to identify those scenes which would be endangered by the usual post-synchronization. They must not be shot outdoors or in

acoustically unfavourable studio spaces. I have always emphasized
that a *Courage* film does not have to be especially imposing,
commercial and cast with well-known film stars. But it does need
taste, talent and diligence and of course good, that is, artistically
oriented, dispositions.

The first attempt failed because the most elementary artistic
demands proved to be incompatible with the technical and
contractual conditions.

[GBFA 23/355–6. Typescript written in 1955.]

On the *Puntila* Script

In its current form the script does not seem right to me. To be sure,
it follows more or less the line that Pozner and I agreed on, but it
has now been implemented so that the *Puntila* story lapses into a
genre that is not comical, but ridiculous. It has become a refined
drawing-room comedy in which the play's crude jokes seem out of
place and simply crude. Nor is it clear *who* tells the whole story and
from what point of view. It appears to be the film company and its
point of view seems to be that of making a film. Naturally the
Puntila stories must be told 'from below', from the common
people's point of view. Then characters like Matti and Eva Puntila
are immediately seen as they should be. In the current script Matti
is a weak and undefined figure. It does not emerge that, despite and
because of his employee relationship, he stands in constant
opposition to his master in every line he speaks. Eva Puntila 'loves'
him not for his muscles – he doesn't need to have any at all – but
because he is a real man who possesses humour and authority, etc.
Naturally he may not believe for a second that Eva is the proper
wife for him or that Mr Puntila would actually give her to him. In
the 'test' he simply plays out Puntila's and Eva's romantic idea ad
absurdum. It must remain a game, otherwise Matti becomes an
idiot.

We immediately sketched out a new outline, since I am aware
that the studio cannot wait. Because the poetic material is already
at hand, a new script could be completed in no time at all. In the
case of the current script under no circumstances would I be able
to transcribe into Puntila-German the new dialogue passages,
which make up half of the total dialogue and are completely
naturalistic, because the situations are naturalistic and in my

opinion not true. Under no circumstances could I let my name or the name *Puntila* be used, if this script is accepted. I certainly do not want to create difficulties, but neither do I want to damage my reputation as a writer. You will certainly understand this.

[GBFA 23/356–7. Typescript written in 1955. In September 1953 Brecht signed a contract with Wien-Film in Vienna, owned by the Soviet Occupation authority, to produce his *Mr Puntila and His Man Matti*, starring Curt Bois, who had played the lead role at the Berliner Ensemble. Brecht commissioned Vladimir Pozner to prepare an exposé in consultation with him and on the advice of Jóris Ivens he commissioned the Brazilian film maker Alberto Cavalcanti to direct. Pozner completed his French-language screenplay in summer 1954, which was then translated into German by Ruth Fischer and, based on comments by Brecht, revised by Pozner and Cavalcanti in February 1955. Brecht was unhappy with this version, in particular with Matti's role, and insisted on a new screenplay version, which Pozner and Brecht's assistant Isot Killian prepared under his supervision. Cavalcanti then prepared a shooting script using Brecht's dialogues and the production was completed in December 1955. Despite his interventions, Brecht was disappointed by the final cut with the new musical score by Hanns Eisler. Meanwhile, the production firm had been transferred from Soviet to Austrian hands and, to avoid counting the film among the export contingent of Austrian productions, the company refused to distribute it. Through Cavalcanti's efforts it was screened publicly for the first time in Brussels three years later on 29 March 1959.]

The Storytelling Women in the Estate Kitchen
[*Puntila* Film]

. . . have two functions in the script:
1. they divide the story into 'the adventures of Mr Puntila'
2. they filter the stories through the servants' perspective, who will tell them many years later like popular legends.

They should have been:
1. staged as conspicuously marked interruptions
2. distinguished clearly from the 'legendary' stories.

A law of the cinema allegedly declares, however, that a film requires continuity and tolerates no breaks. 'The audience should not be pulled too far out of the narrative.'

In fact the estate kitchen is not used for separating but connecting: providing gradual, hardly noticeable transitions. The women do not begin again each time to contribute a new adventure, but rather try to better the previous one. This is primarily a matter of camera and editing technique. The director lacked the courage to halt the editing rhythm and shift to another. The method of photography also does not change noticeably. As everywhere else in the film short, 'exciting', suspenseful editing is used that ends before a situation can be calmly and broadly established. The women's measured work, their exhaustion, the pleasure in telling stories during their nightshift should have used much rougher, calmer shots.

The costumes and sets are constructed in the same style as the 'adventures'.

The small roles of the storytelling women are in part cast with minor actors who simply cannot develop a dialogue into a scene.

As it is, the kitchen keeps getting confused with the adventures, which leads to some curious misunderstandings.

[GBFA 23/357–8. Typescript written in 1955.]

Billiard Room in the Hotel Tavastberg [*Puntila* Film]

The events are *only* comprehensible in the comic exaggeration of their grandeur and importance. The loneliness plaint = Jesus on the Mount of Olives, walking on aquavit = Christ walking on the Red Sea, etc.[24]

These major events appear for the film production only in the text. They are not staged for the story but for a mobile, exciting camera style:

While Puntila complains about being lonely, he constantly dances around on the billiard table and is too busy rather than forsaken. Moreover, the billiard room is just a billiard room and not photographed with the grandeur (long shot) of a battlefield with one lone survivor.

Matti does not enter like a chauffeur who has been waiting for two days and two nights in the car but rather is shown immediately as the film's hero: fresh, elegant, important, shaven (at least it is not apparent that he is unshaven; the stubble is naturalistic and not exaggerated).

Puntila is shocked and falls off the billiard table when he catches sight of the chauffeur. Matti rushes to him and catches him in his arms. Because: the film needs movement. Puntila's motionlessness in front of the 'stranger', the estate owner's mistrust ('Who are you?'), the inspection as if at the cattle market, the invitation to his new friend, in short, the discovery of a person, is sacrificed to constant movement. For example, Matti carries Puntila to the table in his arms during the dialogue 'Who are you?' etc.

Similarly Matti's anger, his reticence, his annoyance at Puntila's assaults on his humanity, Matti's urge to go to bed, are all lost. The impression emerges: two people in a curious situation are joking with each other.

Because the figures in the film are not established in a broad way, because their respective social points of departure are not made clear, the story lines break off already in the first scene.

It was a mistake to delete from the script Matti's long Pappmann story because of concern for movement. Precisely the senseless, impressionistic movement of the photography and editing could have been prevented by this story.

[GBFA 23/358–9. Typescript written in 1955.]

Part II

Texts on Radio Broadcasting

(1926–1932)

[Radio broadcasting began in Germany in 1923 and spread quickly throughout the country with the systematic installation of public broadcasting stations. Dramatic material was used, beginning in 1924 with 'radio plays' produced for broadcast (*Hörspiele*) and after 1925 with 'broadcast plays' of theatre productions (*Sendespiele*). Brecht's own first broadcast took place in May 1925 when he read live from his works in the Berliner Rundfunk. Other plays by Brecht broadcast on radio included in 1926–7 *The Life of Edward II of England* as well as his radio adaptations of Shakespeare's *Macbeth* and *Hamlet*. In 1932 he adapted his *St Joan of the Stockyards* for radio broadcast.]

Young Drama and the Radio

More important than good living is: living in good times.

For a generation whose passion consists in writing plays it is no joy to be confronted with bad theatres, that is, ones unusable for their plays. But the times are good when the production side, far from supplying obsolete, worn-out and apathetic theatres, decides to eliminate this kind of theatre. Indeed, our production for this theatre is the kiss of death. On the other hand, today's theatre distorts our plays to the point of incomprehensibility, even when it works fairly well. Any other reproduction of our stage plays is better for them than that of the theatre. Even a film version would be more intelligible and persuasive.

Therefore the radio – a technical invention that still must create for itself a mass need rather than subordinating itself to an antiquated, exhausted need – is a grand, productive opportunity for our plays.

What I am trying to say is that I anticipated with much greater excitement the production of, say, *Ostpolzug* on the radio than in the theatre.[1]

It is said that our works are only meant for the few or at least they are only suitable for a few. The first is untrue, the second unproven. Our plays are meant for many people, but not for that small elite of snobs who have already 'seen everything' and who claim on every street corner that *they* are the ones intended. The theatre has too long been the property of a small elite that claims to be the nation. It is no accident that today, when this elite clearly *no longer* represents the nation, the theatre is in decline and that an invention like the radio, which in a manner of speaking has a long way to go, is simply attending to the art that was previously the theatre's obligation.

It is said that the radio needs courage to take on art. But if these large, unencumbered, new institutions have no courage, who can?

It is obvious that you will get into an argument with someone more quickly in a conversation about present-day concerns, about some topical issue, than if you listen to transcribed conversations from the past. It is in the nature of *our* plays that they must provoke more opposition than those by people who provoked opposition in other times.

We also hear that the large number of listeners prohibits anything but very general presentations about matters that have already been decided. This sorely underrates the large masses. Naturally it is easier to displease one person among a million than one among ten.

But there are also more who are pleased. And in general it is more important and ethical to please one single person than not to displease one hundred. Usually the masses are considered to be too stupid. They are not stupid. It is probable that only a small minority of the masses understand, say, the theory of relativity. But does that mean it should be communicated only to a few?

Whatever else art may have to rely on, it does not rely on aesthetic training. And whatever else may be necessary to make works of art, naive emotion is enough to appreciate them.

[GBFA 21/189–90. Written in late 1926 and published in *Funkstunde: Zeitschrift der Berliner Rundfunksendestelle* 1 (2 January 1927). Brecht wrote this text, his first theoretical contribution on radio broadcasting, as he was preparing his play *Man Equals Man* for radio broadcast, which was programmed on 18 March 1927 (director: Alfred Braun; music: Edmund Meisel). In a related article written several months later, 'On the Performance on Radio' (GBFA 24: 36–7), and printed in the programme magazine *Rundfunk-Rundschau* (Berlin, 13 March 1927), Brecht begins with the comment:

> When my generation came on the scene after the War, the theatres by no means rejected us. They tried on the contrary to switch their suppliers immediately. For a time my generation saw in the theatres' strong demand a real opportunity. In reality we were the opportunity for the theatres; they had become old and uninspired and while they were still able to exploit the public's habit of attending the theatre, they were unable to justify it. The theatres were no longer able to exploit this opportunity. They were simply too old. The radio is something else and I believe it is better. It is certainly not too old to practise art, rather it is at most still too young. If the radio is perhaps unable to realize some dimensions of the new plays' impact, then – assuming some imagination and a certain general interest for the times on the part of listeners – the essentials can be grasped . . .

In a note written in 1928 Brecht still considered radio broadcasting to be an improvement over the 'old' theatre:

> . . . The radio is a terrifying, living proof of the bad state of current theatre. If the theatre were doing its duty, then you would find only one person ready to sacrifice at least half of the pleasure of a play, which consists of seeing and the feeling of immediacy, in order to get the other half, listening, in a really cultivated way. (See 'Frische Stücke für Theater und Radio', GBFA 21/263.)]

Suggestions for the Director of Radio Broadcasting

1. In my view you should try to make radio broadcasting into a really democratic thing. To this end you would already achieve much, for example, if you were to cease producing only on your own for this wonderful distribution apparatus you have at your disposal and instead allow it to make productive *topical* events simply by setting it up and in special cases perhaps by managing it in a skilful, time-saving way.[2] It is perfectly understandable that people who suddenly get their hands on such a new apparatus immediately want to organize something to provide material for it and invent a new craft to provide them with artificial material. Already in the cinema I have seen with some distress how the Egyptian pyramids and the Indian Rajahs' palaces move to Neubabelsberg in order to be filmed by an apparatus that a man can comfortably slip into his backpack.[3] *In other words I believe that you must move with the apparatuses closer to the real events and not simply limit yourself to reproducing or reporting.* You must go to the *parliamentary sessions* of the Reichstag and especially to the major *court trials.* Since this would be a great step forward, there will certainly be a series of laws that try to prevent it. *You must turn to the public in order to eliminate these laws.* The parliamentarians' fear of being heard throughout the entire country should not be underestimated, since it is justified, but they must overcome it, just like the fear that, I believe, various courts will express about having to announce their judgments in front of all the people. Moreover, instead of dead reports you can produce *interviews* right in front of the microphone in which the interviewees have less opportunity to prepare carefully thought-out lies, as they are able to do for the newspapers. *Debates* between recognized specialists would be very important. You can organize lectures with discussions in large or small spaces. But by means of advance announcements you would have to distinguish clearly all of these events from the run-of-the-mill daily programming of family music and language courses.

2. As far as production for the radio is concerned, as mentioned above, it should be a secondary concern but it should be much intensified. One seldom hears of works by really noteworthy composers for your institution. There is no value in having their pieces played occasionally in concerts and using them occasionally as background music for radio plays. Their works must be performed *on principle* for their own significance and works must be commissioned by them exclusively for the radio. As for radio plays, Alfred Braun has indeed undertaken some interesting experiments.[4]

The acoustic novel attempted by Arnolt Bronnen must be tried out and such experiments must be continued by others as well.[5] For this only the best people should continue to be engaged. The great epic novelist Alfred Döblin lives on Frankfurter Allee 244 in Berlin. I can already tell you, however, that all these recommendations will come to naught because of the laughable, miserable honoraria paid by the 'Funkstunde' for such cultural purposes.[6] In contrast to the very respectable pay for actors and other speakers, the literary fees are so low that in the long run work intended exclusively for the radio will not be written. In time you will have to create a kind of repertoire, that is, you will have to perform pieces at certain regular intervals, say, annually.

3. You must build a studio. Without experiments it is simply not possible to assess fully your apparatuses or what is made for them.

4. Especially for my last two points it is absolutely necessary that you account publicly for the astronomical sums of money radio broadcasting takes in and show to the last penny how these public monies have been used.

[GBFA 21/215–17. *Berliner Börsen-Courier*, 25 December 1927. Under the title 'How can radio broadcasts become more artistic and topical?' Carl Hagemann, the director of the Berlin Broadcasting Studio, published a contribution under the title 'The Director Himself', followed by Brecht's piece. Brecht's recommendations here were not particularly original but rather shared the concerns of many left-liberal intellectuals involved in discussions about radio in the mid-1920s.]

Radio – An Antediluvian Invention?

I can remember how I heard about the radio for the first time. There were ironic newspaper accounts about a virtual radio hurricane that was in the process of devastating America. Nonetheless one had the impression that it was not just a craze but something really modern.

This impression evaporated very quickly as soon as it was possible to listen to radio here too. First of all, we wondered where these tonal productions were coming from. But this wonderment was soon replaced by another one: we were wondering what *kind* of offerings were coming to us from the spheres. It was a colossal triumph of technology at last to be able to make accessible to the entire world a Viennese waltz and a kitchen recipe. An ambush, so to speak.

A phenomenon of the century, but to what end? I recall an old story in which someone demonstrates to a Chinese man the superiority of Western culture. He asked: 'What do you have?' The answer: 'Railways, automobiles, telephones.' 'I am sorry to have to tell you,' the Chinese man responded politely, '*we* have forgotten those already.' As far as radio goes, I immediately had the frightful impression that it was an unbelievably ancient apparatus, long ago forgotten in the deluge.

We have an old custom of getting to the bottom of all things, even of the most shallow puddles, if nothing better is around. We consume an enormous quantity of things of which we can get to the bottom. And we have very few people who are prepared, under the circumstances, to take a step back. In fact, we usually let ourselves be led around by the nose for the sake of *possibilities*. These cities, which you now see rising around us, undoubtedly come as a surprise to the fully exhausted bourgeoisie, used up by its deeds and misdeeds. As long as the bourgeoisie holds them in its hands, they will continue to be uninhabitable. The bourgeoisie judges them only according to the opportunities it naturally can derive from them. Thus the enormous overrating of all things and systems which promise 'possibilities'. No one bothers with results. They just stick to the possibilities. The results of the radio are shameful, its possibilities are 'boundless'. Hence, the radio is a 'good thing'.

It is a very bad thing.

If I were to believe that this bourgeoisie would live for another hundred years, I would be convinced that it will drivel on about the tremendous 'possibilities' to be found, for example, in radio. Those who appreciate the radio do so because they see in it a possibility for which they can invent 'something'. They would be proven right at the moment when 'something' is invented for whose sake the radio – assuming it did not yet exist – would have to be invented.

In these cities every kind of artistic production begins when a man comes to the artist and says he has a hall. At this point the artist interrupts his work, which he has undertaken for another man who has told him that he has a megaphone. For the artist's calling is to find something which later can be used as an excuse for having created the hall and the megaphone without thinking. It is a demanding calling and an unhealthy production.

I strongly wish that after their invention of the radio the bourgeoisie would make a further invention that enables us to fix for all time what the radio communicates. Later generations would then have the opportunity to marvel how a certain caste was able to tell the whole planet what it had to say and at the same time how it enabled the planet to see that it had nothing to say.

A man who has something to say and finds no one to listen is in a bad way. Worse off are the listeners who can find no one with something to say to them.

[GBFA 21/217–18. Unpublished typescript from 1927.]

On Utilizations

1. The questions of how art can be utilized for the radio and how the radio can be utilized for art – two very different questions – must at some point be subordinated to the much more important question of how art and the radio can be utilized at all.

2. If we are right or are judged to be in the right, then this question will be answered in the following way: art and the radio must be put to pedagogical purposes.

3.

The possibility of implementing such a direct pedagogical utilization of art does not seem feasible today because the state has no interest in educating its youth about collectivism.

Art must intervene where the defect is to be found.

If seeing is not involved, it does not mean that one sees nothing, but equally that one sees an infinity of things, 'whatever you like'.

The effects would of course have to remain on the acoustic plane, but precisely this, that the lack of sight into . . .

[GBFA 21/219. Unfinished typescript from 1927; part 3 includes no text, while the last two sections are on a separate page and unnumbered.]

Explanations [about *The Flight of the Lindberghs*]

The Flight of the Lindberghs *not a means of pleasure but of instruction*
The Flight of the Lindberghs has no value if it does not train. It has no artistic value that would justify a performance not intended for this training. It is an *object of instruction* and falls into two parts. One part (songs of the elements, choruses, sounds of water and motors,

etc.) is meant to enable the exercise, that is, to introduce and interrupt it, which is best achieved by an apparatus. The other, *pedagogical* part (the Lindbergh role) is the text for the exercise: the participant listens to the one part and speaks the other part. In this way a collaboration develops between apparatus and participant in which accuracy is more important than expression. The participants speak and sing the text mechanically; they pause at the end of each line of verse; they read along mechanically as they listen to the text.

'In obedience to the principles: the state shall be rich, man shall be poor, the state shall be obliged to have many skills, man shall be permitted to have few, where music is concerned the state shall provide whatever requires special apparatuses and special skills, but the individual shall provide an exercise. Unchecked feelings aroused by music, special thoughts that may be conceived when listening to music, physical exhaustion that easily arises just from listening to music, these are all distractions from music. To avoid these distractions, the individual participates in the music, thus obeying the principle: doing is better than feeling, by following the printed music with his eyes and adding the passages and voices reserved for him, by singing to himself or in conjunction with others (school class).'

The radio not to be served but changed
The Flight of the Lindberghs is not intended to be of use to the present-day radio but to *change* it. The increasing concentration of mechanical means and the increasingly specialized education – trends that should be accelerated – call for a kind of *rebellion* by the listener, for his mobilization and redeployment as producer.

The Baden-Baden radio experiment
The utility of *The Flight of the Lindberghs* and the use of the radio in modified form was demonstrated at the Baden-Baden Music Festival in 1929. On the left side of the platform was the radio orchestra with its apparatuses and singers; on the right side with the score in front of him was the listener, who performed Lindbergh's role, i.e., the pedagogical part. He sang his part to the instrumental accompaniment supplied by the radio. He read the speaking sections without identifying his own feeling with that contained in the text, pausing at the end of each line of verse; in other words, in the spirit of an *exercise*. On the back wall of the platform was the theory being demonstrated in this way.[7]

Why can't The Flight of the Lindberghs *be used as an object of instruction and the radio be changed?*
This exercise helps to teach discipline, which is the basis of freedom. An individual will undoubtedly reach spontaneously for means to pleasure but not for an object of instruction that offers him neither profit nor social advantages. Such exercises only serve the individual in so far as they serve the state and they only serve a state that wishes to serve all people equally. Thus *The Flight of the Lindberghs* has no aesthetic and no revolutionary value independent of its application and only the state can organize this. Its proper application, however, makes it so 'revolutionary' that the present-day state has no interest in sponsoring such exercises.

Performance in a flawed concert application
The following example shows how the application determines the text: the figure of a public hero in *The Flight of the Lindberghs* might be employed to induce the listeners at a concert to empathize with the hero and thus cut themselves off from the masses. In a concert performance, i.e., a flawed one, at least the Lindbergh role must be sung by a chorus, if the sense of the whole is not to be completely ruined. Only *collective I-singing* (I am Charles Lindbergh, I am setting forth, I am not tired, etc.) can salvage something of the pedagogical effect.*

[GBFA 24/87–9. Text written in 1929 and signed by Brecht and Suhrkamp. It was first published in *Versuche* 1 (Berlin: Gustav Kiepenheuer Verlag, 1930), introduced with the phrase 'parts of a music theory'. Co-author Peter Suhrkamp was involved with school music and school operas at the time and worked with Brecht as well on *The Rise and Fall of the City of Mahagonny*, 1930).

Lindberghflug: Ein Hörspiel (*Lindberg's Flight: A Radio Play*) opened at the Festival for German Chamber Music in Baden-Baden on 27 July 1929. The final rehearsal was broadcast on the Silesian Radio Hour (Breslau) on 27 July, followed by broadcasts on stations in Frankfurt am Main (28 July) and Cologne (29 July). Ernst Hardt (Manager of Western German Radio Broadcasting in Cologne) directed the production, and Kurt Weill and Paul Hindemith composed the music, played by the Frankfurt Radio Orchestra. The radio play was developed as a report on the topical event of Charles Lindbergh's pioneer flight over the Atlantic Ocean in May 1927, documenting the event as the struggle of technology against nature (personified in the elements fog, snow and ice) and as the achievement of a collective rather than the triumph of an individual, heroic adventurer. Brecht conceived of the radio play at the festival with the speaker and the

*See *Versuche* 2, *The Mr Keuner Stories*, 'Suggestion, if the suggestion is not heeded' [the reference is to a Keuner story in the first volume of Brecht's *Versuche* (1930)]

listener (playing the role of Lindbergh) entering into a conversation for the radio audience. In other words, the fictional listeners were modelled as active participants by demonstrating how they should listen to the radio. He was not only thematizing the radio in a broadcast presentation but suggesting how the medium itself can transform social communication through its technological advantage: the ear is to become a voice.

Brecht revised the play for publication in 1930 and altered the title to *Der Flug der Lindberghs: Radiolehrstück*; for republication in 1950 he once again changed the title to *The Ocean Flight (Der Ozeanflug)* and the name of the character Lindbergh to the Flier owing to Charles Lindbergh's expressions of sympathy with National-Socialism.]

The Radio as a Communications Apparatus

Lecture on the Function of the Radio

Our social order is an anarchic one, if one can imagine an anarchy of orders, i.e., a mechanical and unconnected disarray of systems of public life that are themselves to a large extent already ordered. Our anarchic social order in this sense enables inventions to be made and further developed, which must then conquer their markets, justify their existence, in short, they are *inventions that have not been prescribed*. Thus there was a moment when technology was far enough advanced to bring forth the radio, while society was not far enough advanced to accept it. The public was not waiting for the radio, but rather the radio was waiting for the public. To characterize more precisely the situation of the radio: the raw materials were not waiting for methods of production based on public needs, but rather production methods were looking around anxiously for raw materials. *Suddenly there was the possibility to say everything to everyone, but upon reflection there was nothing to be said.* And who was everyone?

In the beginning one got by without thinking. One looked around where somewhere something was being said to someone and simply tried to butt in and compete by also saying something to someone. This was the radio in its first phase, as substitute: a substitute for theatre, opera, concerts, lectures, coffeehouse music, the local pages of the newspaper, etc.

From the beginning the radio imitated practically every existing institution that had anything at all to do with the distribution of speech or song. In this Tower of Babel cacophony and dissonance came forth that could not be ignored. In this acoustic department store it was possible to learn to breed chickens in English, accompanied by the strains of the 'Pilgrims' Chorus' and the lesson was cheap as tap water.[8] This was the gilded youth of our patient. I am not sure if it is finished yet but, if so, then this stripling, who needed no certificate of competence to be born, will have to start looking at least retrospectively for a *purpose in life*, just as a person will ask himself in more mature years, after he has lost his innocence, what he is actually doing in the world.

As for the radio's *purpose in life*, I don't think it can consist merely in prettifying public life. For that it has not only shown little aptitude, but unfortunately our public life as well shows little aptitude for being prettified. I am not against the idea of installing receivers in the refuges of the unemployed and in prisons (apparently someone thinks this will prolong cheaply the life expectancy of these institutions), but it cannot be the radio's main task to place receivers under the bridges as well, even if that represented an elegant gesture to provide those who wish to spend their nights there at least with the minimum, i.e., with a performance of the *Meistersinger*.[9] Tact is necessary. Nor is radio in my view an adequate means of bringing back cosiness into the home and making family life bearable again, whereby it might rightly remain an open question whether what it cannot accomplish is even desirable. But quite apart from its dubious function (he who brings much, brings no one anything) the radio is *one-sided* when it should be two-sided. It is only a distribution apparatus, it merely dispenses.

And now to say something positive, that is, to uncover the positive side of the radio with a suggestion for its re-functionalization: radio must be transformed from a distribution apparatus into a communications apparatus. The radio could be the finest possible communications apparatus in public life, a vast system of channels. That is, it could be so, if it understood how to receive as well as to transmit, how to let the listener speak as well as hear, how to bring him into a network instead of isolating him. Following this principle the radio should step out of the supply business and organize its listeners as suppliers. Hence, any attempt by the radio to give a truly public character to public occasions is absolutely positive. Our government needs the activity of the radio as much as our court system does. If government or justice resist such activity, they are afraid and suitable only for the times prior to the invention of the radio, if not even prior to the invention of gunpowder. I know as little as you about the obligations of the Chancellor. It is the radio's responsibility to explain them to me, but among the obligations of the state's highest official is the job of informing the nation regularly by means of the radio about his activities and their justification. The task of the radio does not end, however, with the transmission of these reports.

Beyond this it must organize the collection of reports, i.e., it must transform the reports of those who govern into answers to the questions of those governed. Radio must make exchange possible. It alone can organize the major discussions between business sectors and consumers about the norms for consumer goods, the debates about raising the price of bread, the disputes in municipalities.

Should you consider this utopian, then I ask you to reflect on the reasons why it is utopian.

Whatever the radio sets out to do, it must strive to combat the *lack of consequences* that makes almost all our public institutions so ridiculous.

We have a literature without consequences, which not only sets out to have no consequences itself, but also does all it can to neutralize its readers by depicting every object and situation stripped of their consequences. We have educational establishments without consequences, working frantically to provide an education which has no consequences at all and is itself the consequence of nothing. All our institutions that formulate ideology see their main task in maintaining *without consequences* the role of ideology, corresponding to a concept of culture in which the evolution of culture has already ended and culture needs no ongoing, creative effort. We will not examine here whose interests are served by having these institutions remain without consequences, but when a technical invention with such a natural aptitude for decisive social functions is met by such anxious efforts to maintain *without consequences* the most harmless entertainment possible, then the question unavoidably arises as to whether there is no possibility to confront the powers that exclude with an organization of the excluded. The slightest advance in this direction is bound to succeed far better than any event of a culinary kind. Any campaign with a clear consequence – that is, any campaign really aiming to intervene in reality, taking as its goal the transformation of reality, even if at the most modest points, for example, in the awarding of public construction contracts – any such campaign would secure the radio a quite different, incomparably deeper impact and endow it with a quite different social meaning from the current decorative attitude. As for the *technology* that needs to be developed for all such undertakings, it must work according to the principle that the audience is not only to *be instructed* but also must instruct.

The radio's formal task is to give these instructional under-takings a degree of interest, that is, to make the interests interesting. One part, especially the part oriented towards youth, can even assume an artistic form. The radio's attempt to give instruction an artistic form would support efforts on the part of modern artists to give art an instructive form.

I explained an example of such possible exercises that can use the radio as a communications apparatus at the Baden-Baden Music Week in 1929 with *The Flight of the Lindberghs*.[10] This is a model for a new application of your apparatuses. Another model would be *The Baden-Baden Lesson on Consent*.[11] Here the peda-gogical role that the 'listener' assumes is both that of the airplane crew *and* of the crowd. It communicates with the role of the trained chorus provided by the radio, of the clowns, of the announcer. I will limit myself deliberately to an explanation of the *principles* because the confusion in the aesthetic domain is not the cause of the unparalleled confusion about the functional principle but rather its mere consequence. The error – for some a very useful error – about the radio's actual function cannot be rectified by aesthetic insight. I could tell you, for example, that the application of theoretical insights about modern drama, i.e., about epic drama, could bring about extraordinarily fruitful results in the domain of the radio.

Nothing is less appropriate than the old opera, which aims at the production of an intoxicated condition because it hits upon the individual at the radio receiver and of all the alcoholic excesses none is more dangerous than solitary tippling.

The old drama with Shakespearean dramaturgy is also hardly usable for the radio because at the receiver the lone, isolated individual rather than the integrated crowd is encouraged to invest emotions, sympathy and hopes in intrigues whose only purpose is to give the dramatic individual an opportunity for self-expression.

Epic drama, with its episodic nature, its separation of the elements, that is, its separation of the image from the word and the words from the music, but especially its instructional attitude, would provide many practical tips for the radio. But a purely aesthetic application would lead to nothing more than a new fashion and we have enough old fashions! If the theatre were to capitulate to epic drama, to pedagogical, documentary representa-tion, then the radio could furnish a completely new form of propaganda for the theatre: real information, indispensable information. Such a commentary, closely allied to the theatre, an adequate, worthy complement to the play itself, could lead to completely new forms, etc. Furthermore, direct collaboration between theatrical and radio performances could be organized. The radio could send choruses to the theatres, just as it could transmit to the public from the meeting-like collective performances of the learning plays the decisions and productions of the audience, *etc.*

I won't develop this etc., deliberately not speaking about the *possibilities* of separating opera from drama and both from the radio play or of resolving similar aesthetic questions. I know that you probably expect it from me because you intend to market art by means of your apparatus. But in order to be marketable, art must today first be purchasable. And I preferred not to sell you something, but rather to formulate the fundamental suggestion that a communications apparatus for the general benefit of the public should be made out of the radio. This is an innovation, a suggestion that seems utopian and that I myself admit to be utopian. When I say the radio or the theatre could do so-and-so, I am aware that the large institutions cannot do all they could, not even all they want. They want us to supply, to renovate, to keep them alive through innovations.

But it is simply not our task to renovate the ideological institutions on the basis of the existing social order through innovations. Instead our innovations must get them to abandon this basis. So: for innovations, against renovation! *By means of constant, never-ending suggestions about better applications of the apparatuses in the interest of the many,* we must shake up the social basis of these apparatuses and discredit their application in the interest of the few.

These suggestions, unrealizable in this social order but realizable in another, are nothing more than the natural consequence of technological development and serve the propagation and formation of this *other* order.

[GBFA 21/552–7. Typescript written in summer 1932, partially published in extracts and together with other fragments from Brecht's 'Explanations' about *The Flight of the Lindberghs* (see above) in *Blätter des Hessischen Landestheaters* 16 (Darmstadt, July 1932): 181–4. The typescript has handwritten notations that indicate Brecht had prepared it for oral delivery, but there is no record of when or where.

By this point Brecht's ruminations on the broadcast medium had meshed with his reflections on experiments in other media. The analysis of his radio experiments sustained his conclusions about the functioning of cultural institutions in a class society. The indifference of bourgeois artists to the changing modes of production contradicted the increasing importance of technology for the maintenance and rationalization of capitalist society. His unsuccessful engagement in the filming of *The Threepenny Opera* provided the occasion to examine the implications of this attitude in another medium (see 'The *Threepenny* Lawsuit' in Part IV).]

PART III

Early Screenplays

(1921)

The Mystery of the Jamaica Bar

Film in six acts

[See GBFA 19/53–84. Written between February and early April 1921 (with the work interrupted to complete *The Jewel Eater*), this is the first of several major film script projects Brecht works on during this year in the hope of earning money and providing roles for Marianne Zoff. At first he collaborated with stage designer Caspar Neher, then sought help from the Munich critic, scriptwriter and film agent Werner Klette.

The complicated plot of disappearing party guests, constructed around a cumbersome, carousel-like set that allows the kidnappers to stage mysterious disappearances, reveals Brecht's interest in maximizing the cinematic possibilities by playing with motifs of appearance and reality and cross-dressing. The Munich Stuart Webbs Company produced numerous films with the detective Stuart Webbs in the early 1920s and obviously Brecht was aiming his screenplay at this series. The producer and main actor of the Stuart Webbs series rejected the screenplay, however, and it was never produced.]

Characters:
Paduk, gang leader
Hawk, gang member
Condor, gang member
Griffin, gang member
black servant boy
coat-check lady (Katy Smith)
Mrs Melvil
Mr Melvil
Gayo Perl, millionaire
Brown, coachman
second coachman
Mr Webbs, detective
two teenage girls
society ladies, policemen, servants, etc.

Act I

'The honourable Mr Paduk invites you to his reception at the Pier Plantation.'

Shot 1: *Vestibule.*
Half hidden behind a curtain 'Hawk' and Paduk watch a glass door and the stairs leading up to it. Couples and solitary gentlemen pass through the door; a black boy takes their coats. Paduk comments on certain charms of the female guests with slightly exaggerated gestures: a pretty foot, a deeply cut décolleté in back, swaying hips . . . A few times he mocks their flaws.

Shot 2: *Close-up of the voyeurs.*
Paduk rubs his hands. 'Hawk' pulls out his watch; 'Condor' and 'Griffin' join them, elegantly dressed in frock coats.

Shot 3: *Same as shot 1.*
Hawk leaves quickly through a winged door that the servant closes. Condor and Griffin exit at the side. Paduk enters behind his guests.

Shot 4: *Pier.*
Dark and slender with his collar turned up, Hawk walks on the moonlit, white pier.

Shot 5: *Reception hall.*
Paduk greets his guests too sincerely. *Dissolve.*
    'Meanwhile the overture began at the Opera . . .'

Shot 6: *Lobby for the box seats with the coat check.*
A grotesque old coat-check lady brings Mrs Melvil to her box seat in an overly obsequious manner. Then she waddles upstairs to the public telephone and calls. *Dissolve.*

Shot 7: *Dining-room.*
Paduk and his guests at the table. A black boy brings the table telephone. Paduk writes something quickly on his cuff, leaves quickly . . .

Shot 8: *At the Opera.*
On stage the ballet. Curtain closes, the auditorium is illuminated. Hawk, standing near the stage, scans the box seats.

Shot 9: *Close-up of the box.*
    'Mrs Melvil.'

Shot 10: *Close-up of Mrs Melvil.*
Nervously reads a note she removes from her handbag.

Note: 'Use the enclosed ticket to the Opera and you will learn where your husband spends his evenings . . .'

Shot 11: *Same as shot 9.*
Hawk enters, bows. Mrs Melvil stands up, follows him. The coat-check lady is waiting already with her coat. *Dissolve.*

Shot 12: *Plantation.*
Guests standing at the window. View to the water. Fireworks. An illuminated motorboat glides by. The ladies go into the garden, the gentlemen into the club rooms. At the head is Gayo Perl, the fat millionaire.

Shot 13: *Card room.*
Card tables. Wide windows with thick drapery. Gayo Perl holds the bank; the game begins . . . Vases shake.*

Shot 14: *Garden bench.*
The ladies climb into the motorboat. Short tour. Paduk watches, smiling ironically.

Shot 15: *Pier.*
Condor walks on the pier with a turned-up collar.

Shot 16: *Interior of a coach.*
   'Brown eating dinner.'
The coachman sits in the coach eating cheese and reading the newspaper. Hawk's elegant silhouette appears in the coach window. Brown is startled, packs up his things, crawls out. Mrs Melvil appears at the coach door.

Shot 17: *Motorboat.*
Black boy steers. Ladies tease him: a foolish game. *Dissolve.*

Shot 18: *Elegant hall.*
Condor has been gambling, stands up with a lady:
   'Would you like to join me in the Jamaica Bar . . . ?'

Shot 19: *Shore.*
Paduk waves broadly. The boat lands. Paduk:
   'I just noticed that the club rooms are empty. The gentlemen must have moved on to the next house.'

Shot 20: *Stairs.*
The ladies hurry eagerly up the stairs. They glance into the empty club rooms. Amused, the ladies feign comic horror. Paduk strikes his forehead and grins:

* First, gentle rotating of the revolving stage! See shot 19 for explanation.

'Perhaps a small, innocent orgy in the Jamaica Bar across the way . . . !'

The ladies storm Paduk with questions, who smiles cunningly. He motions to the boy, who precociously stands by, to keep silent and holds back the ladies, who try to coax the boy away with them. All exit except Paduk, who looks at his watch:

Watch face: Five minutes to eleven.

Shot 21: *Interior of a coach. Watch face:*
Five minutes to eleven. Mrs Melvil and Hawk inside; the city glides by nocturnally.

Shot 22: *Pier.*
The black boy leads the ladies, who are walking by threes, arm in arm.

Shot 23: *Interior of a coach.*
The Jamaica Bar's many lights appear in the window. The door is open, all windows lit up.

Shot 24: *Club room.*
Short scene of the inebriated gentlemen. Gayo Perl, completely sober, wins.

'Why in the devil do you always win, Perl?'

'Why in the devil do you always drink, gentlemen?'

Perl pulls a card from his cuff, throws it on the table, and pushes his winnings back to the centre. The gentlemen stare, Perl is amused. The gentlemen drink on. Laughing. *Dissolve.*

Shot 25: *In front of the bar.*
The coach halts. A dispute between Brown and Hawk.

'Come back and fetch us in an hour, coachman!'

Mrs Melvil taps impatiently with her foot, then goes with Hawk into the bar. The coach drives off.

Shot 26: *Entry to the empty club rooms.*
Paduk stands at the entry and pulls out his watch.

'Eleven o'clock.'

Shot 27: *Same as shot 25.*
A car drives up, Condor leads the woman into the bar.

Shot 28: *Club rooms.*
Vases shake, the gentlemen notice nothing, but Perl has noticed.

'Well, are the vases in this house drunk too? It already seemed as if an earthquake . . . '

Exaggerated playfulness: the gentlemen pour whiskey in his

mouth. Paduk enters, plays at being excited, motions the gentlemen out . . .

Shot 29: *Same as shot 25.*
The black boy and the ladies in front of the bar: the boy makes a deep bow, the ladies enter. *Dissolve.*

Shot 30: *Window with view of the lake.*
Parallel to shot 19: Paduk:
'The ladies have gone one house further . . .'
Drunk, the gentlemen look at the empty garden and the gently swaying motorboat. They exit to the garden, Paduk remains where he is.

Shot 31: *Lake.*
The gentlemen are looking for the ladies, one falls in the lake.

Shot 32: *Interior of the bar.*
The ladies look through the window: the road is still visible.

Shot 33:
'Three hours later'
Street. A coach is driving along the street. Arrives at the place where previously the bar was located. A wall is standing here between trees on the left side and water on the right. The coachman's growing dismay: *close-up.*
'So where's the damned bar?!'
Drives on slowly, searching.

Shot 34: *Plantation.*
Completely perplexed, the gentlemen take leave in a momentarily sobered state from the apparently uncomprehending Paduk, who extends his hand to each one individually.

Shot 35: *Winter garden at the plantation.*
Gayo Perl playing chess [with Paduk]: small in a large room. Later Hawk will join him.

Shot 36:
The gentlemen meet up with the coachman – melancholy parallel to shot 22, they interrogate him.
Dialogue:
'Have you seen six ladies, coachman?'
'Nah, but haven't you seen a bar?'
'You're already drunk, coachman!'

Shot 37: *Mr Webbs's morning outing.*
Newspaper boy. Webbs reads a newspaper while riding his horse.

Looks up suddenly: Mr Melvil has stepped in front of the horse. He speaks excitedly:

'My wife has been missing since yesterday evening, help me, Mr Webbs!'

Webbs points to the newspaper, where he reads:

Printed: . . . sensational disappearance of six society ladies . . .'

Webbs looks back and forth from Mr Melvil to the report. *Close-up* of Melvil's knees, which begin to tremble.

'Mr Melvil, I'll be expecting you in one hour at my house!'

Webbs gallops off. Mr Melvil continues to tremble. *Dissolve.*

End of Act I.

Act II

Shot 38: *Winter garden.*

Perl and Paduk are playing chess. Paduk feigns exhaustion, would like to be alone, looks at his watch, goes to the window . . . Perl doesn't let him out of sight. Hawk enters: surprised at Perl's presence. Chess game; Hawk watches stiffly and indignantly. Annoyed at Perl's obstinacy, in wild anger Paduk finally throws the chess board in the air with the tip of his foot. Hawk calms him over-zealously, Paduk grins with a forced excuse. Perl looks at Paduk – *close-up* – suspiciously and tensely. *Fade-out.*

Shot 39: *Fade-in. Bar.*

Morning in the – rotated! – bar. The drapes are closed. The six ladies conclude with their hair arrangements a rather primitive morning dress ritual, nonetheless worthy of a more elegant space. The bar is a grimy tavern decorated with a trashy velvet sofa. The black boy chases fleas in the corner. Movement when the door opens and the coat-check lady from shot 6 enters. She waddles in, mops the floor. Mrs Melvil is sitting apart, still sleeping on a velvet-covered stool. The ladies watch her warily. They storm the coat-check lady with questions, she threatens them grotesquely with her mop. One of the ladies jumps over the wet spot on the floor to the window, holding her dress up. She wants to look out. The coat-check lady and the boy adroitly prevent her, but the pail of water is overturned. The ladies storm over to the window. The boy and coat-check lady cannot hold them back from all the windows.

Shot 40: *Shot from the window of the pier and lake.*

Shot 41: *Same shot as 39.*

The woman clasp their heads.

'Where are we?'

Mrs Melvil is awakened by the noise, calmly joins them. *Dissolve.*

Shot 42: *The city.*

Webbs rides through the city to the plantation. At the wall he finds Brown the coachman, who is looking for the bar in front of it while his horse is grazing. The coachman, unsure because of his nocturnal adventure, addresses Webbs:

'Sir, I have to make a visit to the wall there . . . Could you please keep an eye on the coach for a minute . . .'

With great contempt Webbs climbs on the coach-box, apparently amused by the impertinence. The coachman marches over towards the pier, glances around occasionally, Webbs nods to him.

Shot 43: *Lobby of the winter garden.*

The black boy greets the coachman distrustfully.

'Is this place a wine bar, boy, or is it not?'

The boy exaggeratedly mimics Paduk: throws with one eye a sharp, distrustful glance towards Brown, marches out full of his own dignity. The coachman tosses an insult after him.

Shot 44: *Winter garden.*

Unannounced, the coachman enters behind the boy. Hawk, recognizing the coachman, disappears backwards. Perl toys around with the goldfish aquarium . . . Paduk watches Hawk with surprise, the coachman asks Paduk:

'Are you the innkeeper?'

Paduk shakes his head. The coachman says more impertinently:

'Hand over the woman or I'll call the police!'

Shot 45: *Interior of the coach.*

Webbs finds the note and the theatre ticket (cut briefly to the note from shot 10), puts both in his pocket. Looks at his watch. Ties . . .

Shot 46:

. . . the coach to the wall, *same as shot 42* – after climbing out he attaches a note to the whip, sticks the whip in the ground, harnesses his horse to the coach horse, and drives off in a rush.

Shot 47: *Same as shot 44.*

Paduk shows the coachman out with an imperious gesture, follows him.

Shot 48: *Pier.*

The coachman trots along in a straight line without looking round while Paduk talks to him in an exaggerated but friendly way with large gestures. They move into the distance.

Shot 49: *Same as shot 44.*
Perl moves dreamily around the winter garden. Discovers a door, ascends a circular staircase, encounters the coat-check lady, goes down a corridor with windows and suddenly halts to look outside with great interest. Hawk follows him, watching closely.

Shot 50: *Shot from above. Pier.*
Interrupted by laughing cramps, Paduk continues to talk to the coachman; then Brown discovers the whip stuck in the ground in place of the disappeared coach.

Shot 51: *Close-up of the whip with the note:*
    'Don't have any room at home for your coach, expect you at 34 Long Street. Webbs'

Shot 52: *From below, larger, same as shot 50: pier.*
Paduk turns serious. Paduk fixes the coachman briefly with his eyes, then deserts him, hurrying straight back to the plantation. Perplexed, worried, the coachman watches him, turns round, marches toward the city, scratching his head and turning the whip in his hand, discouraged.

Shot 53: *Staircase at 34 Long Street.*
Melvil rings and rings. *Dissolve.*

Shot 54: *Winter garden.*
Paduk enters in a rush, rings, the coat-check lady enters and says:
    'Quite relaxed now, the dove . . .'

Shot 55:
Paduk interrupts her, gives an order. Gayo Perl and Hawk come down the stairs from shot 49, Hawk and Paduk exchange looks. The coat-check lady brings Paduk his hat and cane. Paduk leaves with Perl.

Shot 56: *Theatre.*
Webbs drives up with the team of horses, disappears into the theatre entrance.

Shot 57: *Watchman's office.*
Webbs shows the note from shot 10. The watchman recognizes the handwriting, shows and compares the receipt book, points to an address.
    'Kitty Smith, box-seat usher, 7 Pier Street.'
Webbs thanks him, exits. The watchman shakes his head.

Shot 58: *34 Long Street.*
The coachman and Melvil ringing . . . Melvil sits down on the steps. Paduk arrives. Close-up of the three waiting for Webbs. The coachman is meek and plagued by his bad conscience, Melvil is reserved, reads his newspaper, Paduk is lost in thought. Then Paduk attempts without success to appear witty:
'Funny to find here a coachman without a coach, and at the theatre a coach without a coachman.
Mr Webbs, who lives here, seems to be a funny bird . . .'
The coachman stands up immediately while cursing. Paduk holds him back:
'Your address?'
The coachman screams it out and stumbles off. They wait. Perl appears as well. *Dissolve.*

Shot 59: *Bar.*
The sequestered women. The somewhat corpulent Condor treats the ladies very circumspectly, takes a mirror from his pocket, which one of the ladies uses first tentatively and then with great eagerness. The others are won over after Condor elegantly serves morning coffee. Mrs Melvil, who is the last to get the mirror, throws it angrily away. It breaks. Condor thanks her with an ironic bow.

Shot 60: *34 Long Street, the façade.*
Webbs drives up. Pats the horses. Enters the house, the stall boy unharnesses the riding horse.

Shot 61: *Webbs's workroom.*
A formal scene: Paduk introduces himself as the owner of the pier platform, Webbs introduces him to Mr Melvil, Perl introduces himself with a bow to Webbs. Conversation. Paduk leads.

Shot 62: *Close-up, split screen.*
In the left half shots 50/51 repeat quickly in small format. Paduk gesticulates wildly, Webb speaks: shot 46. Melvil listens silently and aghast, then follows quickly shot 44 with the intertitle, then Paduk says:
'I beg of you, Mr Webbs, please solve the disappearance of my guests by any means . . . My entire fortune is at your disposal! The coachman has already tried to blackmail me. The man looks harmless, but . . .'
Perl protests.
'The man has an honest face, Mr Webbs!'
Webbs laughs:
'The arguments speak against him, Mr Perl!'

Perl makes a disdainful gesture:
'An honest face is worth more than all the arguments in the world.'
They both smile at each other obligingly. *Fade-out.*

Shot 63: *Theatre square.*
The coachman searches, the coach is not there, he turns back desperately. A moving shot. He sees Long Street from afar, his coach halts, he runs there . . .

Shot 64: *Same as shot 62. Fade-in.*
Webbs speaks, stops suddenly, rushes to the window.

Shot 65: *From above.*
The coachman is just charging off.

Shot 66: *Same as shot 62.*
Paduk nods meaningfully to Webbs. Webbs reflects a moment and asks:
'Do you know the man's address?'
Paduk thinks a moment, shakes his head briskly, takes his leave:
'Then I can expect you at 9 Pier Street?'
Webbs looks at him more attentively for a second and accompanies him politely out the door; he returns, thinks to himself.
'7 Pier Street . . . 9 Pier Street.'

Shot 67: *Coin telephone on the street.*
Paduk is calling.
'You simply buy his house.'

Shot 68: *The coachman's apartment.*
A miserable house. The coachman is discouraged, lost in thought. A vision: alternately the wall . . . the bar . . . the wall . . . the bar.

Shot 69: *Winter garden.*
The police are searching the winter garden. Perl is directing them, the police are not very enthusiastic.

Shot 70: *Pier.*
The coat-check lady waddles along the pier.

Shot 71: *Same as shot 69.*
Paduk enters, looks at Perl hostilely, who introduces the men, Paduk with a cold, exaggerated gesture: 'Search to your hearts' content!'

Shot 72: *Pier.*
Encounter between the unsuccessful police who are leaving, with Perl at their head, and Webbs, who is just arriving. Handshakes.

Shoulder-shrugging in the first instance and Webb's laughter as he enters.

Shot 73: *Entry hall.*
Excited, Paduk greets Webbs.
'You see, now I am supposed to have stolen my own guests . . .'
Webbs calms him, looks around.

Shot 74: *Coachman's apartment. Same as shot 68.*
The coat-check lady enters, lively conversation. Brown shows her around apathetically, writes a note finally that says:
'I sell the house it costs eight thousan . . .'
The coat-check lady and he laugh slyly, she says:
'Much too cheap!'
Which the coachman then doubts. Webbs appears outside the window.

Shot 75: *A comfortable room.*
A lady and gentleman at breakfast. Among the morning mail a letter with handwriting similar to that on Mrs Melvil's note.
'Do you have weapons? Protect your wife. At five o'clock tomorrow climb into the coach at the theatre whose coachman is wearing a white carnation in his hat. Arm yourself as much as you can.'
The gentleman hides the letter, his wife exits, he watches after her, crumples the letter, smoothes it out again, and reads it once more, groaning.

Shot 76: *Same as shot 68.*
The coat-check lady waddles off pleased. Webbs climbs in through the window. Interrogates the startled coachman, who shakes his head, swallows, perspires. Webbs exits, smiling mockingly.

Shot 77: *On the roof of the plantation.*
Perl is smoking a water pipe under a huge umbrella. Giving in to a sudden idea, Paduk kicks the chess board and rushes off.

Shot 78: *Street.*
The coat-check lady waddles down the street. She is smiling broadly. The sun is shining. Webbs follows her, also pleased, he also suns himself . . .

Shot 79: *Theatre square.*
The coat-check lady negotiates with a coachman.
'Be here at five o'clock and drive the gentleman who climbs in to Road Fly. You must have a white carnation in your hat, so that he recognizes you.'

She runs off quickly. Webbs approaches the coachman. *Dissolve.*

Shot 80: *Same as shot 68.*
The sorrowful coachman. Paduk enters. Conversation. Paduk mockingly:
> 'Be at the platform at seven o'clock. Show me the bar that you are talking about.'

Shot 81: *Street in the direction of the plantation.*
Car. Inside, Webbs.

Shot 82: *Market hall.*
Perl follows the black boy, who is pulling a handcart. The coat-check lady goes in, buys with intense enjoyment geese and beef roasts, sausages and veal thighs, a lot of meat. The handcart can hardly hold all the food. Perl is pleased.
> 'Does that old, scrawny Paduk eat all that? He must have boarders!'

Shot 83: *Plantation.*
Webbs is greeted by Condor, masquerading as a house servant. Shows his identification, searches the plantation. The camera follows him around the winter garden (shot 35), full tour, Webbs on the wall, the wall ledge breaks off, Webbs falls in the water.

Shot 84: *In front of the wall.*
Returning, Paduk sees Webbs's car. Sees Webbs in the water. Fishes him out with Condor, handles him with great care, provides him with dry but, of course, much too tight clothing.

Shot 85: *In the countryside.*
Perl arrives at a farmhouse, negotiates with the farmer, pays.
> 'So what if it is only a shed – now I live right next to my friend Paduk.'

Perl exits. The farmer rubs his hands together.

Shot 86: *Same as shot 35.*
Paduk and Condor confer.
> 'They must leave the house, otherwise we'll be in trouble.'

Shot 87: *Bar.*
The black boy enters with the handcart full of vegetables. The ladies begin their feverish activities: peeling potatoes, cutting beans, cleaning asparagus, peeling carrots, etc. At times, however, a knife will lapse in a busy hand, then the yearning eyes focus on a distant point . . . *Dissolve.*

End of Act II.

Act III

Shot 88: *Webbs's apartment.*
He is gathering women's clothing from the cupboards and ties it together in a bundle. *Dissolve.*

Shot 89:
'Five o'clock.'
Theatre square.
Coachman with a white carnation in his hat on the coach-box of coach 1, waiting stoically. Coach 2 comes round the corner, coachman 1 becomes nervous: coachman 2 also has a white carnation in his hat. An angry dialogue, threatening cracks of the whips. Finally coachman 1 drives off cursing. Soon the gentleman from shot 75 enters, climbs in coach 2, which drives off.

Shot 90: *In front of the shed (across from the plantation).*
A delivery car stops. Perl and a servant (in work clothes) unload a huge number of books.

Shot 91: *Interior of the shed.*
Both of them hand books through the window and pile up the entirety of knowledge so hastily in the tiny, narrow room that everything gets mixed up.

Shot 92: *Country road.*
Coach with the gentleman from shot 89 drives along. The gentleman looks out.

Shot 93: *Winter garden.*
The coat-check lady gives Paduk the coachman's note, which is inserted very briefly. The police are again there. Paduk shows the note to the gentlemen.
'The man wants to come at seven.'
One of the gentlemen nods 'aha', Condor (dressed as a servant) approaches, the other police officer laughs:
'He is fetching the ransom for holding his trap.'
Condor rolls up his sleeves threateningly.

Shot 94: *Bar.*
The ladies are bored. Chase flies. Mrs Melvil taps the walls while the others laugh at her.

Shot 95: *Small room.*
Condor changes his clothes: the servant becomes a cavalier.

Shot 96: *Bar.*
Condor as cavalier sails in, bows to the ladies, who have already become friendlier, a short round of roulette. Gaming. Condor exits. Mrs Melvil opens a low, secret door while no one is observing her and sneaks out, unnoticed.

Shot 97: *Room as in shot 75.*
A lady sewing in front of a sewing basket. A maid lets in the curtsying coat-check lady. The lady is surprised, somewhat disgusted.
> 'Your husband has left? You don't know where. You will find out at the Opera. You are an unfortunate woman.'

The lady's anxiety. She nods to the coat-check lady to wait, exits.

Shot 98: *In front of a rural inn.*
Coach from shot 89 halts.

Shot 99: *Interior of the coach.*
The gentleman cocks his pistol.

Shot 100: *Same as shot 98.*
The gentleman descends. The coachman remains sitting in his box. The gentleman looks up quizzically:
> 'What now?'

The coachman's surprise. Conversation. The gentleman angrily pulls his pistol. The coachman as well; he removes his beard with the words:
> 'Allow me to remove my beard.'

To the gentleman's surprise, it is Webbs. With consternation the gentleman gives him the letter. Webbs reads, laughs, takes the gentleman by the arm, looks at his watch, jumps on the box, drives away at full speed. The gentleman remains standing there . . .

Shot 101: *Same as shot 97.*
The lady puts on her coat, the coat-check lady wants to help her, the lady coolly moves back. *Dissolve.*

Shot 102: *Forest.*
On the way to the city Webbs glues back his beard while riding at full speed.

Shot 103: *City. House front.*
The lady leaves the house with the coat-check lady, Webbs and the coach are just coming round the corner. The coat-check lady waves, he halts, both climb in. Sitting straight and seriously on the coach-box, Webbs drives off.

Shot 104: *Same as shot 68.*
The coachman holds a lamp to the clock.
  'Half past six.'
Puts on his hat and leaves.

Shot 105:
  'Evening reception.'
Room in shed.
Perl has arranged things more or less comfortably. Greets friends who look for seats in vain. They climb on the bookshelves. Standing at the window, Perl throws an oblique glance now and again at their sometimes unsuccessful climbing talents.

Shot 106: *Winter garden.*
Paduk once again greets the police. The gentlemen walk over to the . . .

Shot 107: *Pier.*
. . . wall side of the pier and hide in the bushes.

Shot 108: *Small ballroom.*
Dancing course. Griffin is stuffing pralines into the mouths of two teenage girls. They push their way to the door, giggling.

Shot 109: *Street at the pier.*
The coachman is walking along. He weaves somewhat.

Shot 110: *Theatre square.*
Webbs drives the coach up. The lady descends from the coach with the coat-check lady. The lady pays, the coat-check lady rushes ahead. Webbs:
  'Be careful! Your mistrust towards your husband will get you in trouble. When you are picked up, go first into the salon.'
The lady nods. Webbs climbs into the coach, draws the curtain.

Shot 111: *Box as in Act I.*
The coat-check lady curtsies and lets the lady enter. Hawk approaches the lady. *Dissolve.*

Shot 112: *Interior of the coach.*
Webbs changes his clothes: women's clothing.

Shot 113: *Plantation.*
Narrow hallway. Mrs Melvil walks along, touches and taps the walls. Then she climbs up a ladder leaning against the wall.

Shot 114: *In front of the wall.*
The coachman stumbles around. He has been drinking. From the

bushes the beam of a flashlight catches him, policemen approach, he is arrested. Perl emerges from a bush at the side. Paduk looks at him quizzically, he answers:

'From this evening on we are neighbours, Mr Paduk!'

The unimpressed Paduk plays along:

'Enchanted.'

Short interrogation of the coachman, who speaks in his drunken state with large gestures. It is clear what he is saying . . .

Shot 115:

. . . the moving wall, the bar, everything like visions in a fog . . .

Shot 116: *Same as shot 114.*

Paduk shakes the hand of the police commander; the police take the coachman with them. Perl wants to stop them:

'He's not lying, he has an honest face.'

The men laugh loudly. Perl is insulted. *Dissolve.*

Shot 117: *Theatre. The salon in half-light.*

The lady on the arm of the elegant Hawk.

'May I quickly have our coats brought?'

Hawk exits. Webbs (dressed as a woman, now Mrs Webbs) enters.

'Go home immediately. Your husband is waiting for you with great longing.'

The lady nods, backs away. Webbs lets himself be helped into the coat of the lady by the returning Hawk.

Shot 118: *In front of the theatre.*

Mrs Webbs lets Hawk accompany her to a coach.

Shot 119: *Perl's room in the shed.*

Crowded with friends, drinking liqueurs. Perl, always at the window observing, explains.

'The coachman is an honourable man.'

Laughter. *Dissolve.*

Shot 120: *Dancing club.*

Griffin with the teenagers, his finger on his mouth.

'Really a wonderful bakery. Whipped cream and liqueur. But the gentlemen should not notice a thing.'

Whispers. Agreement.

Shot 121: *Interior of the coach.*

Mrs Webbs sitting stiffly next to Hawk in the coach.

Shot 122: *A square.*

The teenagers wait under a lantern. Griffin arrives with two cars, loads them in, drives off.

Shot 123:
'The theoretician.'
Room in the shed, same as shot 119.
Perl lectures.
'Simply observe, my dears, nothing but sharp observation . . .'
They tease him, pull him away from the window, he resists.

Shot 124:
'The practitioner.'
Interior of the coach. Framed in the window: façade of the bar.

Shot 125: *In front of the bar.*
Mrs Webbs climbs out, enters the bar with Hawk.

Shot 126: *Small room, same as shot 95.*
Condor changes his clothes, becomes the cavalier.

Shot 127: *Interior of the bar (side room).*
Webbs is immediately bound and carried to the corner.

Shot 128: *In front of the bar.*
Griffin's two cars arrive with the teenagers. Giggling they enter the
bar. *Dissolve.*

Shot 129: *Room in the shed.*
Perl detaches himself from his friends, runs to the window, the
friends follow him. They see . . .

Shot 130:
. . . the plantation wall. *Dissolve.*

End of Act III.

Act IV

Shot 131: *Plantation. Low roof.*
Mrs Melvil clambers out of a roof window and looks around
observantly.

Shot 132: *Room in the shed.*
The friends, clearly showing the effects of the ample liqueur, are
taking leave. Perl shows them out and returns to his observation
point. He sees:

Shot 133: *Same as shot 131.*
Mrs Melvil on the roof, waving with her long veil.

Shot 134: *Small room in the plantation.*
Paduk and Condor spy through a peephole in the wallpaper.
  'Who is the long bean pole? – A true cavalryman.'

Shot 135: *Bar.*
The ladies and the teenagers are pressed closely together, the latter
still bound, like Mrs Webbs too, who towers over all of them by a
head. Griffin's pralines don't quite work any longer . . .

Shot 136: *Same as shot 134.*
Paduk makes a gesture to 'throw someone out', but Condor calms
him. Hawk enters hastily, reports something. Paduk exits quickly.

Shot 137: *Winter garden.*
Perl is waiting, tells Paduk gently when he enters:
  'A lady is sitting on your roof, Mr Paduk, and is waving and
  screaming!'
Paduk is startled, controls himself, and smiles weakly. Hurries out,
brings Perl the wrong hat, in order to keep him there, then presses
him to sit down . . .

Shot 138: *Hallways.*
Hawk hurries through.

Shot 139: *Same as shot 131.*
Hawk sticks his head out of a roof window. Conversation with Mrs
Melvil.

Shot 140: *Small room.*
Hawk hurries in, hollers through the peephole.

Shot 141: *Bar.*
Griffin listens, exits. Mrs Webbs breaks a mirror and rubs the ropes
with fragments of glass.

Shot 142: *Roof.*
Hawk climbs out, chases Mrs Melvil, who escapes but then falls
into the water from the pier.

Shot 143: *Same as shot 107, the pier.*
Condor and Griffin fish Mrs Melvil out. They bind her and pull her
into the bushes.

Shot 144: *Winter garden.*
Tired of the delays in shot 137, Perl puts a hat on Paduk and
accompanies him out. They see . . .

Shot 145:
. . . the empty roof.

Shot 146: *Pier.*
Paduk shakes his head angrily, Perl unbelievingly.
  'Do you often suffer from these hallucinations, Mr Perl?'

Shot 147: *Bar.*
The young girls, released by Webbs, comb their hair. Webbs, gathering up his skirts, leaves the room through the low, hidden door.

Shot 148: *Same as shot 1.*
Paduk alone, musing. Then Griffin enters from the club rooms. They look at one another silently. Gambling. Condor and Griffin bring the wet and bound Mrs Melvil. The coat-check lady, waddling more quickly than usual, hurries in, cries out what must be a warning, for Condor and Griffin pull Mrs Melvil hastily away. The police enter. *Dissolve.*

Shot 149: *Bar.*
A lady sneaks behind Webbs through the hidden door. The coat-check lady enters, the ladies hide the door like a flock of hens.

Shot 150: *Winter garden.*
Paduk, leading the police, gesticulates:
  'The only person who lives in the area is a certain Perl . . .'

Shot 151: *Hallway, leading downwards.*
The lady traverses it, finds herself in a small

Shot 152: *cellar room.*
Its door closes automatically behind her. Rats are crawling on the floor, sniff at her; she pulls her skirts together, jumps with a scream on a bed. *Dissolve.*

Shot 153: *Winter garden.*
Paduk is becoming nervous, the police listen. Someone bends down to the floor.
  'Didn't someone scream there?'
Paduk smiles weakly, shakes his head slowly.

Shot 154: *Bar.*
The coat-check lady listens, rushes through the hidden door, leaving behind terrified faces.

Shot 155: *Cellar room, same as shot 152.*
With astonishing speed and grotesqueness the coat-check lady masters simultaneously the rats and the screaming lady. She leads her out while holding her mouth closed.

Shot 156: *Winter garden.*
The police are still listening. In vain. Paduk shows the men out.

Shot 157: *Room in the shed.*
Perl at his post at the window, tired. There is a knock, the door opens. Police. Perl is arrested, handcuffs.

Shot 158: *Small room.*
Paduk, the Paduk gang. Animated discussion. Paduk:
'I'd have to have too many people arrested. The whole bunch must be gotten rid of.'

Shot 159: *In front of the shed.*
A police car stops. Policeman load the bound, fat Perl.

Shot 160: *Roof.*
Webbs's head emerges from the roof window. Looks around. He sees:

Shot 161: *From above. The pier.*
Condor and Griffin start up the motorboat.

Shot 162: *From above. The shed, from afar.*
The police car drives off.

Shot 163: *From above. In front of the plantation.*
The women are loaded into a zoo cage on wheels. Condor directs the loading of the cage with a rifle, assisted by the coat-check lady. The cage on wheels rolls on its own from the hill down to the beach.

Shot 164: *Close-up, concave mirror shot.*
Webbs's face becomes longer and longer.
'And from the roof with sly and cunning
Looks Mr Webb, half-man, half-woman.'

Shot 165: *Beach.*
The cage on wheels stops, the women are loaded into the motorboat.

Shot 166: *Same as shot 160.*
Webbs sets the wig straight, climbs desperately out of the window on to the roof, getting caught up in his skirts.

Shot 167: *On board the motorboat.*
Condor and the women look up at the roof in horror.

Shot 168: *Roof.*
Mrs Webbs's giant hulk. Waves violently with her white scarf.

'By God, there is another one who wants to come along!'

Shot 169:
The motorboat turns around, docks. The coat-check lady goes back to the plantation.

Shot 170: *Beach.*
Hawk and Griffin lead the weakly resisting Mrs Webbs to the arms of the coat-check lady.

Shot 171:
The motorboat taking off. Mrs Webbs towers over the other women by a head and a half. Day breaks.

End of Act IV.

Act V

Shot 172:
'It is dawn.'
Motorboat, the interior of the tiny cabin.
Through the window one sees the boat is moving. The kidnapped women, pressed together, are wringing their hands, Mrs Webbs wrings her hands as well.

Shot 173: *Same as shot 172, but shot from inside.*
Consultation. Webbs:
'We can't get out, so we must turn back.'
Condor is piloting; while he looks away for a moment and the women look at Webbs with astonishment and expectation, he throws a mirror against the boat's back wall; Condor jumps to the spot, from where he cannot see into the cabin. Webbs grabs an anchor and slams it quickly and violently against the flooring. Condor rushes in, Mrs Webbs points to the hole in the floor through which water is already leaking.

Shot 174: *Hallway at the plantation.*
Paduk watches through a window the boat moving away.
'Thank God, they are safe.'
Suddenly he is shocked because he sees . . .

Shot 175: *Water.*
. . . the boat is turning around.

Shot 176: *Boat.*
It fills quickly with water; the women surround Mrs Webbs, once

again wringing their hands. Condor gets the situation under control:

'Don't scream so god-awfully! You will all be rescued!'

Webbs agrees and points straight ahead:

Shot 177: *Front of the plantation.*
Very small above the surface of the water, but growing quickly.

Shot 178: *Look-out at the plantation.*
Paduk's observation is interrupted by the coat-check lady, who waddles in. He hurries out with her, she points through a window.

Shot 179: *The beach, from above.*
Paduk sees from the window in the wall that the husbands of the kidnapped women from Act I are marching towards the plantation. He leaves with the small whistle in his mouth.

Shot 180: *Motorboat is sinking.*
Condor pulls off his jacket, the ladies are fighting for the only life-belt.

Shot 181: *Harbour pier, from below.*
Paduk greets the gentlemen with compliments, guides them somewhat hastily into the house, enters last himself, looking back at the water. He just catches a glance of

Shot 182: *The motorboat landing.*
Griffin and Condor, pulling their revolvers, force the women into the cage on wheels.

Shot 183: *Winter garden.*
Paduk guides his guests in. Gambling.

Shot 184: *Interior of the cage.*
Mrs Webbs whispers to Mrs Melvil:

'Wait for me on the roof.'

She nods. In front of the cage's bars the three 'birds' are negotiating excitedly. Condor points to Mrs Webbs, who is fished out somewhat more impolitely than usual.

Shot 185: *Winter garden.*
The gentlemen want to leave. Paduk tries to stop them, sweating profusely. The black boy brings in huge trays with liqueurs. They push their way out.

Shot 186: *A club room.*
Mrs Webbs is being bound, rolled in a white sheet and tied to a board.

Shot 187: *In the front room.*
The gentlemen at the windows, where Paduk does not wish them
to be.
'What kind of wild animal cage is that, Paduky? Do you have
such large animals at the plantation?'
Paduk makes a face, trying to smile. He goes with the gentlemen –
the camera travels along – through the hallway into the club room
of Act I.

Shot 188: *Beach.*
With great effort the 'birds' push the wheeled cage up the beach.
The coat-check lady at the shaft of the cage succeeds in steering
with abundant comical effects.

Shot 189: *Club room, same as shot 187.*
The gentlemen lose patience and demand to be let out. Paduk
backs off through the glass door, outside a heavy drape falls down
and conceals him. The gentlemen tear away the window drapery
and see a smooth, white wall . . . Ceiling lights are turned on by an
invisible hand. The gentlemen look at each other. *Dissolve.*

Shot 190: *Entry hall.*
Paduk gives instructions to the 'birds', who are just dragging in the
women.

Shot 191: *Club room 2, same as shot 186.*
Mrs Webbs unwinds herself from the linen sheet and ropes.
Takes off her woman's clothing, is now Mr Webbs again, bundles
up the clothes, goes to the window, passes through the glass
door.

Shot 192: *Police headquarters.*
Perl is being interrogated. He describes what he saw; vision of shot
133. The police laugh.
'Fraud, my good man! You are the suspect, not Mr Paduk!'
Perl is led out.

Shot 193: *Hallway.*
Paduk sees with a shock that Mr Webbs is approaching him slowly
from behind.
'Ah, Mr Paduk, could you accompany me to the exit! You can
really get lost here!'
Worried, Paduk leads him first to wall-hangings, but Webbs smiles
and pushes him on. Paduk looks through a window.

Shot 194: *From above, the small entry.*
The last women are being brought in by the 'birds'. The coat-check

lady is sitting on the wheeled cage and directs it down to the boat storage.

Shot 195: *Docking point.*
Relieved, Paduk leads Webbs out. Webbs examines the boat, points to the leak.
'May I help you a bit with the repair?'
Paduk thanks him but shakes his head energetically. Webbs takes his leave, the bundle under his arm. He leaves slowly, smiling. Close-up of Paduk: hate, mistrust, satisfaction:
'Thank God, I have got rid of him!'

Shot 196: *Bar.*
The women are being pushed as quickly as possible into the bar. Hidden behind a group of them, Mrs Melvil immediately crawls through the hidden door.

Shot 197: *Pier.*
Webbs strolls over to the pier, smoking.

Shot 198: *Same as shot 196.*
The coat-check lady pushes her way through the women, locks with a murderously large key the hidden door. A smile lightens up several of the women's tear-stained faces.

Shot 199:
Mrs Melvil climbs out of the roof window. Waves.

Shot 200: *Pier.*
Webbs looks around, goes to the water, wades, swims over to the wall. Between the wall and the water a willow is growing on a narrow piece of earth. Webbs climbs it and pushes himself up to the roof where Mrs Melvil is waiting. He changes clothes with Mrs Melvil, exactly as follows: Webbs steps behind the chimney, Mrs Melvil crawls into the fireplace. The clothes fly in and out from the top of the chimney, then Mrs Melvil steps out disguised as Webbs and greets with great seriousness Mrs Webbs.

Shot 201: *Small room.*
Paduk, the 'birds'. Rapid scene: consultation.
'As soon as the boat is clear, we'll beat it. The plantation will blow up . . .'
The 'birds' exit quickly. Paduk alone, grins desperately, pockets a revolver.

Shot 202: *Split screen:*
on the left Webbs – dressed again as Mrs Webbs – climbs as a lady

back through the roof window, same as shot 199; on the right, clothed as a man, Mrs Melvil jumps into the water and swims to the pier.

Shot 203:
'That evening.'
The boathouse, interior.
The 'birds' repair the boat completely. Exit. The cage on wheels opens, Mrs Webbs slips out gracefully. Seems not to take things so tragically any longer and with pleasure drives another hole through the boat with the anchor.

Shot 204: *Beach.*
The 'birds' are walking up to the house immersed in a lively conversation.

Shot 205: *Shed.*
Perl's friends arrive, speak with the guard posted there, learn of Perl's arrest, laugh uncontrollably.
'Arrested?'

Shot 206: *Pier.*
Mr Melvil crosses the pier.

Shot 207: *Club room 2, same as shot 186.*
Paduk enters, does not see Mrs Webbs, is startled, goes to the window, sees from above:

Shot 208: *Same as shot 204.*
Mrs Webbs comes up the beach.

Shot 209: *Hallway.*
Paduk comes running, meets up with the 'birds', pushes them, runs on, they follow.

Shot 210: *Beach.*
Webbs sees the four of them coming from the plantation running towards him, turns round, goes to the right. Chase in the evening dusk. Back to the boathouse, they follow, Webbs jumps in the water, wades, swims. Hawk and Condor follow. He arrives at the same place seen in shot 200, climbs the tree, jumps on to the roof, which Hawk and Condor do not see because they are swimming more slowly. They climb up on the pier:
'She couldn't have gone into the plantation!'
Consultation:
'She wouldn't dare!'
They stand on the pier, perplexed. *Dissolve.*

Shot 211: *Beach.*
Paduk shakes Griffin by the shoulders, who plucks at his beard while musing.
'I am sick and tired! Away with them! I'd rather guard a sack of fleas than half a dozen women!'
They walk away.

Shot 212:
Mrs Melvil in Webbs' clothes walks along the wall toward the city. *Dissolve.*

End of Act V.

Act VI

Shot 213: *Club room 1.*
The gentlemen are investigating the floor, walls and ceiling, kneeling, crawling, climbing on each other's shoulders.

Shot 214: *Boathouse.*
The 'birds' want to float the boat, they see the leak, go back to work cursing.

Shot 215: *A narrow shaft.*
Following a complicated system of cables that she does not touch, Mrs Webbs lowers herself on a rope.

Shot 216: *Police headquarters.*
Mrs Melvil enters in Webbs's clothes. Explains the situation quickly.
'Webbs says that you are to land a police boat at the water's edge.'
The police chief leaves with Mrs Melvil. Perl enters, led in by a policeman. He has been released! Looks around in amazement, slowly exits, lost in thought.

Shot 217: *Same as shot 205.*
Perl's friends drinking liqueurs with the guards, a car drives up. Perl enters breathing heavily. They surround him, he shakes them off, goes stiffly to the window, takes up his position there, looks straight ahead out the window.

Shot 218: *Wooden tunnels (travelling camera!).*
Dressed in Mrs Melvil's torn evening dress, Webbs crawls through, hops over rolls of cable, comes to the control room.

Shot 219: *Beach.*
The coat-check lady and Condor are pulling the wheeled cage up the beach again.

Shot 220: *In front of police headquarters.*
A police car leaves. Mrs Melvil is seated next to the driver.

Shot 221: *Travelling shot: bar, hallways, winter garden.*
The coat-check lady and Condor lead the girls out of the bar into the winter garden. Suddenly there are too many: some of them remain in the bar. Paduk joins those in the winter garden. The following is seen through a mirror:

Shot 222: *Same as shot 218.*
Webbs sees Paduk with the girls through a telescopic mirror. He pushes various levers.

Shot 223: *Boathouse beach.*
The 'birds' leave the boathouse, carefully lock the door and hurry to the plantation.

Shot 224: *Plantation wall.*
The police car drives up. Police go to the pier. Mrs Melvil is not with them!

Shot 225: *Club room 2, same as shot 186.*
The gentlemen break the window panes, find only white walls, are shocked, begin to fight with each other.

Shot 226: *City pier.*
A police boat takes off. Next to the pilot stands Mrs Melvil, in woman's clothes.

Shot 227: *Telescopic mirror.*
Webbs sees, as in shot 222, the 'birds' enter the winter garden. They wave; like a school class the troupe of girls begins to move together with the coat-check lady. Webbs smiles calmly, moves a large lever. *Dissolve.*

Shot 228: *Shed.*
Perl at the window starts, looks more closely, waves his friends over. Through the window:

Shot 229: *Framed in the window.*
The bar, rotating gently, appears. The illuminated windows pass by and disappear, punctually like the blinking light of a lighthouse. It is a majestic view.

Shot 230: *Water.*
The police boat shoots through the evening dusk.

Shot 231: *Winter garden (directly)*.
Paduk suddenly stops in his tracks, then the 'birds' too. They grasp their heads, stand motionless. *Dissolve.*

Shot 232: *Club room 1.*
With shock the men watch the wall move away, a view of the front room from shot 1 appears and then passes by.

Shot 233: *The front of the plantation.*
Police push their way in, and, reaching the entry hall, they see how . . .

Shot 234:
. . . the illuminated club room glides by.

Shot 235: *Telescopic mirror, same as shot 222.*
Webbs watches the pillars of salt in the winter garden. Laughs.

Shot 236: *Winter garden (directly)*.
The ladies scream. Paduk rushes to the door. The 'birds' follow. 'The devil take it! That's Webbs! We'll never get out!'

Shot 237: *Shed.*
Perl runs out without his hat.

Shot 238: *View from the shed window.*
The plantation carousel turns faster. (Possibly from this point on instead of a slowly turning trick shot, a model that also shows the roof construction of the plantation!)

Shot 239: *Beach.*
The police boat docks. The police run to the plantation.

Shot 240: *Hallways.*
Everything is shaking, trembling, pictures are swinging on the walls, fall off. The Paduk gang and Paduk himself stumble through the hallways.

Shot 241: *Hallway between the front room and the carousel.*
The police bump into each other.
   'We can't go in as long as the carousel turns like this!'
They see:

Shot 242:
Behind the flying windows the Paduk gang runs by. *Close-up* – their pale faces stare straight ahead.

Shot 243: *Hallways.*
Paduk and his gang rush through.

Shot 244: *Roof rim of the bar.*
Wall ledge; the Paduk gang balances along it.

Shot 245: *Deep in the tunnel.*
Webbs is thinking to himself:
'Have the police arrived yet? This little carousel of mine is running damned fast by now!'

Shot 246: *Street in front of the plantation.*
Perl runs in. He sees: the bar with the women sails by, club room 1 with the men sails by. He is startled when he suddenly feels a heavy hand on his shoulder: coachman Brown is standing behind him. *Dissolve.*

Shot 247: *Deep in the tunnel, same as shot 245.*
Yellow clouds of smoke are rising from the machines.
'The ball-bearings are overheating!!'
Webbs grasps at his collar, he works the levers, he is frightened.

Shot 248: *Small room.*
Paduk is working feverishly at the control panel. It doesn't work! His face is distorted.

Shot 249: *Hallway between the club room and the front room.*
Perl meets up with the police, confers and leaves with a small troop.

Shot 250: *Deep in the tunnel.*
Surrounded by yellow clouds, Webbs works like a possessed man at the levers.

Shot 251: *Trick shot.*
Short circuit! The fuses blow in the control room, the spark travels along the cables, sparks fly from everywhere, there is crackling throughout the plantation.

Shot 252: *View from the shed.*
The carousel turns more slowly.

Shot 253: *Street.*
Perl with the police. They see how the carousel slowly stops. They hide in the bushes.

Shot 254: *Hallway.*
The police. The carousel has stopped!

Shot 255: *Club room 1.*
The gentlemen, some frozen by fear in their club chairs, some gesticulating excitedly, crawl out the broken windows as the police at the same time push their way in.

Shot 256:
Webbs in the control room, almost suffocated.

Shot 257: *Hallways. Bar.*
The Paduk gang runs through; they are caught by the police as they go outside. The women crawl after them out of the bar.

Shot 258: *Winter garden.*
As they exit, the women meet up with Mrs Melvil, who enters at the head of the policemen. They explain something to her, gesturing wildly:
'Webbs is in danger!'

Shot 259: *Plantation.*
Begins to fill up with smoke. Wild search of the rooms for Webbs. The women compete with the police, that is, they get in the way.

Shot 260: *Deep in the tunnel.*
Webbs climbs up a ladder, half unconscious he keeps falling back.

Shot 261: *Side wing of the plantation.*
Begins to smoke threateningly. The police boat sprays thick, short streams that naturally do not reach.

Shot 262: *At the bottom of the shaft.*
Fighting for air, Webbs is showered with water by the women from above, then pulled up by a rope.
'The women rescue their rescuer.'

Shot 263: *Winter garden.*
The men and women sink into each other's arms with laughter and weeping. With a bright and a tearful eye they examine their more or less ruined evening clothes. In the centre of the confusion Webbs, the most ragged of all in the torn, dripping gown borrowed from Mrs Melvil, shakes each of his female rescuers' hands while half choking and coughing. The fat Perl comes towards him, pulling coachman Brown with him, and says:
'An honest face is worth more than all the arguments in the world!'
Brown grins.

Shot 264: *Beach.*
The cage on wheels rolls down, above the policemen, with the worthy Mr Paduk and his 'birds' inside. Behind, however, led by the largest policeman, the melancholy black boy trots along and the coat-check lady waddles after, completely disconcerted.

The end.

78

The Jewel Eater

[See GBFA 19/84–105. Written in mid-March 1921, when work on another screenplay, *The Mystery of the Jamaica Bar*, was interrupted, this is the first screenplay completed by Brecht. He probably borrowed the motif of the swallowed jewel from Friedrich Hebbel's comedy *The Diamond* (1841), enriched by set pieces from adventure and gangster genre films of the early 1920s. The screenplay was never produced.]

Characters:
Stick, the orange seller
Anna, his girlfriend
Fatty, her brother
the innkeeper
Flophouse Fritz
Sticky Fingers Herman
Buttercup
Jezebel, an old slut
the young gentleman
the lady
the police commissioner
the over-dressed woman
police and hotel guests

The 'Crocodile' flophouse is an old, worm-eaten, wooden building located on the canal of a harbour town. It has no wallpaper inside, its hallways are narrow, slanting, uneven and crooked, and there is almost nothing in the rooms except a table and a chair. The vermin–wicked and coarse lads, rather crude and lazy – have their fun with devilish seriousness. Nothing especially unusual happens the night this story takes place – the brutal, disgusting joke of a sot – there is no trace of exceptional horror. This is precisely the story's uncanniness.

The introduction of the main characters as a prologue

1. In front of a white-washed wall: Orange Stick, motionless, with oranges on a plank buckled around his belly, on the plank is a sign, 'Orange Stick'. He fades out.

2. In front of the wall: a wooden bench without a back. Next to one

another, facing the camera – Anna, Flophouse Fritz, Sticky Fingers Herman, Jezebel, Buttercup, the innkeeper, Fatty. Their names hang like signs over them. They swill from a brandy glass, one after the other, moving from left to right with rapid gestures. Then they all fade out, except:

3. Anna and Fatty. The latter turns his head quickly and barks something crude. They fade out.

4. A gentleman in a top hat, lighting a cigarette: from bottom left to top right a series of rapidly moving letters spells out: *The gentleman who will be murdered.* He looks as if he has been crossed out. He fades out.

5. The young gentleman and the lady, sitting on a bed, facing the camera. On the headboard is written: *The lovers.* They fade out.

6. In front of the wall a commissioner and two policemen herd a pack of barely dressed couples from right to left. The shot fades out.

7. Orange Stick. Anna runs to him, embraces him. Fatty pulls her away with a rapid grip.

The very first shot: Narrow, outlying road.
An elegant gentleman in a top hat comes forward. It is evening.

Shot 1: *Blue: parkway with bushy, high trees.*
A lady dressed in bright colours with a white veil hiding her face walks forward quickly. She looks back once in a while, as if she is being pursued, she walks in a zigzag and stops for a moment in mid-range with her hand at her eyes, searching. Then an elegant car drives up, and a young, refined gentleman in a frock coat jumps from the running board and helps the woman into the vehicle. Both look back once again and the car leaves.

Shot 2: *Narrow street of a harbour town.*
An orange seller, Stick, a large, strong person with a mean look, is selling oranges from a handcart. It is evening. The street lanterns are lit.

Shot 3: *Country road, frontal shot.*
The car speeds by. It is possible to make out inside the young gentleman next to the woman. He is holding her hand. Their faces are somewhat immobile.

Shot 4:
A ragged lad, Flophouse Fritz, pulls Stick to the side, whispers

something in his ear. Stick nods, sells oranges. Flophouse Fritz runs off.

Shot 5: *Another narrow street.*
The elegant gentleman is mugged and beaten by three ragged characters (Flophouse Fritz, Buttercup and Sticky Fingers Herman). They bend over him.

Shot 6: *Street corner.*
A policeman. Listens, looks around, whistles. Rushes out.

Shot 7: *Another street.*
Two policemen walk along slowly. They stop, listen. Walk on.

Shot 8: *Street, same as shot 2.*
Stick is selling oranges.

Shot 9: *Street, same as shot 5.*
The policeman appears, the characters flee. First, however, Flophouse Fritz pulls a ring from the finger of the beaten man. The lifeless body lies on the black asphalt. *Dissolve.*

Shot 10: *Canal bridge, at an angle.*
The car drives over the bridge.

Shot 11: *Street, same as shot 2.*
The three characters trot by Stick's handcart. Flophouse Fritz appears to buy oranges but actually passes Stick the ring. He walks on.
    'Put the little jewel in an orange, Stick!'

Shot 12: *Narrow streets.*
The three policemen, two of whom are carrying the gentleman.

Shot 13: *Street, same as shot 2.*
Alone for a moment, Stick breaks out (*close-up*) the jewel from the ring, presses it into an orange, throws away the ring, pushes his cart on.

Shot 14: *Street, same as shot 2.*
The policemen walk by. One of them looks around and stares at Stick, who offers him an orange with a grin.

Shot 15: *Street.*
The car pushes its way forward, rocking.

Shot 16: *Other streets.*
The three characters saunter homewards. They see

Shot 17: *in front of the Crocodile flophouse*
a car stopping that fills the entire street. The two young people step
out of the car and sneak rather quickly into the flophouse.

Shot 18: *Telephone conversation.*
Script on the image, thin and delicate, appearing word for word
between the police commissioner and an old man:
> 'My daughter Gertrude has been taken away in a car by a young
> man unknown to me.'

The old man on the left fades out, the commissioner rings, a guard
enters into what only now comes into focus as a guard room.

Shot 19: *Same as shot 17, in front of the flophouse.*
The car drives off. The characters, snooping after them, enter the
flophouse making exaggerated gestures that mimic the pair.

Shot 20: *In front of the police headquarters.*
The commissioner climbs into a car with two policemen. Drives
off.

Shot 21: *Street.*
Stick examines the oranges, one by one. He can't find the jewel.

Shot 22: *Lounge in the Crocodile.*
An old slut, Jezebel, tipples in the corner. Anna, the barmaid, goes
to the window. Fatty, her brother, gets up from the table cursing:
> 'If you don't sack that orange dandy, I'll knock out your teeth.'

Anna walks out muttering. He follows slowly. He bumps into the
three characters who are merrily trotting in. She pushes them aside,
exits.

Shot 23: *Same as shot 17, street.*
Stick at his cart is examining the oranges once again, but he finds
nothing. He has a scowl on his face. He whistles with two fingers in
his mouth.

Shot 24: *Corridor in the Crocodile.*
Anna enters and goes to the door on the left. Meanwhile the old,
fat innkeeper and the pair climb up the stairs. A wicker trunk
remains in the corridor.

Shot 25: *Same as shot 17, street.*
Anna walks toward Stick, who is impatient. She pushes the cart into
the corridor. Stick follows her, keeping a close eye on the oranges.

Shot 26: *Same as shot 24, corridor.*
Anna pushes the cart, Stick watches the pair, his hands in his
pockets. At the top of the stairs the lady turns round to look.

Shot 27: *Close-up.*
The lady's face.

Shot 28: *Same as shot 24, corridor.*
Anna speaks to Stick, who turns away:
  'Why don't you just steal the jewel? Then we can get out of here!'
Stick, with an angry look:
  'Do you think I know where it's hiding in this rotten fruit!?'
Anna grasps Stick's arm as Fatty enters. Stick turns to the cart
apathetically, shoves oranges in his pockets. He gathers the rest in
both arms and hands. Enters the lounge.

Shot 29: *Same as shot 22, lounge.*
The three characters at the table pound with their fists and feet for
the waitress. Jezebel holds her ears, protesting. Stick enters with the
oranges. Buttercup comes his way, embraces him emotionally. The
oranges roll to the floor.

Shot 30: *Small room with an alcove bed in the Crocodile.*
Small, white curtains on the alcove windows. Low ceiling. Electric
chandelier. Upholstered door. The innkeeper and the pair enter.
The cavalier gives the innkeeper money so that he keeps his mouth
shut. The innkeeper looks coldly, impassively at the corner of the
room. Takes the money and stomps out. The cavalier shakes his
head. The lady sinks on to the bed, sighing with relief. He goes to
her, throwing off his coat.

Shot 31: *Same as shot 24, corridor.*
Anna leans the cart against the wall. Fatty intervenes, scolds her.
The innkeeper comes down, does not look at them, walks past:
  'I don't like you playing around with the orange dandy. I'll get
  the bucks even if I have to sell my skin. I'll get you out of here.'
Anna shakes her head, pulls herself away from him, runs into the
lounge. He stomps in angrily after her.

Shot 32: *Lounge, same as shot 21.*
The characters ask Stick about the jewel. Exaggerated, with soft
gestures:
  'Where is the little jewel?'
Stick plays ball with the oranges. They ask more impatiently. He
juggles. One of the oranges hits the innkeeper on the nose. Stick
grabs it with exaggerated quickness because Jezebel wants to take
it. Anna and Fatty enter.

Shot 33: *Enter.*
The police car driving along. It halts in front of a hotel. The

commissioner goes inside.

Shot 34: *Room, same as shot 30.*
The cavalier stretches out both arms pleasurably. She smiles up at him.
    'Now the old man can take his time searching the hotels! The boat tickets will arrive any minute now.'
He kisses her.

Shot 35: *Lounge, same as shot 22.*
Excited negotiations. Stick points to the oranges, puts them on the table, examines one after the other, shrugs his shoulders. Flophouse Fritz pulls a knife from his bag. Anna rushes over to him, but Stick takes it from him calmly, looks him straight in the eyes, looks sceptically at the knife, wipes it off on his jacket lining, cuts into an orange. All of them stare greedily at him.

Shot 36: *Hotel lobby.*
Travellers at the porter's desk. The police commissioner walks up. He takes the guest register, studies it.
    'Hans Storm and sister No. 47'
The commissioner points to it, grins, walks with the porter to the elevator.

Shot 37: *Hotel room.*
A half-dressed pair sits happily on the bed. There is a knock. Great confusion. Finally he goes to the door. The police commissioner. Exchange of words. The young man does not have his identification papers in order, especially those of his sister. The commissioner grins threateningly. He takes both with him.

Shot 38: *Same as shot 33.*
The pair climb in the car. The commissioner follows. The car drives off.

Shot 39: *Room, same as shot 30.*
The young man leads the lady to the window. Pressed against each other, they look out. They look at the

Shot 40: *canal.*

Shot 41: *Same as shot 39 and 30.*
She wraps her arms around him. *Dissolve.*

Shot 42: *Lounge, same as shot 22.*
Still arguing. Then they grab the oranges, sit down along the wall, and bite into the fruits. All chew on the oranges except the innkeeper, who is leaning on the ceramic heating stove, and Anna,

who is standing behind Stick. They throw halved oranges, peels, seeds at Jezebel, crawl after rolling oranges under the benches.

Shot 43: *Close-up.*
Stick sees something.

Shot 44: *Close-up.*
Fatty blinks his eyes, swallows, looks around.

Shot 45: *Lounge, same as before.*
Everyone is eating and searching.

Shot 46: *Close-up, same as shot 43.*
Stick looks coolly, intensely at

Shot 47: *Close-up, same as shot 44.*
Fatty's body, and now Fatty has become transparent. The slightly illuminated oesophagus appears, like a vision, with a black object being swallowed. Then only the stomach is illuminated with the object (black) in it.

Shot 48: *Lounge, same as shot 22.*
Fatty lays his orange aside, stands up slowly. He goes slowly to the door. Stick watches him.

Shot 49: *Lounge, same as shot 22, the door.*
Fatty saunters toward the door, and his stomach is transparent.

Shot 50: *Lounge, same as shot 22.*
Stick stands up and follows him slowly. Anna watches both of them. Upset, she brushes her forehead.

Shot 51: *Room, same as shot 30.*
The lady half lies on the bed, the young man listens for sounds from downstairs. He goes to the wall and opens an upholstered door, looks out, shakes his head, looks then at the lady, who pays him no attention. He closes the door quickly, returns.

Shot 52: *Corridor, same as shot 24, dark.*
Fatty, moving slowly, his stomach transparent, behind him Stick.

Shot 53: *In front of a hotel.*
The police car drives up.

Shot 54: *Long, dark corridor, uneven, windows at back.*
Fatty and behind him, as earlier, Stick.

Shot 55: *Hotel corridor.*
The police commissioner with the porter knocks at three doors one after the other, enters the first.

Shot 56: *Corridor in front of the windows.*
Fatty opens the window, wants to lean out, dries the sweat on his brow, hears Stick, turns round. They look into each other's eyes.
'Watch out that you don't get sick and vomit out the window!'
Fatty smiles painfully and vaguely. They go back.

Shot 57: *Hotel lobby.*
The police commissioner leaves the hotel with two pairs of lovers.

Shot 58: *Room, same as shot 30.*
The lady and the young man in an embrace on the bed.

Shot 59: *Lounge, same as shot 22.*
Flophouse Fritz thrusts his knife in the table. Tensely:
'Orange Stick stole the little jewel.'
Anna screams back at him. The innkeeper brings whiskey. Buttercup gets up slowly.
'Stick never steals, you steal . . .'
They throw themselves at each other, fight. Fatty enters. Thin smile.

Shot 60: *Corridor, same as shot 24.*
Stick meets up with a messenger boy dressed in red, takes an envelope from him. Gives him a coin. Opens the envelope, holds two tickets in his hand:
'The Kaiser Wilhelm II. Luxury cruise Hamburg – New York. First Class Cabin No. 74.'
Stick looks up. He sees the wall fade out, and he sees

Shot 61: *the ocean.*
Shot 62: *Same as shot 60.*
He speaks to the boy:
'Call a taxi.'
The boy lifts his cap, exits. Stick stands there musing. Goes into the

Shot 63: *lounge,*
where a real fight is going on. They throw orange peels at Stick, who goes over to the innkeeper, takes several whiskey bottles from him. Together with Anna he fills five or six glasses, pushes them over to those fighting.
'Bottoms up for the digestion! The devil has taken the jewel!'
Buttercup drinks, lying under Sticky Fingers Herman, half surrendering.

Shot 64: *Streets.*
Police car, illuminating house fronts with its headlights.

Shot 65: *Corridor, same as shot 24.*
Stick pulls Anna into the corridor:
> 'Dance. Make them drunk. Help me get rid of them! I've got to
> be alone with your brother, do you hear!'

She hugs him passionately. He pulls her roughly into the lounge.

Shot 66: *Hotel room.*
A couple in a double bed sit up, look at the door. The man climbs
out.

Shot 67: *Another hotel room.*
Ditto.

Shot 68: *Dark, obscure, an entire series of hotel rooms.*
Couples jump out of bed, one after the other.

Shot 69: *Lounge.*
The men are getting drunk. Stick pours more. Anna dances,
starting up the electric piano time and again. Fatty goes out, still as
if in a dream.

Shot 70: *Corridor.*
Fatty tries to spit into a basin. Suddenly Stick is standing behind
him. They return to the lounge.

Shot 71: *A bare hotel room, rather dark.*
Filled with half-dressed pairs of lovers. More and more arrive. The
gentlemen hold their identification papers in trembling hands. In
front of the glass door, outside in the brightly-lit hallway, a large
policeman.

Shot 72: *Stairway at the Crocodile.*
Fatty ascends the stairs. Halfway up he looks round. Descends,
goes to the door. Stick is standing in front of it. Fatty looks at him,
ascends again. He is transparent again.

Shot 73: *Lounge.*
Wild dancing. Jezebel is dancing with Anna.

Shot 74: *Row of windows from the exterior.*
Fatty's sweating, pale face is visible peering out. It appears at one
window after another.

Shot 75: *Corridor without a window.*
Fatty halts, listens. He hears:
> 'He's crazy enough to send the police after us! Then the scandal
> is sure – and goodbye New York!'

Shot 76: *Room, same as shot 30.*
The pair. He paces back and forth. She stretches her arms out towards him.

Shot 77: *Same as shot 75.*
Fatty thinks. Goes to a window ledge. Scribbles something on a piece of paper. Opens the window.

Shot 78: *Street seen from above.*
A young, somewhat over-dressed woman passes by, looks up.

Shot 79: *Window seen from below.*
Fatty makes hand signs, throws the notepaper down, the over-dressed woman bends down.

Shot 80: *In front of the hotel.*
Car with spotlight. Couples swell forth from the brightly-lit interior of the hotel. The police commissioner bends over to the chauffeur.
    'Only love! No identification papers!'
He stuffs papers in his breast pocket.

Shot 81: *Streets.*
The over-dressed woman is running with the notepaper.

Shot 82: *Lounge.*
Stick takes Anna aside.
    'I've got to deal with your brother alone. I'll get rid of your guys.'
Everyone is pretty drunk. They smash a lamp, for which Buttercup has to climb on the shoulders of Sticky Fingers Herman. They organize a cockfight. Then Stick has an idea. He points upwards. Everyone grins.
    'A great trick.'
Everyone looks at Anna, who leads the way. The others follow. Stick moves to the window, looks out. He sees

Shot 83: *the canal*
and across from it a two-storey house with darkened windows . . .

Shot 84: *Hallways in the Crocodile.*
Anna goes upstairs, enduring the characters, followed in a wild chase by Buttercup, Sticky Fingers Herman, Flophouse Fritz, the innkeeper, and Fatty slowly stumbling behind them.

Shot 85: *Lounge.*
Stick looks out at

Shot 86: *the canal*
that flows by slowly and darkly.

Shot 87: *Anna's small bedroom.*
The whole gang spills drunkenly into the room. Sticky Fingers
Herman immediately discovers a picture of the Madonna above
Anna's bed. He breaks out in loud guffaws. Anna shows the others
a dressmaker's dummy lying under a pile of junk; they pull it out
and leave the room while hamming it up. Anna is alone for a
moment, looks forlornly at the wall with the picture, then Fatty,
who was standing by the wall behind her, moves toward her with
fear in his broad face. She moves away from him, he makes a half-
begging gesture so that she stops, somewhat touched, and twists up
her face. He says something, probably without making a sound.
She stares at his face with curiosity, but he points with his short,
bent index finger to his body, which becomes transparent where
the stomach is located. In the dimly-lit stomach lies the small,
black jewel. This does not last a second. And Fatty, his finger still
pointing to the body which is no longer transparent, talks on
soundlessly. But Anna turns away with disgust and walks out. Fatty
follows her quickly.

Shot 88: *Corridor, same as shot 84.*
Fatty grabs at Anna's arm, breathing fast. He says, close to her
face:
    'See to it that you get to the Butchers' Bridge! The police are
    already there! You have to get them, Anna. At least seven men,
    Anna!'
He makes the gesture of cutting off his head. Anna stares at him,
uncomprehending.

Shot 89: *Lounge.*
They drag in the dressmaker's dummy, make a head from wadded
rags, Sticky Fingers Herman dances with her, Flophouse Fritz even
kisses her, but Stick pulls her from them and examines it with a
professional gaze. Stick sends Flophouse Fritz upstairs. Meanwhile
they give the dummy whiskey to drink.

Shot 90: *Same as shot 88.*
Anna and Fatty. Close to his face, she bends her own face back,
looks at him coolly, shrugs her shoulders, turns round, goes off
calmly. He watches after her with a stupid expression on his face,
leans back on the wall suddenly with a shiver, closes his eyes for a
moment. *Dissolve.*

Shot 91: *Room, same as shot 30.*
The lady is lying on the bed, the young man is sitting on his wicker
trunk, his top hat lying in front of him on the floor. He loosens his

necktie and smokes. The upholstered door opens. Flophouse Fritz stands there for a while and watches the idyll, quite touched. When the young man notices him, he moves forward with an oily smile and invites him downstairs.

'Sir, downstairs there is a boy with tickets!'

The young man follows him reluctantly, knotting his tie, while Flophouse Fritz watches him with amusement. The lady asks the young man not to leave her alone. He quickly reassures her and hastily steps out, in front of Flophouse Fritz, who makes a most obliging bow towards her.

Shot 92: *Streets.*

The over-dressed woman comes panting to the police station, bumps into a policeman, who brusquely pushes her away, intimidates her, and asks for her identification; then he pulls her into the station, despite her sudden resistance.

Shot 93: *Lounge.*

Anna is collecting glasses. Fatty walks around restlessly. Sticky Fingers Herman is dancing with the dummy, Jezebel moves the chairs aside so that he has room, Buttercup pounds the beat with his foot and claps his hands. The young man enters, led by Flophouse Fritz with a deep bow. They all greet him with bows, show him the dummy, which he notes with great amusement, then Stick throws his arms around him from behind and pushes a gag into his pretty mouth. The others grab him, as he courageously defends himself, and tie him up like professionals, while Stick and the innkeeper calmly exit.

Shot 94: *Room, same as shot 30.*

The lady is waiting at the window. Stick and the innkeeper enter without looking at her. They look around a bit, then Stick points with his chin to the trunk. At this point he and the innkeeper drag the trunk out. When they have reached the door, the lady steps forward, and Stick turns round to her, looks at her coolly.

Shot 95: *Close-up.*

The lady, very worried.

Shot 96: *Same as shot 94.*

Stick, bent over, looks past the lady, their profiles fade out quickly and dissolve to

Shot 97: *water (the ocean).*

Shot 98: *Same as shot 94.*

Stick controls himself, he points briefly with his chin towards the door. They drag the trunk completely out. The lady moves anxiously after them to the door. She sees from above

Shot 99: *on the stairs, same as shot 24,,*
both of them dragging the trunk down and then Fatty going from the wall to the door.

Shot 100: *A corridor.*
Fatty passes through.

Shot 101: *Anna's bedroom.*
Fatty enters, looks around with a blank expression, stomps out anxiously.

Shot 102: *Corridors.*
Fatty looks through the window at

Shot 103: *the canal.*

Shot 104: *Police station, bare room.*
Filled with pairs of lovers; the gesticulating commissioner examines their identification papers. All the detainees are shivering, the girls are crying, dissolved in tears, some barely dressed. The image is cluttered and disorderly. The large policeman pushes the over-dressed woman into the room, who, sobbing, hands the note to the commissioner.

Shot 105: *Lounge.*
They place the young man on his feet, hold his arms and pull off his jacket and tie. Jezebel pours whiskey in his face, Anna stops her, dries him off. Stick and the innkeeper set down the trunk. Stick removes the key from the young man's vest pocket, opens it and pulls out underwear, clothes, toiletries, the others join in the rummaging, and Jezebel greedily collects the flying pieces of underclothes. With hoots and hamming they bind the young man and throw him in the trunk, which they close.

Shot 106: *Room, same as shot 30.*
The lady paces anxiously back and forth.

Shot 107: *Police station.*
The commissioner pushes out the couples who are clustered around the door. He is very excited, waves the notepaper. He looks at it:
'To the Commissioner!
If ya wanna catch a rich couple who's afraid of tha police, come to the Butchers' Bridge right away, fast, at least seven men, I'll meet ya there.'
Exits.

Shot 108: *Lounge.*
While the characters try on the underwear, including fine women's lingerie, Stick pounds a large nail in the trunk because he threw away the key and cannot find it. He and the innkeeper drag the trunk out again, up the

Shot 109: *staircase, same as shot 24.*

Shot 110: *Room, same as shot 30.*
The lady hears the noise, opens the door. They place the trunk back in the corner, exit without a sign of sympathy. At the door they both turn their faces towards her. Then they leave. The lady regards the nailed trunk with surprise.

Shot 111: *Same as shot 103.*

Shot 112: *Lounge.*
The same commotion. Now the dummy is dressed in the young man's tuxedo. Stick has entered and looks at the work of art. Jezebel cheek to cheek with the handsome puppet-boy in a tuxedo and flowing shirt. Stick leads them to the small windows at the back. All of them look out, he explains something. They laugh drunkenly. Stick looks around for something, leaves quickly.

Shot 113: *Corridor, same as shot 24.*
Fatty and Anna. Fatty desperately shakes the locked entry door. Anna argues with him, her arms on her hips. She laughs contemptuously for a moment. Suddenly Stick walks up to them. Fatty, filled with fear, notices him. Stick, who says something to Anna, looks at the door, through which the characters, the innkeeper and Jezebel drag the dummy. They have poles. Stick informs them:
'I'll toss it! You can watch from outside. But fish the dummy back out!'
Stick takes the dummy from them, nods to Anna, who takes from her apron the door key and unlocks the door.

Shot 114: *Close-up.*
Fatty watches her. He dries the sweat on his brow, takes a step forward.

Shot 115: *Corridor, as before.*
Fatty stands in the middle of the entrance hall, cowering. The characters stand at the door, when suddenly something occurs to Sticky Fingers Herman. He pulls Buttercup over to the wall, climbs on his shoulders and plays with the wires above.

Shot 116: *Room, same as shot 30.*
The lady listens at the door. The light goes out.

Shot 117: *Corridor, same as shot 24.*
Stick grabs Fatty by the arm. Standing at the door, Anna looks over, the others are now outside. Anna closes the door, turns the key. Fatty walks alone to the lounge, surrendering to his fate, his shoulders pulled in. Stick talks to Anna.

Shot 118: *In front of the Crocodile, same as shot 17.*
The whole gang (Flophouse Fritz, Buttercup, Sticky Fingers Herman, the innkeeper and Jezebel) stagger drunkenly up the street.

Shot 119: *Lounge.*
Fatty enters. Halts. Goes to the window, as if in a dream, dries the sweat on his brow, bends out of the windows, sees

Shot 120: *the canal, same as shot 86.*

Shot 121: The canal dissolves and Fatty sees in a vision the police car being driven by the policemen.

Shot 122: *Lounge.*
Stick comes in, behind him Anna. Fatty is startled, spins around.

Shot 123: *Same as shot 30.*
The lady, almost desperate, rings violently, runs out, comes back, sinks with sobs on to the trunk. The trunk becomes transparent. The young man is lying in it in his shirt sleeves, dressed only in his trousers. He turns his face, he seems to be listening. The trunk is once again opaque.

Shot 124: *Streets.*
The police car at top speed.

Shot 125: *Lounge.*
Stick approaches Fatty, not letting him out of sight. Standing in front of him, he points imperiously but calmly with his hand to the corner where Anna has placed a bucket. Fatty, completely cowed, stares at him first full of hate. Then, trembling with fear, he shuffles over to the bucket. Stick follows him with a wide knife in his hand.

Shot 126: *Wooden bridge.*
The gang pounds its way over the bridge.

Shot 127: *Lounge.*
Stick and Anna tend to Fatty, who is trying to vomit, sticking his finger in his mouth, etc. He bends over the bucket and sees

Shot 128:
at the bottom of the bucket the Butchers' Bridge (in stone) on which seven policemen are standing with their faces turned upstream.

Shot 129:
Suddenly Stick grabs him brutally and drags him into the corner, kicking the bucket away and pounding him on the head with his fist. Anna tries to prevent him from beating Fatty, so that he is able to pull himself away, making a stumbling jump sideways, and run away as fast as he can. Stick turns in a rage towards Anna, lifts his hand to strike, but angrily lets it fall, and runs after Fatty.

Shot 130: *The Butchers' Bridge.*
The police car halts. The police jump out.

Shot 131: *Hall, stairs, corridors.*
Chase. Stick is after Fatty.

Shot 132: *Row of windows from outside.*
Fatty's face, pale and sweaty, rushing by.

Shot 133: *A corridor.*
Stick at a small window, Anna chases him past it.

Shot 134: *View from the window. Canal and earthen bank directly across.*
The five are standing on the bank, whistling and hollering, they wave at him.

Shot 135: *Same as shot 129.*
Stick returns, cursing, goes down the stairs.

Shot 136: *Corridor.*
Fatty runs into Anna's room.

Shot 137: *Anna's bedroom, same as shot 87.*
Fatty, breathing heavily, pushes up against the door.

Shot 138: *Lounge.*
Stick lifts up the dummy, drags it out.

Shot 139: *Same as shot 137.*
Anna pounding at the door. The door gives way. She dashes in.

Shot 140: *Room, same as shot 30.*
The lady has heard the commotion. She goes from the door to the window and from there to the door again. She stops in the middle of the room, and now she listens.

Shot 141: *Canal and bank.*

The five are whistling at the top of their lungs with their fingers in their mouths.

Shot 142: *Corridor in front of the room from shot 30.*
With long strides Stick jerks the dummy along behind him.

Shot 143: *Same as shot 30.*
The lady, cowering in horror, stares at the door flying open. From the dark corridor Stick enters, dragging the dummy behind him. The lady looks at it for a moment and collapses without a sound because she recognizes the dummy as the young man. Despite his haste Stick manages to toss the dummy out of the window with calm and composure. He is standing two steps away from the window, and the dummy shoots elegantly out of the wooden window into the dark like a very slender torpedo.

Shot 144: *Bank on the other side, same as shot 141.*
The raving five splitting their sides with laughter.

Shot 145: *Canal.*
The dummy flows downstream quickly.

Shot 146: *Room, same as shot 30.*
Stick roughly picks up the collapsed woman from the floor, drags her to the window, shakes her; she begins to resist, he pushes her towards the window and she screams because she thinks he wants to push her out.

Shot 147: *Same as shot 141.*
The gang suddenly stops laughing, and then begins again because they see

Shot 148: *at the front of the Crocodile towards the canal*
the lady through a window, as if she wants to leap after the dummy while Stick is holding her back.

Shot 149: *Anna's bedroom, same as shot 87.*
Fatty kneels before Anna, begging with raised arms. She shakes her head, goes to the window in the background. He crawls after her on his knees, all the time looking at the door. She looks out. She sees from above the

Shot 150: *bank of the canal*
and the five who are drunkenly fishing for the dummy with their poles.

Shot 151: *Corridor in front of the room, same as shot 136.*
Stick appears with a knife. He stops for a moment (*close-up*), presses his lips together, looks at the floor, which disappears and sees

Shot 152: *rushing water.*

Shot 153: *Bedroom, same as shot 87.*
On his knees Fatty points to the picture of the Madonna, Anna's face becomes softer, she wants to pull him up by his arm. She says: 'Come!'
He half stands up, but suddenly turns round because Stick appears at the door. Immediately Stick jumps (*the image should be shot from a different angle*) on Fatty so that Anna falls back against the wall. Stick fights with him, pushes him to the corner of the bed alcove, and now he twists with his left hand the left part of the brown curtain into a thick rope and strangles Fatty with it. At the same time he pushes him back on the bed, and now, as he stretches out his right hand with the knife, all the bed curtains fall over the two of them. Anna rushes to them, but then stumbles back. *Dissolve.*

Shot 154: *The bank of the canal from below.*
The five pull the dummy out of the water.

Shot 155: *Bedroom.*
Stick unravels himself ponderously from the drapery, stands upright, throws the knife back on the bed, looks coolly at the jewel, sticks it calmly but hastily into his vest pocket. Anna has half stood up, looks up at him full of dread. He looks past her, and the wall dissolves, and he sees in a vision

Shot 156: *water.*

Shot 157: *The Butchers' Bridge.*
The police waiting.

Shot 158: *Corridor.*
Stick drags Fatty's corpse behind him, wrapped in bed sheets.

Shot 159: *Room, same as shot 30.*
In the dark room there is a white spot, the unconscious lady. Stick appears as in shot 137 and drags the corpse to the window. He lifts it up and sees through the window

Shot 160: *the house directly across the canal*
light up.

Shot 161: *Wooden bridge.*
Swaying drunkenly and howling the characters carry the dummy triumphantly on raised arms over the bridge.

Shot 162: *The house directly across the canal.*
People in night clothes stare out of the windows.

Shot 163: *House front of the Crocodile seen from the bank of the canal.*
A heavy body is thrown out from the window. It falls with a splash
in the

Shot 164: *canal,*
while (*camera turns*) the people in the windows of the house directly
across the canal step back and (*camera turns*) the five disappear over
the bridge.

Shot 165: *Bedroom.*
Bent over the bed, Anna sees the blood stains on the bed and the
knife on the floor. *Dissolve.*

Shot 166: *Canal.*
Fatty floats downstream.

Shot 167: *Street in front of the Crocodile.*
A car stops in front of the flophouse. The characters push their way
past it and enter.

Shot 168: *Corridor, same as shot 24.*
They arrive with the dripping dummy. They stumble into the
lounge just as Anna comes down the stairs, as if exhausted.

Shot 169: *Lounge.*
Stick is sitting behind the bar, immobile and huge, he stares coolly
at those entering. They point with their thumbs back over their
shoulders, go to the window, point outside. Stick rises slowly, he
looks through the window and sees

Shot 170: *in the street*
the car.

Shot 171: *From the house directly across the canal*
people with lanterns emerge and go first to the canal, then to the
bridge.

Shot 172: *Lounge.*
Making a joke, Stick pulls the jacket off the dummy, wrings out the
water, puts in on to the great mirth of the others when the people
from across the way enter. He shows the excited, gesticulating
people the dummy. They leave, and he goes out behind them,
swaying. The flophouse people throw orange peels after him.
Leaning on the door, too weak to stand on her feet, Anna follows
him with a tired gesture.

Shot 173: *The Butchers' Bridge.*
The police at the stone balustrade, seven faces, just as Fatty saw

them in the vision in the water bucket. Movement. The commissioner points impatiently at the note, he has pulled out his watch.
'I'll meet ya . . .'
Suddenly a policeman raises his arm, points to the water.

Shot 174: *Canal.*
Fatty floats by.

Shot 175: *Stairway.*
Stick ascends.

Shot 176: *The Butchers' Bridge.*
The policemen fish Fatty out of the canal.

Shot 177: *Lounge.*
The characters sit along the walls and swill. Jezebel is sitting on Buttercup's knees. And Anna is dancing with Sticky Fingers Herman, cheek to cheek, slowly and apathetically.

Shot 178: *Room, same as shot 30.*
In the corridor (the door is still open) Stick appears in the tuxedo of the young man, but scowling and threatening. Lying on the floor with her upper body leaning on the bed, the lady looks up impassively, almost without surprise. Stick picks up the top hat, grabs the frock coat and looks around for her fur coat. Meanwhile, she stands up as if sleepwalking and wraps herself, half-stumbling, in the alcove drapery. But Stick has found the fur coat and approaches her. He simply helps her into the coat. She submissively lets it happen and exits submissively on his arm. *Dissolve.*

Shot 179: *Riverbank.*
The policemen run upstream.

Shot 180: *Stairway.*
Stick drags the woman downstairs.

Shot 181: *Lounge.*
The people are looking out of the window and, except for Anna who is sitting at a table holding her head in her arms, they see

Shot 182: *in front of the Crocodile*
Stick and the lady (*both from behind*) climb into the car. It drives off, pushing its way through the street.

Shot 183: *Lounge.*
Turning back from the window, they see Anna rise calmly and go out of the door, exhausted. She does not respond to the innkeeper's call.

Shot 184: *A street.*
Police peering from house to house.

Shot 185: *Corridor with stairs.*
Anna, her head leaning on her chest, ascends.

Shot 186: *Corridors.*
Anna passes through.

Shot 187: *Bedroom.*
Anna enters. She looks uncomprehendingly at the bed, exits. She leaves the door open so that the muslin curtains on the window billow.

Shot 188: *Corridor in front of the room, same as shot 136.*
Anna goes to the stairs, looks down, bent forward, returns, looks at the open door of

Shot 189: *the room from shot 30*
and goes in.

Shot 190: *In front of the Crocodile.*
Police ring.

Shot 191: *Lounge.*
The characters, completely drunk, listen, Jezebel goes to the window, looks out, looks back slightly, everyone freezes. Then a wild chase to reach the door begins, through

Shot 192: *the hall, stairwell and corridors.*

Shot 193: *Same as shot 190.*
The police pound with their pistols on the wooden door. It is forced open.

Shot 194: *Room, same as shot 30.*
Staggering in, the characters see Anna, lying on the trunk, pounding on it with her fists as if demented, sobbing and weeping. They fill up the dark room, they run to the trunk, tear it open, lift out the bound and lifeless young man, stare uncomprehendingly at his face. He opens his eyes and stares straight ahead. A large policeman is standing at the open door.

Shot 195: *Bridge.*
A car drives over. Inside, Stick is sitting next to the lady. Stick twists up his face, he looks through the window (*fade to*)

Shot 196: *the Crocodile flophouse.*
It turns into water.

The end.

Three in the Tower

[See GBFA 19/16–35. Written in July 1921 together with Caspar Neher, the script probably reflects Brecht's jealous reaction to Marianne Zoff's affair with Oskar Camillus Recht, Brecht's rival for her attention. The dramatic situation was inspired by August Strindberg's *Dance of Death* (1904), which Brecht saw in Munich in 1919. He adapted from it the isolated tower, the militaristic milieu and the motifs of a bad odour as well as the wife's estrangement from her husband, but he transformed the marriage tension into a love-hate relationship between the lieutenant and the woman. The screenplay incorporates traits of the Expressionist chamber film with its restricted number of characters, the emphasis on interior space (including corridors and winding staircases) and motifs of tortured marriage relations. In fact it resembles more a self-consciously amusing horror film that plays off the preoccupation with phantoms and the disastrous psychological tension of the Expressionist cinema. In November 1922 Brecht saw an opportunity to get the script accepted at the newly established company Kunst-Projektions-GmbH (Kupro), but it produced only one film, *Mysteries of a Hairdresser's Shop* (*Mysterien eines Frisiersalons*, 1923), starring the Munich comedian Karl Valentin, which Brecht ostensibly wrote and co-directed with Erich Engel. Lasting twenty-eight minutes, it is a series of surreal, grotesque episodes of torture perpetrated by barbershop employees on their customers.]

Characters:
Captain Gland
his wife
Lieutenant Seegers
young valet
Commander
soldiers, cavalry, officers
young cavaliers
the madam
three young men

Act I

'Last supper of the crocodiles' or '3 – 1 = 2' or 'What's biting me?'

Shot 1: *Huge, massive tower, blue.*
It is night. *Fade to*

Shot 2: *upper room in the tower with low, wide windows, white drapes; the windows are open.*
The captain moves slowly to the window, dragging his feet, closes it, lets the blinds down and looks around suddenly to his wife, who is rocking like a child in the rocking chair. The young valet lights candles on the table and sideboard, goes to the door, hears no further orders and exits. Walking over to the sideboard, the captain continues to read the newspaper.

Shot 3: *Circular staircase.*
The lieutenant quickly ascends, his left shoulder slightly pulled in. He hangs his sword and belt on a hook (*the camera moves with him*) and with lowered head hesitates in front of the glass door. It is covered with a curtain, but flickering lights can be seen through it.

Shot 4: *Same as shot 2 (dining-room).*
The captain heard something: he folds the newspaper, half closes his eyelid, looks coolly at his wife, who is looking at her hand. He walks calmly to the door.

Shot 5: *Same as shot 3 (circular staircase).*
The lieutenant looks up, at this moment the curtain behind the glass door is pushed apart and the captain looks at him: he straightens up, they look into each other's eyes, the captain opens the door, the lieutenant quickly enters, stooping again. *Dissolve.*

Shot 6: *Same as shot 2 (dining-room).*
The captain carries a candelabrum from the sideboard to the table and looks into the faces of both, who are already sitting. He turns round; goes very slowly to the window (his arms akimbo), opens the blinds a crack with his finger, looks out, turns round, sees his wife stroking the hand of the lieutenant sitting stiffly at the table. The captain half closes his eyelid, turns round. The lieutenant looks over at him, pulls back his hand abruptly, pulls at his collar, he looks fixedly at the rigid face of the woman, who is afraid, and he stands up abruptly, as if driven, and hits the table lightly with the flat of his hand. The captain has turned towards them again, his arms still akimbo, he opens his eyelid and looks at his wife. The lieutenant moves his head imperiously, the woman rises calmly,

moves a little way towards her husband but then remains silent and exits, with lowered head. The men follow her with their eyes; as the white curtain closes behind her, the lieutenant bends forward and says with a distorted face:

'You or I! One of us must have her! We could ask her – if only she knew . . .'

With his face twitching, the captain walks restlessly back and forth. The lieutenant stands still and continues to speak.

Shot 7: *Same as shot 3.*
The woman leans on the door, clasping her head in her arms.

Shot 8: *Same as shot 2.*
The lieutenant says no more. The captain has gone to a cupboard with a curtain, bent over, fished out a pistol case (80 × 40 cm) and frowning, shrugging his shoulders, throws it on the table with both hands. The lieutenant sets upright one of the knocked-over candelabra, he has a helpless look, resists with his hands. He says:

'You or I! We don't need a casualty in the house.'

The captain has moved to the glass door, he stops, pulls at the curtain, thinks again, releases his hand, turns round, looks at the lieutenant: the lieutenant closes the pistol case and glances towards him. Then he makes the gesture of cutting off his head and appears to say, holding his hand at his throat:

'Even if she doesn't know, she should decide. Fetch her! Whomever she toasts first will simply disappear . . .'

The captain walks slowly to the window, looks out through a crack, turns round and nods quickly towards the lieutenant. Relieved, he then goes to the servant's bell (made of material, hanging on the wall) and rings.

Shot 9: *Same as shot 3.*
The valet passes by the woman, who is leaning over the banister and straightens up as he goes by. The door remains open, the captain comes out, offers his arm to the woman, they go back in. *Dissolve.*

Shot 10: *Same as shot 2.*
The valet comes towards the two, holding the pistol case. The woman is startled, she looks at the lieutenant, who bows. They watch each other, waiting, the valet brings glasses and wine from the cupboard.
Close-up of the three around the table.
The lieutenant pours, he pushes a glass to the woman, his hands tremble, the captain steadies his hand. Then he suddenly stands up

calmly, goes to the window while furtively glancing at his wife in passing, opens it, breathes in the air, as one can see from his back, he turns round and is startled: his wife has stood up after she once again stroked the lieutenant's hand amicably and now she goes to the captain with their two glasses. He drinks his glass in one gulp while watching her and walks by her, coolly half closing his eyelid, in order to put his glass on the sideboard. The woman turns, follows him with her eyes, looks at the lieutenant, drinks to him as well, the lieutenant smiles painfully. Meanwhile the captain has taken a candelabrum from the sideboard. He holds it in his hand, he stands indecisively at the door, the two drink to each other, they do not look at him. He turns round and exits through the glass door. They notice only as the curtain closes behind him.

Shot 11: *Same as shot 3, but seen from below.*
The captain descends, but actually only the lights of three candles are visible. They are trembling.

Shot 12: *Guard room.*
Four soldiers are playing cards near the wall. They jump up. The captain has entered. He has four bottles under his arms. The soldiers stand at attention. One reports. The captain nods to stop. He stands there calmly and seems to be looking into the distance with cool self-control. *Dissolve and fade-in.*

Shot 13: *Same as shot 2.*
The two are bent towards each other. The woman places her hand on the lieutenant's. *Dissolve.*

Shot 14: *Same as 12.*
Slowly the captain comes to, attends to the bottles and pours a glass of wine for each of his men, one after the other. He moves from one to the next and they stand at attention. So he pours the wine in their mouths. Then he places the three full bottles on the table and slowly walks to the corner of the room. He says something over his shoulder, at which point they stand at ease. Turning round a second time after he has already reached the corner, he says:
  'Lie down!'
He looks at the wall clock. It is eleven o'clock. He bends over the sofa and busies himself. Then he shoots into his body. There is smoke, the soldiers jump up, run to him, place him on the table, tear open his coat. Then one of them waves from the door, they exit after him.

Shot 15: *In the courtyard*

they fetch the horses.

Shot 16: *Same as shot 12.*
The valet, left behind, giddy at the door, walks fearfully over to the lifeless body, looks at him, covers him with a guard's coat, exits as if drunk. The coat moves. The captain stands up. He presses his hand against his chest, with a jolt he straightens. Presses his handkerchief between his teeth, exits.

Shot 17: *Same as shot 3.*
The valet leans against the banister, does not dare to enter. Shocked, he watches the captain walk by him into the room. Once again he carries the candelabrum, from below the valet watches him drift up the stairs.

Shot 18: *Same as shot 2.*
The two are drinking. The lieutenant listens, goes to the window, sees

Shot 19: *in the courtyard*
a rider galloping off.

Shot 20: *Same as shot 2.*
The captain is standing in the door. He takes the candelabrum, he says:
    'Good night!'
Turns round, steps through the curtain. They follow him with their eyes, they look at each other. The lieutenant looks at the wall clock. It is eleven o'clock.

Shot 21: *Corridor.*
The captain shuffles along, holding himself very upright, very laboriously. He throws the handkerchief away, opens his jacket collar. Then he has an idea. He removes his jacket, throws it over the banister.

Shot 22: *Guard room.*
The valet is emptying the wine bottles, completely drunk.

Shot 23: *The captain's bedroom.*
He enters slowly. He walks to the mirror. His image in the mirror. Pale, uncharacteristically rigid. Still holding the candelabrum in his hand. Near his heart a dark stain on the shirt:
    'We don't need a casualty in the house.'
He grins slightly.

Shot 24: *Same as shot 2.*
With her face lightly covered in perspiration, the woman reaches

her glass half over her shoulder to the lieutenant, who is standing behind her and kissing her neck, stops suddenly and turns very pale. She stands up, seems to be listening, walks to the sideboard, takes a candelabrum from the table and while the lieutenant pours wine, drinks and clumsily touches her, she lights the candles, lost in thought. The lieutenant blows out one of the candles, but she goes to the door with it. *Dissolve.*

Shot 25: *Entry hall below.*
Enter two soldiers; they watch the woman with the candelabrum come down the stairs. She immediately rushes over to the jacket and grabs it. The soldiers drag out the drunken valet and watch the woman run back up the stairs: she has the bloody jacket in her hand.

Shot 26: *Same as shot 23.*
The captain moves towards the bed. He places the candelabrum on the floor and lies down. (Goya.[2])

Shot 27: *Corridor as in shot 21.*
The woman comes swaying along the wall.

Shot 28: *The captain's bedroom.*
Stretched out on the bed, the captain lifts his head and listens. He sits up and falls partly off the bed, overturning the candelabrum that extinguishes. Night. Wind billows the drapes at the window. The captain, visible in his white shirt (and the dark spot on it is visible as well), crawls towards the clothes cupboard. Darkness swallows him.

Shot 29: *In front of the door*
the woman is listening, wants to open it, becomes frightened, pulls her hand from the door handle and goes back.

Shot 30: *In the dining-room, same as shot 2,*
the lieutenant is drinking while standing at the table, still listening. Pulling apart the curtain on the door, the woman enters, stops, almost collapses and stands there with the uniform jacket. The lieutenant goes to her, pulls the jacket away, stares at it soberly and walks out. The woman follows him with her eyes, completely pale. *Dissolve.*

Shot 31: *Bedroom, same as shot 28. Dark.*
The lieutenant enters, lights the candelabrum on the floor, the room is empty, the woman, standing in the door, sees it too. The two look at each other. *Dissolve.*

Act II

'Toiletries in the house of death' or 'Lime is not enough' or 'A corpse in the lovers' bed'

Shot 1: *The tower, grey.*
Morning, the sky is clearing.

Shot 2: *Guard room.*
The soldiers stand in a row at the white wall, facing the camera. Above them the round clock with a swinging pendulum. In front of them, astride a chair, the lieutenant with his arms casually swung over its back. The woman, with drooping shoulders, bent forward, staring at the floor, sits on a bench along the wall behind the soldiers. She watches. The soldiers take their turn speaking. The lieutenant shakes his head impatiently. The woman raises her face and looks at him. The lieutenant stands up slowly, stretching. He paces back and forth, arms akimbo, and gestures to the soldiers to leave. He stops in front of the woman, he looks at her face. It is white, like the clock face he sees above. The clock hand moves towards eleven, then towards a quarter, then back to eleven. The lieutenant knits his brow. *Dissolve.*

Shot 3: *A cubicle attached to the guard room.*
The valet in a fever on the camp bed. Soldiers with hanging heads (large figures) pressed round the bed. One of them opens his mouth and the others all look at the whitewashed, plank door.

Shot 4: *Guard room.*
The lieutenant walks to a corner, looks round because the woman wearily stands up and slowly exits with lowered head, leaving the door open. The lieutenant follows her with his eyes, presses his lips together, turns round, discovers four or five wine bottles near the stove. One is smashed, lying in a pool. The lieutenant swings round, looks again at the wall clock, moves to the writing stand and rings loudly. The guards rush in and stand at attention. Turning his back to them, he writes a message at the stand. A soldier takes it and exits. After a moment of reflection the lieutenant exits.

Shot 5: *Dock.*
The soldier rides off.

Shot 6: *Circular staircase. Same as Act I, shot 3.*
The woman leans on the door with the curtain. She listens, she looks out and sees (*from above*) in the

Shot 7: *hall on the main floor*

the lieutenant step out of the guard room. He encounters the valet, who is carrying three large suitcases and a laundry bag. He goes up the stairs in front of him.

Shot 8: *Upstairs.*
The lieutenant, in passing, preoccupied with the suitcases, opens the glass door for the woman. He holds the key chain in his hand and continues on his way. The valet trots along behind him, weighed down. Standing calmly at the doorpost, the woman has observed the lieutenant with some surprise, she watches him – her brow slightly creased (*see Act II, shot 6*) – as he moves away and goes calmly through the door into the dining-room.

Shot 9: *Hall on the main floor.*
Two soldiers without jackets and a currycomb for the horses in hand look up at the landing. One grins bitterly and pushes the other. They tumble into the guard room.

Shot 10: *The captain's bedroom.*
The lieutenant enters with the valet. He pulls the bed covers off and throws them into the valet's arms. Pushes open the windows.

Shot 11: *Guard room.*
Soldiers with half-opened uniforms guzzle the wine remaining in the bottles; card game. The two from shot 8 enter, imitate the suitcase scene. The soldiers listen, they run to the door, one waves with a bottle. They look out, up.

Shot 12: *Above in the corridor*
the lieutenant enters and goes into the dining-room.

Shot 13: *The dining-room.*
Everything like the previous evening, the blinds down, the table full of glasses and the woman sits in the middle of the darkened room at the table. The lieutenant at the door nods with his head. He still has his hand on the door handle, but when she does not move, he goes to her, bends over the table (*always seen from behind*) towards her, pushes the glasses away, looking into them. Then he places the flat of his hand somewhat heavily on hers. She looks up quizzically. Then she stands up and walks right past him through the glass door, as he watches her with a somewhat concerned look.

Shot 14: *Corridor.*
The woman removes linens from the cupboard. She hands them over to the lieutenant who, arms akimbo, taps with his right foot and watches her. He turns his head and whistles over his shoulder. The valet runs in; the woman calmly gives him the linens after she

looks coolly at the lieutenant. *Dissolve.*

Shot 15: *An outlying road.*
Two soldiers ride in, stop in front of the commander's house.
Dismount. One enters.

Shot 16: *The lieutenant's bedroom.*
The valet prepares the toiletry articles, sniffing at the small bottles.
Makes the bed in the alcove. The lieutenant enters and examines
the soiled linen on the chair. Finds a blood stain. Washes his hands.
Throws the water from the basin out the window, goes in his shirt
sleeves into the

Shot 17: *corridor,*
does not find the woman and descends

Shot 18: *the circular staircase.*
He opens the door to the

Shot 19: *guard room*
and looks through the other open door of the cubicle to the woman,
who is standing inside by the valet's camp bed. The soldiers watch
with hardly disguised astonishment how the lieutenant with a dark
mien nods at the woman to come to him. The woman looks at him
aloofly and turns back again to the camp bed. He exits angrily,
slams the door shut. One of the soldiers, a tall one with a Dutch
pipe, steps in front of the stove, follows the lieutenant with his eyes,
nods with understanding. Now the woman emerges from the
cubicle, motions to him with her eyes and asks the soldiers at the
stove something. Two of them stand at attention and say:
 'He talks about a corpse that gets up.'
The woman nods her head, exits slowly.

Shot 20: *Hall.*
The woman comes out, the lieutenant has been waiting for her, he
has his jacket on, a scarf over his arm which he puts round her
shoulders. Both are strangely aloof. Why? They exit.

Shot 21: *A path in the vineyards on a hill.*
They walk next to one another, separately. They stop. He looks
around, his arms akimbo. The wind blows. He says:
 'He will never return. He swam away.'
She was looking straight ahead as he said this, but now she looks
him straight in the eyes. She says:
 'Where is he?'
His face darkens, he says between pressed lips:
 'You no longer love me!'

She shakes her head, she does still love him, but he should tell her. She approaches him, rather close, she grasps like a child at a button near his neck, she asks more urgently:

'For God's sake, I beg of you, just tell me where he is.'

He shakes her free. She stands there startled, she lets her head sink, her face recedes into the shadow. He looks over the hill. Then he makes an angry gesture with his shoulders. He speaks with his hands. He says something like: How can you believe I would know more than you? Then he clumsily tries to grab her. But she looks at him coldly and moves away. At first startled, he then throws back his head (who cares!) and seizes her again, she resists with her hand and walks slowly with lowered head into the dunes. He stands there, half ashamed, half glowering, straightens his collar and turns round. *Dissolve.*

Shot 22: *Guard room.*
Soldiers clean their rifles, as the stooping, exasperated lieutenant passes by – visible through the window. The soldiers have angry looks on their faces.

Shot 23: *In front of the wooden gate.*
The woman emerges from the darkness, moving slowly. She passes through the gate.

Shot 24: *Guard room. Evening.*
The soldiers sit together round the stove, playing cards. One of them looks at the clock, which shows eleven. At that moment the door opens and the woman enters. The soldiers put their heads together, two want to stand up, the others recede. The woman notices nothing, she calmly walks to the plank door, she has a glass of milk in her hand, she disappears into the cubicle.

Shot 25: *Cubicle.*
The valet tosses and turns on the camp bed. The woman bends over him, she places the milk on a small table. Behind her, in the doorway, the tall soldier with the Dutch pipe appears. He looks in suspiciously.

Shot 26: *Guard room.*
The soldiers watch the tall one, who motions to them with his head. They all look into the cubicle. The Dutchman enters.

Shot 27: *Cubicle.*
The woman straightens up, looks round, sees the soldiers behind her. The cubicle is filled with them.

Shot 28: *The commander's house.*

A table, a lamp with shade. The commander bent over papers. (The guard soldier enters right and delivers the lieutenant's note.) The commander reads:

'Captain Gland allegedly shot himself yesterday evening between 11 and 11.15 in the guard room of the tower. Corpse disappeared. Awaiting orders. Lieutenant Seegers.'

He stands up and rings.

Shot 29: *Cubicle.*

The woman is still kneeling at the camp bed, but she looks round and when the Dutchman motions with his chin (not removing his pipe from his mouth) for her to leave, she stands up with composure and looks the soldier straight in the face. A commotion arises among the soldiers, several point to the door, point with their thumbs over their shoulders to the ceiling and then one of them even grabs her by the arm and wants to throw her out. She tears herself loose, jumps to the wall, where, crouching like a tiger, she holds back the crowd with her look. Suddenly she relaxes her posture. She walks towards the Dutchman; she grasps him by a button on his uniform. He says with his head bent back, as if in fear:

'Because you are running around with the murderer . . .'

She releases him, she reconsiders, several of them grab her now by the arm, almost as if they want to support her, but . . . she pulls herself free and runs like a hunted animal through the group that forms a path for her.

Shot 30: *Guard room.*
She runs through.

Shot 31: *Circular staircase from below.*
She calls up, then runs up the stairs.

Shot 32: *Bedroom.*
The lieutenant lies on the bed next to the candelabrum, clothed, reading the newspaper; he listens.

Shot 33: *Circular staircase.*
Halfway up the woman calls again and then continues to climb.

Shot 34: *Bedroom.*
The lieutenant sits up as the door opens, the woman tumbles in and, straightening her hair, calls to him anxiously. He immediately takes his sword and exits past her. Standing in the doorway, she follows him with her eyes, then follows.

Shot 35: *Outlying area.*

Three officers with twenty cavalrymen galloping!

Shot 36: *Guard room.*
The soldiers enter from the cubicle. At the same time the
lieutenant rushes in, he makes an imperious movement of his head,
perhaps he says: 'Attention!' One stands at attention, the others
gesticulate and shout:
'What do you care about the woman?'
The lieutenant points with his sword as if he were going to jump
into the crowd. At that point the Dutchman, with his pipe in his
mouth, pushes aside the soldier standing at attention, coolly steps
up to the lieutenant and says sharply:
'You are a murderer!'
The lieutenant wants to strangle him, but the others jump on the
lieutenant and pull him down. They throw the bottles and kick at
him with their boots. Tie him up, lay him on the table. Meanwhile,
the woman has crept in, walking in a slouch, she is pale, standing
at the wall, and shudders slightly at the word 'murderer'. Now in
the stillness they all look at her and she goes to the lieutenant. With
composure she walks over to him, she stares right into his face,
once again she has the crease on her brow and she suddenly turns
round and exits. The soldiers follow her with their eyes, puzzled,
and she disappears through the door into the darkness. The
Dutchman looks up and it is 11.15 p.m.

Shot 37: *Courtyard scene. It is dark night.*
The woman stands in the doorway, brightly lit, she takes a step out
and collapses sluggishly, unsteadily and without a sound. Two
soldiers run out, bend over her . . . *Dissolve.* (The entire detach-
ment of cavalry, riding elegantly like a tidal wave and very fast,
recedes into the distance . . .)
Then very quickly

Shot 38: *Dock.*
three officers, followed by about twenty cavalrymen, gallop over
the dock. They dismount in the courtyard. An officer lifts up the
woman, who lies like a white stain on the stones. They push their
way into the tower.

Shot 39: *Guard room.*
The bound lieutenant, a soldier with a cocked pistol. He hears the
cavalry, runs to the window, runs to the cellar door, shouts down.
The commander in the doorway looks with astonishment at the
bound lieutenant . . . the cavalry behind him flood into the guard
room, then down the cellar steps.

Shot 40: *Cellar.*
Among the barrels and bottles the half-drunken soldiers crawl round in shirt sleeves. They are apprehended and each one is escorted up by two cavalrymen with drawn swords.

Shot 41: *Circular staircase.*
The lights of three candelabra ascend the stairs. The woman is being carried up on the arms of one of those lighting the way.

Shot 42: *Dining-room. Dark.*
Enter the commander and the officers. The lieutenant; one of them carries the woman, places her on the chaise longue. The lieutenant clears the glasses from the table. The adjutant begins to write. The lieutenant reports. The lieutenant paces back and forth. He opens the window, all three see from above

Shot 43: *in the courtyard*
the soldiers carry out a table. (*Continues from below.*) The four officers come through the tower door very quickly and go to the table. They sit down. A knee-high, four-cornered paper lantern (Goya[3]) is placed on the ground.

Shot 44: *Dining-room. Half dark.*
The lieutenant watched the soldiers from the door. Now he strolls secretively over to the chaise longue and bends over the woman. She awakens, recognizes him, slips out from under him, pulls herself partially from the sofa to safety, staring at him all the while. Standing erect, ready to flee, she says to his face:
  'Don't you dare kill all of them! Because they know what you have done to one of them.'
He wants to attack her, she pulls away from him, slips out. He shakes the door, then leaves abruptly through the glass door.

Shot 45: *The woman's bedroom.*
She still holds the door closed, then relaxes her grip. Absent-mindedly arranges her hair, goes to the dresser and packs, suddenly like a wild person, underwear and clothes in baskets. Occasionally she stops, breathing fast, hand on her brow, absent.

Shot 46: *In the courtyard.*
The rebels are brought out, assembled in front of the table. Several tremble, one bawls. They stand in a line. The commander rises, says something. The rebels are surrounded and pushed towards the back. The commander and his officers quickly go into the house. The lieutenant, large and brutal, becomes visible for a moment alone (the rebels have been pushed into a dark corner of the

courtyard), as he carries the paper lantern to the back.

Shot 47: *The woman's bedroom.*
The woman hears something, she runs to the window and looks down. She sees the paper lantern move through the courtyard.

Shot 48: *At the wall*
the rebels stand in the shadows. They are waiting for something. They watch the paper lantern come towards them. The lieutenant emerges from the darkness, he places the lantern on the ground, he reads the judgment. The rebels stand rigid. The lieutenant swings the lantern, the soldiers form a line, they aim their rifles. The scene has a ghostly light from below owing to the lantern.

Shot 49: *The woman's bedroom.*
The woman rushes from the drapes. She runs out.

Shot 50: *Courtyard.*
The lieutenant raises his dagger. At this moment something white enters, the woman running from the right. The lieutenant lets his dagger fall. The soldiers shoot. Almost simultaneously the woman stops in her tracks. She comes to herself, then moves four steps in the direction of the lieutenant, she emerges from the darkness, she looks at him. Soldiers want to remove the lantern, but the lieutenant kicks the lantern so that darkness prevails. *Dissolve.*

Shot 51: *Tower entrance.*
The officers emerge. As the woman passes by, she halts, says something, bends her head, continues on her way. After saluting, they wait. The woman goes into the house.

Shot 52: *Circular staircase.*
The soldiers carry out trunks.

Shot 53: *Courtyard.*
Soldiers pull an ancient travelling carriage out of the coach house and harness the horses. The woman approaches it, seen from behind. The officers have mounted, they hold the horses and carriage. Then the lieutenant emerges again from the shadows with the lantern. The woman looks at him and climbs into the carriage without a word. Then the carriage begins to move.

Shot 54: *Courtyard corner.*
Soldiers gather the bodies of the executed rebels.

Shot 55: *Courtyard.*
The lieutenant is still standing there with the lantern in his hand. He watches the carriage depart. For a long time the woman does

not turn round, but at the gate she stands up and turns towards him, without a gesture. Her face is empty, large, clouded over. The lieutenant brushes his brow, he drops the lantern. It extinguishes.

Act III

'The year of mourning' or 'The wonderful life' or 'The Madonna among the animals'

Shot 1: *Night.*
Two paper lanterns (attached to the front of the carriage) emerge from the background. The woman is sitting in the carriage. The carriage swerves and halts. Three gentlemen in frock coats appear in the background. Waving. The woman descends, one of the paper lanterns changes into a chandelier and illuminates a small marble table in a

Shot 2: *restaurant private booth.*
The woman joins the cavaliers at the table. The carriage has disappeared. A waiter brings drinks. A thin, delicate cavalier strokes the woman's bare arm, she ignores him. She toasts another one who has an aster in his buttonhole, and he disappears. Trembling, she stands up, stares after the man who disappeared, the glass falls over, the thick, dark liquid flows over her dress, she is confused. The thin man offers her his arm, a black, elegant carriage glides in, she steps in with the cavalier. One of them stays behind. He tosses round banknotes, grins, fades out. The chandelier extinguishes. The carriage lights glide through the darkness, stop. In the carriage the woman and the thin man stand up, see an obstacle in front of the horses: a bundle of elegant men's clothes, a top hat, a large aster, the carriage moves on, very springy. It halts.

Shot 3: *At an entrance.*
The woman descends and enters

Shot 4: *a brightly-lit ballroom.*
She is caught up and dances away with a huge, spindly, elegant young man. Her companion fades out. The dancer has a pockmarked face. For quite a while they dance alone under the chandelier. While dancing, they pass a long silk drape; he pulls it back and drags her out; they flee through

Shot 5: *a draped corridor,*
and then she leans half-drunken in his arms, in

Shot 6: *a carriage,*
which fills up, for suddenly two other men are in it who attempt to
get her drunk by force, putting filled glasses to her lips. She resists,
but one of them throws her back, he is fat, sweaty, one of his eyes
is glued shut, the other opened too wide by a large monocle. She is
lying on a

Shot 7: *white ottoman,*
and the man moves behind her. He disappears. But the corner of
the room changes into

Shot 8: *the corner of the tower courtyard,*
and under the trees the lieutenant is walking alone, back and forth,
his arms akimbo. He stops at the gate. The tree there begins to
move, apparently there is a wind, its leaves fall. The lieutenant is
still standing at the gate, the leaves fall on him, he is completely
covered by wilted leaves. Now he disappears.

Shot 9: *At the canal.*
The leaves continue to fall, the woman walks among them towards
a canal, her dress is torn. A ragged man walks next to her; they
climb

Shot 10: *stairs*
through

Shot 11: *crooked streets, narrow like house corridors, with washing hung
out to dry above.*
She runs away from him to an

Shot 12: *attic room,*
sits down with her hands in her lap, bent forward . . . It is raining
outside. *Fade to*

Shot 13: *the bedroom in the tower.*
The lieutenant is lying fully clothed in bed among many
newspapers. He arises from the newspapers, suddenly lets one fall,
looks at the ceiling, stands up, shuffles through the

Shot 14: *corridor*
to the glass door, which he opens with a key and enters

Shot 15: *the dining-room,*
which is dark, as if devoured by moths. He goes to the drapes,
looking at the table where the glasses have been standing for a year
already. He opens a crack in the drapes, as the captain once did.
He looks out. It is raining.

Shot 16: *Attic room. Evening.*
There is a ring, the woman looks up. An old woman waddles in, rubs her hands. She is a madam. Enter the fat, black cavalier (Daumier[4]). He has a dress over his arm. He places it over the chair. The old woman examines the cloth, exits. The woman sits bent forward, her elbows on her lap, she looks aloof and somewhat exhausted, turning her head towards the dress. She glances at the cavalier, stands up slowly, looks in the mirror, slides her fingers down her sides, releases the clip over her shoulder and walks fatalistically with the dress behind the dressing screen, while the cavalier lights a new cigarette in a flash. She emerges immediately in her evening gown. He looks her up and down, grins. He has bad teeth. *Dissolve.*

Shot 17: *A carriage*
drives through the evening with its lights on to

Shot 18: *the Bats' Cabaret.*
Musicians with long Spanish guitars sit on velvet cushions. Swollen, the cavalier enters with the woman, who looks tanned, racy. They are still standing in the middle when the room fills up with costumed people (four or five). The woman dances with all of them on the carpeted floor. Drapes in the background fall away, the room changes into

Shot 19: *the lieutenant's bedroom.*
The closed drapes in the alcove are pulled open. The lieutenant wakes up. He has had a nightmare. Sitting in bed, he lights a cigarette, he shakes his head ponderously, he lies back. Drapes fall.

Shot 20: *The ballroom*
comes once again into sharp focus. A knife-battle is taking place. The lamps are broken, someone grabs the woman and pulls her out to

Shot 21: *a carriage.*
Wretched, with a limping horse. The new cavalier kisses the woman brutally, bends her back, she drives on alone. The coach driver throws her out of the carriage because she cannot pay and strikes her with his whip. She stands

Shot 22: *next to a street lantern,*
and gentlemen in frock coats pass by. She holds out her hand. Then three drunken young men come by and drag her along through the

Shot 23: *street with drying laundry, narrow like house corridors,* and carry her, when she collapses,

Shot 24: *up the stairs*

Shot 25: *to the wallpapered attic room, same as shot 12.*
They throw her on the bed and leave with a suitcase. The drapes
billow in the wind, it is black outside the window. Snow falls.

Shot 26: *Snow falls on trees that have now lost all their leaves.*
The trees become smaller, *fade to*

Shot 27: *the lieutenant's bedroom.*
And the lieutenant stands at the window and looks at the trees. The
captain's valet clears up the meal. Many newspapers are strewn
about, everything looks messy. The lieutenant walks down the

Shot 28: *corridor,*
lethargically, his hands in his trouser pockets, to

Shot 29: *the dining-room door.*
He turns round, he cannot decide to go into the dining-room, he
turns and goes back to

Shot 30: *the bedroom.*
He sits down and smokes. Throws the newspapers in the fireplace,
pulls open the windows, sprays perfume round the room, sniffs. He
looks at his frayed sleeves, curses. Then he pulls open drawers,
rummages among the underwear, changes clothes. He cleans up,
combs his hair, poses at attention in front of the mirror. He has
taken off his old boots. Then he goes to the door without his
helmet, pulling on his white gloves.

Shot 31: *Courtyard.*
The travelling coach has pulled up, the valet hands the lieutenant
his coat and the helmet with long feathers. He climbs in and drives
off. Snow is falling. The trees are still, two of them change into

Shot 32: *the wallpapered attic room*
with the woman at the window, while it snows outside. The room
has looked until now very impoverished. The woman presses her
face to the glass. The old, dirty woman brings food on a tray, leaves
again rapidly. The woman had glanced round, she now looks out
of the window again. Then the door opens and the lieutenant is
standing there. He takes off his helmet with the feathers. The
woman looks round, sees the lieutenant, she stumbles towards the
wall. The lieutenant shrugs his shoulders, he looks at her with a
serious expression. Then she calmly moves a step towards him, she
invites him to sit down on the only chair, looks at him again. He

once again makes the gesture of not-being-able-to-do-otherwise. Then she calmly walks to the right to the screen, the lieutenant looks out the window from the middle of the room. She comes out again immediately in the dress from the beginning of the act. She passes by him to the door, her head somewhat lowered, one shoulder pushed back towards the lieutenant. He follows her out, stooping slightly, since the door is too low for him. *Dissolve.*

Act IV

[Shots 1–9 are missing in the typescript.]

Shot 10: *Cubicle. Evening.*
The valet pulls the captain's jacket from the bed and dusts it off, tries it on in front of the small window, combs his hair, shuffles out in his work trousers. He imitates the captain.

Shot 11: *Guard room.*
The young soldiers are playing cards at the stove. The valet walks by, his right hand in his jacket (à la Napoleon and the captain). The soldiers laugh and continue to play cards.

Shot 12: *Hall, same as shot 9.*
They have all been drinking and this has animated them. They tell jokes and laugh uproariously. In their midst the woman, completely passive, with a pale, immovable face. The commander stands up and toasts:

'Our young friend, the young captain, has just revealed to me that he wishes to go before the altar and it is to be with the beautiful wife of our old friend, the old captain!'

Uproarious laughter. The glasses are lifted. The woman has half stood up and suddenly the table becomes dark, across from the woman sits the captain, heavy and black, in front of the fluttering white window drapes. He has calmly rested his arm on the table and he is playing with something in his hand. It becomes brighter. The officers rush to the woman, who has fallen over the table. *Dissolve.*

Shot 13: *In front of the glass door in the tower.*
The valet, seen from behind, enters the dining-room.

Shot 14: *A country road between dark hills at night.*
In the closed but transparent glass coach the lieutenant and the woman. Wretched and miserable. He removes his helmet, dries his brow. She looks at him with an unfriendly stare. Why?

Shot 15: *In front of the glass door.*
The lieutenant pushes the woman in before him. He calls something down the stairs.

Shot 16: *The dining-room.*
The woman catches sight of the valet at the table who is playing the captain, reading the newspaper and smoking, getting drunk. He is startled and collapses. The woman makes a few uncertain steps towards the table. She has lowered her head, but looks straight ahead and almost smiles. The lieutenant, following her, sees through the bluff and slaps the valet, throws him out. The woman falls into the rocking chair. *Dissolve.*

Shot 17: *The lieutenant's bedroom. Evening.*
The lieutenant enters, he throws his jacket on the bed, pushes open the window, sprays perfume round the room.
    'This constant stink in the room!'
At this moment he hears something, he goes to the door, takes a pistol, leaves, walks across

Shot 18: *the corridor,*
looks down and walks with a candelabrum that he takes from

Shot 19: *the dining-room.*
Only his arm can be seen.

Shot 20: *Circular staircase.*
The lieutenant walks down and sees below

Shot 21: *on the stone floor*
the woman, spread out, kneeling where one year ago the bloody jacket lay. The lieutenant lifts her up, he leads her back upstairs and he says to himself:
    'But now the wedding, for God's sake, before you land in the mad house.'

Shot 22: *Arrest cell.*
The valet. Catching fleas. The sliding window opens. A soldier's fist pushes in a bowl. The window closes and slides open again and a woman's hand pushes fruit in.

Shot 23: *The country road with trees that are budding again.*
The woman walks along. A man comes towards her. She halts; it is the captain. He looks very calm, he is smoking. He walks by her, nodding. *Dissolve.*

Shot 24: *The woman's bedroom.*
Kneeling on the floor, the woman folds linen. The lieutenant

stands behind her. Suddenly she clasps her hands in front of her face and lets her head fall with great sobs on the piles of linen. The lieutenant behind her shakes his head, laughing maliciously.

Shot 25: *Guard room.*
Yes, soon the wedding will take place. The men are cleaning the room with mops and rags. They change clothes, slick their hair. The lieutenant enters; he sticks a thick cigar between the buttons of each of their jackets. They grin.

Shot 26: *Courtyard.*
Coaches arrive. The lieutenant, behind the gate, receives the guests. The four officers and the commander arrive. They enter the house.

Shot 27: *The hall below*
is decorated with flags and so on. An oval table is almost breaking under the weight of fruit bowls, mounds of plates, baskets of tableware. Between the upholstered chairs are ice buckets with bottles. The woman sits at the table. The officers enter. Formal greetings.

Shot 28: *Guard room.*
The soldiers, in gala uniform, are pasting together the paper lantern from Act II. One of them stops another, who knocks it, salutes and says:
  'Watch out, kids, people were shot under it.'
The soldiers grin, salute the lantern.

Shot 29: *The hall.*
The drinking is in full swing. The woman – calm, with charming grace – is serving the guests. Then the chairs are pushed back, they rise. A soldier appears at the wall, he plays the accordion. The officers dance with the woman. The lieutenant drinks alone at the table. And now the officers begin one after the other to change back into the cavaliers. One of them has an aster in his buttonhole, one has a pockmarked face, one pushes a monocle in his eye and all of them are aggressive and fresh. She begins, however, to dance ever more wildly and shamelessly; she laughs freely, then her face freezes up completely, only to laugh again. Two cavaliers drag her to the table, empty the glasses into her mouth, while the lieutenant watches with a threatening look. One of them strokes her arm, the lieutenant jumps up and strikes the table. But fortunately the commander is still just able to make a toast at the head of the table. And while everyone seeks glasses to toast, there appear above

Shot 30: *in the corridor*
three drunken soldiers who lower the paper lantern.

Shot 31: *Hall.*
In the middle of the toast the lantern lowers on to the table, the woman jumps with a start out of the arms of the cavaliers, the lieutenant stares at her with horror. She turns her face slowly; he follows her gaze and in the place of the commander stands the captain, toasting. After a moment of horrified gazing, the woman grasps a glass, reaching far over the table, and throws it at the one who is toasting. She pounds on the table while laughing wildly so that the glasses dance; she jumps up crazily and rushes past the drunk officers to the captain and (*close-up*) the commander shoves her arms away coolly and aloofly. Leave-taking. The officers go to the window, look out. Time to leave.

Shot 32: *Courtyard.*
The coaches are harnessed. The guests rush out to the coaches. The coaches rush out of the gate.

Shot 33: *Hall.*
Not overturned! The lieutenant stands in the middle of the hall and, apparently with great calm, shoots with his pistol at the lantern. The woman, sunken into the commander's chair, waves her foot, stares at the wall. Bowed over her, the lieutenant has one hand on the chair back, one on the table and beside himself with anger tells her what she does not hear. He straightens up, looks darkly at the tablecloth, smashes a glass on an ice bucket and walks to the bell. He rings.

Shot 34: *Guard room.*
The soldiers, drunk, half-dressed, hear the alarm bell, grab their clothes. The door opens abruptly, the lieutenant steps in, stomping with his foot, they rush out.

Shot 35: *Hall.*
They stand in formation, at attention, half-dressed, completely drunk. The lieutenant gives orders. They rush to the table, each takes a glass. They run back to the formation, when the lieutenant beats with his sword on the table, they must drink on beat. Suddenly he grabs the woman's arm roughly while she continues to stare into the emptiness, but now she looks at the soldiers. And then she begins to laugh so hard that she shakes. It is completely unnatural, she is transformed, she has seen the emptiness and now she jumps up on the table and dances and everyone watches her. But at this moment the valet, completely drunk and standing in the

door wearing the captain's jacket, can no longer hold the rope to which the paper lantern is attached; he releases it and it falls on the woman, who is immobilized, holding it in her hands. And the valet, startled, rushes to the table and then everyone laughs loudly in unison. The woman lets the lantern fall on the valet and sinks down, the soldiers catch her. But she holds on to the tablecloth and, freeing herself from them, with the tablecloth in her grip she walks to the stairs, trailing it behind her. The lieutenant, however, rushes over to the valet. Suddenly he straightens up, looks round as if ruined, takes a few steps towards the woman and stops. *Dissolve.*

Shot 36: *The captain's bedroom.*
Sitting on the bed, a dark and bulky profile, the captain smokes calmly. *Dissolve.*

Act V

'The evil child digs up a corpse' or 'The flesh-eating plant' or 'Through the broken defence the black waters break'

It is night.

Shot 1: *The woman's bedroom.*
The captain goes from the bed to the door.

Shot 2: *Circular staircase.*
Unclear, as if a bundle of clothes, the woman rushes down the circular stairs.

Shot 3: *Gate.*
The woman runs towards the gate. Pounds at it like a mad woman, the gate gives way, she runs out, the gate stays open.

Shot 4: *Night in the hills.*
The woman walking.

Shot 5: *More hills.*
The woman walking towards the camera more slowly, hours have passed.

Shot 6: *The lieutenant's bedroom.*
The lieutenant is sleeping restlessly, then he pulls away the alcove drapes and gets up. In his shirt sleeves he goes to the door and walks into

Shot 7: *the corridor,*
where he knocks on the door of the woman's room. Then he enters.

Shot 8: *The woman's bedroom.*
The lieutenant enters, he lights a candle, illuminates the bed. The woman is gone. He is slightly startled; he goes with the candle to the window, then back again. He appears to be thinking.

Shot 9: *In the hills*
the woman is wandering. She appears to be tired.

Shot 10: *The woman's bedroom.*
On the chair next to the woman's bed the lieutenant is seated and has fallen asleep. His shoulders are slumped and ragged, he looks remarkably old. Then he twitches and awakens. He looks again at the bed, leaves with the candle.

Shot 11: *Corridor.*
The lieutenant gives the alarm. He looks down and sees

Shot 12: *in the hall*
the half-dressed soldiers stumbling out.

Shot 13: *The hall, same as Act IV.*
The soldiers stand in formation. They see the lieutenant with the candle. He steps up to them, strong but as if ruined. He counts them with the candle in his hand, absent-mindedly, then he turns round and leaves to go upstairs again. They stare stupidly after him. *Dissolve.*

Shot 14: *In the hills*
the woman is wandering, and behind a hill the captain joins her. He calmly walks at her side, smoking. She walks slowly next to him, like his slave, she dares not look at him.

Shot 15: *The lieutenant's bedroom.*
The lieutenant enters, he looks at the room like a stranger; he has lived there for a year, it was not a happy year. He lies down on the bed, half-dressed, stiffly.

Shot 16: *Guard room.*
A lazy, sleepy soldier sits at the table. He lifts his head from the tabletop, through the window he sees the woman creeping home. She is fatigued, dishevelled, she has sand in her hair and walks like an animal.

Shot 17: *The woman's bedroom.*
The woman enters shyly. She lets down her hair, falls on her bed as if dead. The captain in black is sitting on the chair and watches her.

Shot 18: *The tower from outside, day breaks.*
A window opens. The lieutenant, in shirt sleeves, looks out with a scowl. He looks at the sky.

Shot 19: *The woman's bedroom. Dawn.*
The captain has disappeared. The lieutenant enters, he stands in the door, glances at the bed, wants to come in, thinks again, turns round, shuffles out.

Shot 20: *Circular staircase.*
The lieutenant descends slowly, carrying the wide pistol case. A soldier (the guard) salutes at the bottom. He does not see him, walks into the

Shot 21: *courtyard*
and shoots at targets on the wall.

Shot 22: *Guard room and cubicle.*
The plank door is smashed. The soldiers are lounging on torn straw mattresses, one is still guzzling, several are sleeping. Half-closed metal blinds through which pale light shines. One of them hears shooting. He turns over. No one gets up.

Shot 23: *Dining-room.*
It looks as if it has been devoured by moths. The woman moves round, dragging her feet. She sets the table. She looks out, glances from above

Shot 24: *into the courtyard*
where the lieutenant is target shooting. He is supporting his right arm with his left hand.

Shot 25: *Dining-room.*
The woman has no expression on her face. She sets the table calmly: two place settings, then, hesitating, a third one. The lieutenant enters. He sees the third place setting. Passing by, he takes it in his fist, apparently with calm, one arm akimbo, and throws it in the corner. Sits down. Goes to the window, looks out through a crack. The woman sits down. The valet serves. This is the morning after the wedding, the lieutenant thinks to himself and looks at the woman. But she is looking at the third chair, because the captain is sitting there. The lieutenant sits down now, suddenly he notices the woman's gaze, he leans forward, he stares at the scene with great concentration, he sees nothing, he goes to the window, he pulls up the blinds. The woman pushes her plate to the one who is invisible to the lieutenant, and – smiling strangely – like a servant, gives him her salt shaker. The lieutenant is uneasy, why

does she smile that way? No, this is unbearable. He moves around her in a wide arc, he goes to the door and exits. *Dissolve.*

Shot 26: *Guard room.*
The half-dressed soldiers sit around the table and eat their mash. The door opens and the lieutenant saunters in. He scowls, he has stray hairs on his shoulders, has not washed, even his jacket is open. He does not notice the mess, or even how lazily they stand up. He sits down at the table and lets them eat. They continue to eat, their skulls deep in their plates, squinting at him from the side. He does not eat. He stares at nothing and plays with a knife. *Dissolve.*

Shot 27: *Fade-in, guard room.*
The lieutenant is standing at the window, his back to the camera, the soldiers no longer pay him any attention, he looks out. And you see nothing through the window except

Shot 28: *the black-leafed trees in the courtyard*
that shake in the evening wind. And

Shot 29: *in the courtyard*
the lieutenant stands and looks at the sky.

Shot 30: *The sky*
with moving clouds.

Shot 31: *Courtyard.*
The lieutenant turns round and shuffles into the house.

Shot 32: *Guard room.*
The men are eating again. The lieutenant enters, sits down with them. Eats nothing.

Shot 33: *Dining-room.*
The woman kneels at the fireplace, she is cold, she stretches her bare arms over the fire, her clothes are torn. The captain is rocking in the rocking chair. The woman stands up, says something to him, leaves slowly. She begins to run, at the door already. The captain fades out. The empty chair continues to rock.

Shot 34: *The hall.*
The woman takes in passing some bottles from the table.

Shot 35: *Guard room.*
The woman enters with bottles under her arms. She places them on the table. The lieutenant hardly looks up. The woman fills the soldiers' glasses, they toast her. Everyone drinks, the woman too, who sits cowering on a chair across from the lieutenant, who is not

drinking; he looks at her briefly. She is looking fixedly at her husband, as if examining – like a child who thinks slowly – the face of a strange man. Her strange husband. He then drinks hastily. Now a soldier plays the accordion. It is warm here. There are people. Here it is better than elsewhere. One of them asks the woman to dance, the soldiers are already waltzing with each other. Why not? She waltzes as well and watches the lieutenant constantly and it goes well, the lieutenant even tries to smile at her. But why does she get that small crease on her forehead? The lieutenant stands up and exits.

Shot 36: *Courtyard.*
The lieutenant comes out. He shuffles over to the gate, closes it. He begins to look strangely alone. He shuffles further to the corner of the courtyard, finds the pistol case, lifts it up and takes it under his arm. Lost in thought he searches the targets for hits, then he turns round, walks back to the house, sunk in thought. *Dissolve.*

Shot 37: *Guard room.*
The woman waltzes. The lieutenant stands in the doorway. He looks at the woman, turns round, shuffles out. The woman halts, stares after him.

Shot 38: *Hall.*
The lieutenant drinks while walking. The woman comes in. Somehow she is revived, she walks up

Shot 39: *the stairs*
somewhat more freely.

Shot 40: *Dining-room. Dark.*
The lieutenant guzzles from a bottle. He waits. The woman enters. The lieutenant guzzles, throws away the bottle, holds himself up by the white drapes. He speaks hoarsely, wildly, choking:
    'I'll wait no longer.'
The woman wants to leave, simply to turn round. The lieutenant springs like a tiger. He catches her at the glass door, smashes it in the process, drags her back in. She resists, she bends back her upper body like a supple animal. He throws her to the table, which she holds on to and stares at him. He pulls a pistol from the case, he thrashes around with it, he points it to his temple. She raises her hands, she clearly is afraid, she says something with pale lips, very few words, he listens, she has said nothing for so long. He goes towards her, takes her face in his two hands, he has thrown the pistol on the table. But she looks at him like a stranger, despite everything. He releases her, this can't go on, he has started and is

going to take care of things, whatever the price, he'll put an end to these ghosts. He walks to the windows, pushes them, they break, the white drapery billows into the room. He throws the table at the wall, he's taking care of things. He tears down a drape, bundles it up, throws it out of the window, follows it with his eyes, grins over his shoulder, he is drunk, he is becoming bizarre. She has been watching him calmly from the table, now she smiles, pale and bloated in the shadows, she smiles. She moves from the table to the door, free, light, but extremely tense, she looks out, she is somewhat crazy, but that doesn't matter. She too goes to the window, always stooped now, she looks out. Then, as she turns round beside the lieutenant, she sees the captain emerge from her bedroom door, large, massive, apparently sunk in his thoughts or as if he had forgotten something in the room. The woman touches the lieutenant's sleeve, she stares at the apparition, the lieutenant begins to move, he walks through the room with heavy steps, he stops, looks at her to see where the ghost is located, then he raises his hand and drops it right through the captain, with his whole arm. The captain has stopped, now he continues to move, he grins slightly. But the lieutenant sees how the woman laughs, she is beginning to laugh, her special laugh for this, she has experienced all the misery of the earth; now she is laughing, she is laughing it off. She goes around the table and laughs. She straightens the tablecloth, she runs her hand over the drapery. She laughs the whole time. The lieutenant has had enough, he is seized by the horror, this is too much, he is only a human being and not a particularly bright one at that! He bends down to the pistol case, fixing the woman with his stare, he takes out a pistol and moves in front of the woman, seizes her right hand with his left. He aims with his right. He determines where he must aim by looking back at her. He shoots where she is looking. He shoots three times. Each time it whizzes through the captain and the captain continues to walk. And the lieutenant shoots in the new direction. But after the third shot his arm sinks and the horror seizes him even more strongly. He grasps at his throat and runs out. The woman follows him with short steps, then stops, laughs and turns round; she laughs again.

Shot 41: *Corridor. Rapid timing.*
The lieutenant runs through

Shot 42: *the lieutenant's bedroom.*
The lieutenant enters, panting. He leans against the dresser, throws clothes about. He fetches suitcases from under the camp bed, throws his clothes in, he takes his uniform jackets from the

hook and throws them in the suitcases. He rings like a madman until he is trembling. He is at his wits' end. Then he shakes the clothes cupboard. Nothing, it doesn't move. The devil take it, that too! The lieutenant smashes the cupboard with a chair. It breaks open and the lieutenant jumps back. (*Close-up.*) In the cupboard there is a half-decayed corpse wearing uniform trousers and a shirt! The captain. And it falls slowly out of the cupboard. And when the lieutenant sees it, he bends down, lifts the left arm, runs to the door, through the

Shot 43: *corridor*
in a wild chase to the

Shot 44: *dining-room,*
where the woman comes towards him, calls something at the door, turns right round, but she stands there as if rooted to the spot. He rushes back in, pulls her with him by the hand.

Shot 45: *The lieutenant's bedroom.*
They rush in, they hurry to the clothes cupboard, the lieutenant bends down, lifts up the corpse, carries it to the bed, throws an end of the sheet over it, looks round at the woman. But she has straightened up, catches her breath, pulls a strand of hair from her eyes, lifts up her arms, falls over the lieutenant, who catches her in his arms. They stand upright for a moment in the black bedroom, the drapes billow into the room; then the lieutenant throws her violently and wildly on the bed and falls over her. *Dissolve.*

The end.

Part IV
The *Threepenny* Material
(1930–1932)

The Bruise – A Threepenny Film

[GBFA 19/307-20. Nero-Film Company purchased the adaptation rights to Brecht's and Weill's musical on 21 May 1930, hoping to capitalize on what had become the most popular play in Weimar Germany. On Brecht's insistence, Nero-Film negotiated a further agreement, signed on 3 August, that allowed him to write a scenario with his theatre collaborators Caspar Neher and Slatan Dudow, as well as Leo Lania. Though the agreement accorded Brecht the right to demand changes if the final cut did not follow their scenario, it also obliged them to follow the original play's text both in style and content. While Brecht and his team were writing the film treatment in southern France, Nero-Film had resold the rights to Tobis-Klang-Film and Warner Brothers in anticipation of an international release by the celebrated director Georg Wilhelm Pabst. Nero-Film proceeded to rent studio space and hire the casts for both a German and a French version. When the production company realized that Brecht's screenplay differed in essential points from the stage play – he had introduced, for example, an entirely new motif, the bruise of the title, as a visual element to connect structurally the three antagonistic groups: Macheath and his gang, Peachum and his beggars, and chief of police Tiger Brown and his men – it sought an accommodation, which Brecht refused. The production began nonetheless, with a new script written by Béla Balász and Ladislaus Vajda (see Brecht's footnote 17), whereupon Brecht went to court (see 'The *Threepenny* Lawsuit'). An English-language version of Pabst's shooting script – not identical with the final cut – can be found in *Masterworks of the German Cinema* (New York: Harper, 1973), pp. 179–263.

For 'The Bruise', Brecht basically took from the play the characters and the Victorian setting in order to construct a much more radical image of struggle between class interests. This modification of the storyline affected the sequence of scenes and songs as well as the play's message. In a typically Brechtian interpretation of the Hollywood happy ending, the three main enemies discover their common interests when confronted with the threat of a revolt by the mass of exploited beggars. Thus, Brecht and his collaborators not only revamped the story to sharpen the political message, but also took into account the cinematic medium for which they were writing, integrating parallel montage sequences and conventions of the American gangster and romance film genres. The numbered footnotes are from Brecht's original text.]

First Part
Polly Peachum's Love and Marriage[1] [2]

Love at First Grasp

Old Oak Street, a winding row of dilapidated warehouses, granaries and apartment houses, overlooks a dirty canal criss-crossed by several wooden bridges, the largest of which is St George's Bridge. Stepping out one early afternoon from the Drury Lane Swamp, the brothel located in this street, Mr Macheath catches sight of a girl fetching beer who will bring him within a few hours to the marriage altar and to a close call with the gallows before many days have passed.[3] He looks at her only from behind. He begins to follow her immediately and knows: he will marry this charming bottom. A small crowd of people round a shabby ballad singer at the end of the street provides him with an opportunity to approach Miss Polly Peachum more familiarly. The ballad's content is a sketchy report about the alarming misdeeds of a certain Mac the Knife, which seem even more alarming because of their unprovability. At a particular point in the song, when this unprovability is regretfully and admiringly emphasized, Mr Macheath allows himself a very questionable trick: standing behind the captivating girl, he suddenly reaches round the nape of her neck for the slender throat with his thumb and middle finger – the all-too-practised grasp of a seducer on the docks. In response to her shocked look, he repeats with a smile the ballad's last verse – 'Nothing can be proven against him'. Immediately the victim turns round to leave, he follows on her heels – she will no longer escape him. But now the crowd shrinks back from him as if he were a wild animal, heads press together behind him and malicious whispering follows the figure hurrying after the girl with the beer stein.[4]

1. Sound films have the deplorable habit of forgoing intertitles. The titles in the *Threepenny* film are long shots of an entire section's intellectual site. They do not only serve to clarify what follows. In certain instances they can claim a value in themselves: in this case their function would consist simply of being seen. Beyond that they ensure the epic flow by dividing the film into chapters. To leave them out would be idiotic.
2. At the beginning the entire cast sings 'You gentlemen who think you have a mission . . .', *The Threepenny Opera* [see 'Second Threepenny Finale', Act II, Scene 6].
3. See *The Threepenny Opera*, 'The Ballad of Sexual Obsession' [Act II, Scene 4].
4. In this first part, which portrays a free love unburdened by earthly interests, it will be effective to awaken a certain *suspicion* about Mr Macheath – who is so thoughtlessly, so instinctively married here – by means of all sorts of improbable and witty ideas.

Where There's a Will, There's a Way

The same day; the Macheath Gang – already numbering over 120 members from various social strata around 1900[5] – has organized for the evening hours an energetic visit to the National Deposit Bank, the fourteenth such undertaking. The appropriation of the old, honourable bank will take place differently from what was planned for this evening. Polly Peachum's first love and Mr Macheath's final marriage will bring about the great transformation. We come across Mr Macheath once again as he notes with satisfaction the contents of the store window display that Miss Polly finds worthy of her interest: an engaged couple in wax. Discovering the reflection of her pursuer in the window glass, she moves on in a huff. But the Octopus Hotel, which she enters to fetch the beer, already anticipates the first resolution: in the crowded, cramped confusion of the mazurka, danced by the prostitutes, maidservants and loafers in front of the bar, Polly suddenly, but not exactly unexpectedly, feels herself pulled by her pursuer into the swirling entertainment. She hardly resists. Her destiny is sealed. Without a word she leaves the pub with him – although she does not know him – from the other side, exiting to a different street (they have not danced more than half a round) and, crossing the courtyard, they pass by amorous, embracing couples and then make their way past the factories along the canal over which the moon is just rising.[6] Meanwhile her companion still found time to tell several gentlemen waiting in two cars parked in front of the hotel that the bank visit planned for that day is to be postponed and instead a wedding, which had just been decided upon, is to be organized.[7] In the meantime she waits patiently for him with the filled beer stein in her hand. She says: 'I'll only go a short way with you.' Then two hopelessly infatuated lovers move through the night in carefree and blind love,[8] while the revolver shots of the thieves in the car echo through the city's shopping street, for a wedding trousseau must be collected. No less than twenty major robberies bring together all the necessities, from the marriage bed to the toothbrush and, most importantly, a rich selection. The lovers take a boat,[9] while three cars block a sidewalk,

5. At some later point in the film this 'club' can be shown in a photo in the style of certain choral society portraits.
6. One or two moons will suffice.
7. He names a banquet committee and sets the wedding for 11 p.m. sharp. The place: the absent Duke of Somersetshire's stable.
8. See *The Threepenny Opera*, 'Lovers' Dialogue' [end of Act I, Scene 2].
9. With her at the oars.

several masked men break a store window and steal a toothbrush. Meanwhile a blind beggar snitches on four men, who are arrested by the police as they steal a grandfather clock, while behind the gate of a factory entrance the bride quickly pulls on the wedding dress (which, wrapped in newspaper, was shoved under the groom's arm).

A Social Event

Mr Macheath's wedding with Miss Polly Peachum takes place in the fourth hour of their acquaintanceship in the stable of the Duke of Somersetshire. Since this gentleman is at present not in London, it is only a matter of twisting the arms of two domestics to 'rent' a banqueting hall that holds 150 guests. At eleven o'clock sharp it is filled to the last seat. Under the banquet manager's clever direction, the wedding couple finds the stable already transformed into a huge parlour. The first impression might be of a somewhat conventional occasion: these good, rather stout men have brought their women; but if a marriage licence were required of them, some would certainly be embarrassed and the bride may herself offer the fruit bowl to certain of the women whose social function she perhaps suspects but can never approve. All in all, this wedding is a social event. Prominent members of society who are in attendance include:[10] the High Judge from Drury Lane, a general, two members from the Upper House of Parliament, three well-known lawyers, the vicar of St Margaret's; noted in particular was the presence of Chief of Police Tiger Brown, an old war buddy of the groom, as was whispered among the guests. The banquet meal – in the yard a complete butchery has been set up for the entire duration and proceeds to prepare not less than three entire oxen – is embellished by the performances of several of the groom's musically endowed colleagues. The bride, too, outdoes herself with a short ballad for which she receives ample applause.[11] A brief, unpleasant episode is of no further importance: towards the end of the banquet, which lasts into the early morning hours, three of the men report to their gang leader Mac the Knife that a beggar snitched while they were making 'arrangements' for the celebration and they barely escaped the

10. It can be indicated that this chapter is a newspaper report by copying a newspaper page over it. Single sentences from the society page, such as 'noted in particular', can be highlighted with bold-faced type.
11. 'Barbara Song', *The Threepenny Opera* [Act I, Scene 3]. During the ballad Polly, the actress, stands small and alone in the huge space.

police. This beggar is a member of J.J. Peachum's Beggars' Trust.[12]

Second Part
The Beggar King's Power

The Dull Routine
The next morning members of Macheath's gang, undoubtedly coming directly from the banquet, break into Peachum's costume house for beggars and leave with the contents of the cash register. Upon entering his office, the 'Beggar King' sees on the door, written in chalk, 'Receipt for 40 pounds 6 shillings 2 pence for the purchase of a grandfather clock'. Soon he has the explanation. Business is just getting started – simply, but decently, dressed people are transformed into pitiable wretches – when a beggar delivers the one-pound reward for having prevented the theft of a grandfather clock. At the same time he reveals a huge bruise on his head from a recent thrashing by the thieves in front of the store for having snitched on them. Mr Peachum slaps his face. How stupid of him to have brought the Macheath Gang down on him! A bit later he discovers that his daughter was out the entire night – as she tells him in so many words – and married to a man whose name she does not even know. Mr Peachum knows it. And straight away he knows, too, that it can only be a fight to the finish. He pulls the man with the bruise from the corner. He raises him up like a monument to public injustice. He promises his employee to avenge immediately and most cruelly the injustice meted out to one of his own in the service of the police. He goes to the police.[13] The man with the bruise accompanies him.

In the office of the police commissioner he finds an unfamiliar

12. The first part – 'Polly Peachum's Love and Marriage' – is divided into three chapters with their own titles. Each chapter demands its own technique in terms of photography, rhythm of events and images, and the particular camera shots they require, etc. The first chapter should flow without editing and cuts. (The spectator does not see Polly Peachum's face before Macheath does.) The second chapter introduces two regularly alternating and mutually qualifying activities: the falling-in-love (soft focus, indolent) and the organizing of the trousseau (sharp, montage editing). The third chapter shows single, unconnected still lives; the camera searches for motives, it is a sociologist.
13. Not without having complained beforehand in the first 'Threepenny Finale' about the 'uncertainty of human relations'. This finale can be presented in the form of a family fight; Polly sulks in her room behind the door she has slammed shut, her mother whines on the stair landing, and Mr Peachum argues at the bottom of the stairs.

gentleman engaged in a confidential discussion with the chief of
police. (Apparently they are discussing certain files about a Jimmy
Beckett alias John Miller alias Stanford Sills who was condemned
to death in Southampton and Newcastle and Dover, files that
incriminate this gentleman and are to be delivered to him that
afternoon – a belated wedding present from the chief of police.)
This gentleman – Mr Macheath – dismisses Peachum's complaint
against the gangleader Macheath with the statement: with such
accusations he could call for the arrest of London's mayor. The
Beggar King stands silently next to his employee, who has once
again been insulted, then silently leaves police headquarters with
him. Ringing laughter follows them. Who is this Mr Peachum?[14]

Who is Mr Peachum?
The events during the inspection of the renovated Old Oak Street[15]
quickly demonstrate to the police chief (this very same afternoon)
who Mr Peachum is. Since the Queen must pass by Old Oak Street
in the harbour after her arrival (scheduled for the coming Friday),
this eyesore is being transformed by the police into a charming
garden street – several gallons of whitewash do wonders,[16]
dumping places become children's playgrounds, the women
inhabitants of the Drury Lane Swamp leave their workplace under

14. After Mr Peachum and Macheath depart, Mr Brown sings the following
strophes to the melody of 'Mac the Knife' [see *The Threepenny Opera*, trans. Ralph
Manheim and John Willett (London: Methuen, 1979), additional songs]:

> Oh, they're such delightful people
> As long as no one interferes
> While they battle for the loot which
> Doesn't happen to be theirs.
>
> When the poor man's lamb gets butchered
> If two butchers are involved
> Then the fight between those butchers
> By the police must be resolved.

15. Especially at this point the stage play is left behind, not the meaning but its story.
To film elements from the stage play with only slight changes would be pure
nonsense.
16. The police sing while whitewashing, 'The Song about Whitewash':

> Where something's rotten and walls are crumbling
> Then something must be done to set it right
> And the rot is growing so frightfully
> If anyone sees that, it's just not good.
> There's already another new
> Spot on the wall
> It's just not good! (No good at all!)
> We need whitewash! Whitewash is what we need!

police guard with howls of protest so that on the Friday yearned for by the entire nation it can pretend to be a home for fallen girls. Just as Mr Peachum transforms his employees into wretches, here a wretched street is transformed into a pretty and restful scene. At the inspection of the completed renovation by the Prime Minister, Mr Peachum demonstrates his art: masses of beggars have left the inner city, they creep forth from the centres of the metropolis, and among the newly planted flower beds between the freshly whitewashed houses appear the faces of the professional beggars, corroded by vice and misery.[17] No one has attempted, and rightly so, to camouflage the children of this quarter. Here any attempt to disguise things is hopeless: no velvet suit can hide the thin bodies wracked by rickets. And what would be the point in using police kids if suddenly a real child is smuggled in among the imported ones and, in answering the question of the fat, rosy-cheeked Prime Minister as to his age, says 'sixteen' instead of the 'five years old' one might expect from his size? The festive tour ends in other words on a shrill dissonance. Returning from this flop, the police chief – who very clearly saw Mr Peachum standing silently at the first corner, next to him the man with the bruise – can only advise his friend Macheath, who impatiently demands his wedding present, to disappear as quickly as possible. 'Macheath, we are dealing with adversaries who know nothing about morality or even the most primitive forms of human decency,' he says to him. He does not even mention the files.

>When the pigsty collapses, it's just too late!
>Give us whitewash and we're willing
>To do everything to make it right.
>Give us whitewash, don't make such a fuss!
>It's not our fault, we're ready to work!
>Give us whitewash, then everything'll be new
>And then you'll have your new times.

[This is an early version of 'The Whitewashing Song' in *Round Heads and Pointed Heads*, interlude between Scenes 2 and 3.]

17. They scream out:

>You! There's something rotten! The walls are crumbling!
>Is it not possible to do something about it?
>You! The rot is growing so fast!
>If anyone sees us, it's no good! (No good at all!)

(We did not work out additional suggestions since at a certain point the sight of those who were supposed to follow our suggestions and complete the film robbed us of our illusions. Immersed in our work, we had forgotten: it was already September 1930.)

Departure and Plans . . .

The carefree attitude of a young girl has brought Miss Polly Peachum one day of unmitigated happiness; already the next morning she is desperate after her father's horrible revelation about her husband, the next evening suddenly thoughtful, sober and a decisive Mrs Macheath. Immediately after the terrible scene in the parental home, she has rushed to seek help at the scene of her nocturnal joy. Among a crowd of curious onlookers, attracted by the strange scene, she watches with her face pressed to the fence as eager police carry furniture – her furniture! – out of the Duke of Somersetshire's stable onto the lawn. Three fully packed travelling carriages indicate the return of the palace's owner. At this very moment, when all her illusions are collapsing, she feels on her neck an all too familiar grip: thumb and middle finger of her lover! 'Poor Polly, you can learn something!' They immediately leave together. Once again the pair takes a walk, only the second one, but how different from the first! He tells her that he must leave, right away. She tells him that she cannot approve of his work, she weeps. 'Can't you become something decent?' she asks. She glances at a street sign: National Deposit Bank. It is the same bank her father works with. 'Can't you become a banker, or something?' – 'We've long had our eyes on this bank,' he says. 'No, not like that,' she says and weeps. 'You can always buy it,' he says with irritation. 'Can I do that?' she says. 'You see, if we could buy the bank where my father's money . . .' and they continue on their way, immersed in an enthusiastic conversation. At a corner they take leave of one another. 'Now I know everything,' she says, 'for now we can do without you. It's better if you hide in the Drury Lane Swamp, as you intend.'

Third Part
Playing with Fire

The Historical Change of Ownership of the National Deposit Bank
While the prostitutes from the West India Dock read the 'wanted' leaflet in which the police describe a fugitive named Mr Macheath, the Macheath gang's general meeting is taking place in a restaurant's banquet room. With Mrs Macheath presiding, they decide to assume control legally of the National Deposit Bank. Justification: the new times. Astonished, Mr Macheath is just passing through the completely transformed Old Oak Street, while the general meeting is dismissing by means of retirement

allowances those members whose social standing is so low that it would prevent them from participating in the important changes. The Macheath gang's buy-out of the venerable National Deposit Bank can be best illustrated with an image: emerging from their stolen cars,[18] moving towards the modest entrance of this old, renowned house that awakens nothing but trust, approximately forty gentlemen cross over an imaginary line on the sidewalk. Before the eyes of the unbelieving observer they are transformed at the moment of crossing over from the bearded robbers of days of yore into the sophisticated managers of a modern financial market. – And Mr Macheath walks with a light step in the direction of the West India Dock, resolutely moving towards the Drury Lane Swamp, while humming a few new verses of a ballad that has just become obsolete . . .[19]

The Struggle for the Head of Macheath

On this morning Mr Jonathan Jeremiah Peachum enters police headquarters together with the man with the bruise. Seven lawyers accompany him. For the first time during this discussion with the

---

18. While they arrive in four or five cars, they sing the 'Song to Inaugurate the National Deposit Bank' [see translation by Manheim and Willett, additional songs]:

> Don't you think a bank's foundation
> Gives good cause for jubilation?
> Those who hadn't a rich mother
> Must raise cash somehow or other.
> To that end stocks serve much better
> Than your swordstick or biretta
> But what lands you in the cart
> Is getting capital to start.
> If you've got none, why reveal it?
> All you need to do is steal it.
> Don't all banks get started thanks to
> Doing as the other banks do?
> How did all that money come there? –
> They'll have taken it from somewhere.

19. [See translation by Manheim and Willett, additional songs.]

> How's mankind to get some money?
> In his office, cold like snow
> Sits the banker Mac the Knife, but he
> Isn't asked and ought to know.
>
> In Hyde Park behold a ruined
> Man reclining in the sun
> (While down Piccadilly, hat and cane, just think about it)
> Strolls the banker Mac the Knife and
> God alone knows what he's done.

chief of police the threat of the 'demonstration of misery', which causes so much dread, is explicitly mentioned . . .[20] Once again Tiger Brown envisions the horror of the slum dwellers, who would do anything for a piece of bread. Mr Peachum demands point-blank the head of Mr Macheath, alias Jimmy Beckett. 'My friend Sam,' he says, 'insists that the man be hanged.' Mr Brown can only reply that the police do not know the whereabouts of the notorious bandit. 'You will find that out,' Mr Peachum promises.

The arrest ensues under racy circumstances during a picnic outing by car under God's free heavens to which Mr Macheath has invited the ladies from the Drury Lane Swamp. In the police car that pursues him, the prostitute Jenny Diver, an old acquaintance of Mr Macheath, sits by the side of Mrs Peachum. Among ageless oaks in a circle of shady ladies the poor devil receives the kiss of Judas from this person. After a speedy chase (for the turn of the century) – a car full of police charges after a car full of prostitutes – Mr Macheath is apprehended. 'Please come along, Mr Macheath, it's only a formality.'

Half an hour later a deputation of bankers and lawyers led by Mrs Macheath enters police headquarters. In the ensuing conversation with the chief of police the directors of the National Deposit Bank demand point-blank the release of their boss. The chief points out to the gentlemen that in the slum districts a demonstration is being planned against the police's handling of the case of the banker Macheath that – in view of the Queen's expected arrival – would make him fear the prospect of unpleasant incidents.

'The police are too weak, gentlemen, against the misery that is too great.' – 'Sir, then it is our duty to undertake something against this misery.' – 'And?' – 'We will strengthen the police.'

The ensuing deliberation about the means to be put at the disposal of the police, a conversation that increasingly takes on the character of a philosophical debate about the state, provides Mrs Macheath with an opportunity to seek out her husband. She enters his cell in order to declare her unwavering love despite events and sees there her rival, Jenny Diver, who in a fit of remorse has visited him. Once again: the struggle for Macheath.[21]

Returning exhausted from this unpleasant scene – Diver, happy, was led out – Mrs Macheath meets the gentlemen who are coming down the stairs. Their comments about the chief of police's attitude appear to be so depressing that Mrs Macheath falls in a faint.

20. Peachum's story about the police chief of Semiramis. *The Threepenny Opera* [end of Act II, Scene 6].
21. The 'Jealousy Duet' [Act II, Scene 6].

With Macheath's arrest events begin to unravel. Towards evening Mr Peachum stands at a street corner and reads a newspaper announcement to a man with a bruise which reports that in the city there is an enormous tumult because of the completely unfounded arrest of the National Deposit Bank owner. Influential circles were warning the police about submitting to the demands of the riffraff in the streets. The banker's release was now expected that evening. In a gateway Mr Peachum carefully removes his companion's hat in order to examine the bruise. 'It's getting smaller,' he cries out angrily. 'I can't help it,' the man replies incredulously. 'Well,' says Mr Peachum and hits him forcefully and cold-heartedly on the disappearing bruise. 'Now,' he states, 'they can release him this evening.'

Fourth Part
The Mounted Messengers of Mr Macheath

A Turbulent Night
This evening five or six beggars pass through the slums of the West India Dock, one of them carrying a placard on a pole. In their midst is a man without a hat who has a large bruise on his head and the placard reads: 'Justice for poor Sam!' They go from bar to bar and show the bruise to everyone who has a sense of justice. It turns out that in this district there are a lot of people who either have a sense of justice or a sense of humour and therefore are prepared to meet at St George's Bridge the next morning at seven o'clock in order to show the high and highest authorities poor Sam's bruise.

And no matter how small the bruise is, the fear of those above will make it larger, their bad conscience will see to that.

During this expectant night the chief of police nervously rides one more time through the streets, which the next day will be a place of joy or maybe of other feelings. Passing over St George's Bridge, which – closed off by the police – lies there empty and tidy under waving flags, he believes that he hears noises. Getting out, he notices *under* the bridge dark, formless heaps: naked misery itself that is just lying down to sleep. This misery is entirely unfamiliar not only to Mr Peachum . . .

Mrs Polly Peachum keeps watch over her husband in jail. The greying morning will bring the hour when she will don black clothes, hastily, just as no more than three days ago she put on her wedding dress . . . Did the couple not consider during the night whether they should separate after all?

The house of Peachum's Beggars' Trust is fully illuminated in the light of dawn. Do Mr and Mrs Peachum have a reason to laugh? Here forty or fifty persons await instructions from the boss, kept awake with cigarettes and coffee; they are the messengers to the countless masses in the slums, naked misery itself. In the business premises some of them are already painting impressive placards for a demonstration that will certainly be successful in 'those dark holes that London tries to forget'. Will the decision be made here? What ideas will a rather illogical but substantive speech by Mrs Peachum – drunk as usual – awaken in her husband, who in any case fears for his business. 'You are a genius, Peachum,' she says, 'don't go too far! You want to summon the misery, but remember, the misery is great.' – 'I will tell them, it is time to settle accounts,' he says gently. 'You can do that,' she suggests, 'they will settle, but with whom will they settle? Can you arrange it so that they don't also settle accounts with us? They will come forth from the slums, why not, but for whom will they come? They will hang Mr Macheath, lynch the chief of police, do who-knows-what to the Queen, will they spare us? What will happen when they come, Jonathan?' Will he not say suddenly: 'I must reconsider, perhaps it would really not be very pleasant . . .'

Now, no matter what this whole society cooks up, one thing is sure: it is supposed to save this society. And one question will unavoidably be raised at this point: from whom?

A dream of the chief of police will answer some questions.

The Dream of the Chief of Police

Towards morning the chief of police has a dream: he sees a bridge from below, a small piece of earth surrounded by raging river water. But on this small site under the flags something is moving that spreads out quickly, no one knows from where they come, there appears to be something even deeper here below; in any case there are already crowds moving up now, up the banks and over the freshly painted railings, onto the bridge itself directly under the flags. Yes, this small site spews forth many, innumerable, steadily. Once it has begun, it never ceases; of course, there are police, they are standing over there, they will block the bridge, there are tanks, they will fire, there are soldiers too, they will – but the miserable are already there, they are coming together, they are marching, their ranks are closed, as wide as the streets, they fill everything, like water, they seep through everything, like water, they have no substance. Of course, the police throw themselves against them, of course, batons are flying, but what's this? They strike right through the bodies: in a wide wave the miserable march through the police towards the sleeping city, through rolling tanks, through fenced barriers, silent and mute through the police calls to halt and the rattle of the machine guns and they pour into the houses. Teeming misery in a mute march, transparent and faceless, they march through the palaces of the wealthy, they march through the walls of art galleries, the royal residence, court chambers, parliament.

Such dreams have consequences.

The Messengers Ride Forth . . .

When morning dawns, the men and women from the West India Dock are standing on St George's Bridge, waiting for poor Sam with his bruise. But through the tolling of the bells that greet the Queen's special train, past the honour guards, under waving flags, the chief of police rushes to the Old Bailey to sacrifice his friend Macheath and halfway there he meets, coming from the opposite direction, Mr Peachum, who is turning in his friend Sam, *for the same reason.* They have realized that they have the same enemy – the people waiting on St George's Bridge.

And Mr Macheath? Fortunately he is also not exactly hard up: mounted messengers, or rather, cars of the National Deposit Bank guarded by armed police, are just delivering the bail for the hero. Arm-in-arm, Mr Peachum and the chief of police enter the death-row cell to release the bandit and lock up the man with the bruise. After all, unity makes for strength: after an embittered struggle a unified society greets in its midst the banker Macheath and waits with him for the Queen.[22]

22. Closing verses of the 'Mac the Knife' ballad [see translation by Manheim and Willett, appendix]:

> So we reach our happy ending.
> Rich and poor can now embrace.
> Once the cash is not a problem
> Happy endings can take place.

> Smith says Jones should be indicted
> Since his business isn't straight
> Over luncheon, reunited
> See them clear the poor man's plate.

> Some in light and some in darkness
> That's the kind of world we mean.
> Those you see are in the light part,
> Those in darkness don't get seen.

No Insight through Photography

You don't have to doubt whether the cinema is up-to-date! Photography is the possibility of a *re*production that masks the context. The Marxist Sternberg, for whom you surely share my admiration, explains that from the (carefully taken) photograph of a Ford factory no opinion about this factory can be deduced.

Even when the sociologist comes to the same conclusion as the aesthete, his conclusion is infinitely more useful.

[GBFA 21/443–4. Manuscript written around 1930. Fritz Sternberg was a Marxist-oriented sociologist and philosopher whom Brecht met in late 1926. The photograph of a Ford factory alludes to a similar passage in 'The *Threepenny* Lawsuit' (Part III, Section 2).]

On the Discussion about Sound Film

The *Threepenny* lawsuit demonstrates how far the process of transforming intellectual values into commodities has progressed. To preserve the formal and socially critical features of *The Threepenny Opera* in the sound film, we ourselves wrote a version of the screenplay. To protect this version against the anticipated neutralization by the industry, we signed a contract. To implement this contract, we went to court. What happened? For the version of the screenplay we were offered money so that we would not write it. It was a commodity. For the contract, which was completely ignored, we were offered 25,000 Marks right there in the courtroom, just so that we would sell it. The contract too was a commodity. The lawsuit, which in part we lost because our witnesses were not called, must be appealed through all the courts, which is very expensive, so that we must buy it at an unreasonable price. The lawsuit – also a commodity. According even to Cicero, who was an attorney, the system of law costs either justice or money. For justice waits behind many doors that can only be opened with money. What then can be learned from the *Threepenny* lawsuit? When you buy a ticket to a sound film, you have learned and you know that what you are about to see was produced exclusively as a commodity in a world consisting exclusively of commodities. If you intended to buy art with your ticket, then you have not learned that the art sold to you in the sound film first must be marketable in order to be sold.

[GBFA 21/444. Written in November/December 1930, published in *Der Scheinwerfer 7* (Essen, December 1930). Brecht refers to the Roman orator Marcus Tullius Cicero, who was a practising lawyer. A typescript of the text includes a handwritten addition following the last sentence:

> If then you buy a ticket for the sound film *Threepenny Opera*, in so far as there will ever be such tickets to buy, then you must know that this *Threepenny Opera* fell into a huge machine whose function it is to make commodities out of artistically formed works at enormous expense.]

Meddling with the Poetic Substance

All changes undertaken in the process of adapting existing stage plays for sound films are no longer simply transformations from the acoustical to the optical medium necessitated by technological considerations. Rather they are to an extent a form of meddling with the poetic substance of the work itself.

Here, then, the rights that the author has in the theatre must be extended to the sound film. This question has not yet been clarified legally. The lawsuit concerning *The Threepenny Opera* has created a precedent. As Brecht had explicitly demanded in his contract, the screenplay was supposed to be written in consultation with him. He sold his play to the company only on condition that he could control the adaptation for the sound film. This clause was a major component and a major right of the contract. Yet from the beginning, so Brecht explained to us, the company violated it, at first mainly because of lack of time. They wanted to use the studio space that had been rented too early.

The few conversations with the director Pabst afforded absolutely no artistic perspective but rather were limited to issues of authority (whether Brecht could decisively influence the screenplay or not, etc.), and from Pabst's side came the repeated advice that one must take into account the backwardness and stupidity of the film audience.[1] In these discussions Brecht already suspected that any serious and artistic work would face enormous obstacles.

Brecht said that he did everything possible to avoid a botched job and produced the material for a *Threepenny* film very quickly. This provided the film company, in its own opinion, with the opportunity simply to ignore the contractual rights of collaboration by fabricating a legalistic delay. He was supposed to deliver the material on 15 August. The legal delay consisted, in the film company's opinion, in the fact that he had indeed delivered to Leo

Lania the material as contractually agreed on 15 August, but not in the form of a medicine that Lania could easily swallow.[2] Lania and Brecht had planned a series of discussions in which they would work on the stylistic adaptation of the material into the final script.

Three days after delivering his material, Brecht received written notice that he was legally overdue and that the film company was no longer obliged to work with him. 'I tried continually,' he said, 'to get an overview of what was happening in the studio. But I did not even succeed in getting a look at the shooting script. However, I did hear from a third party that two other authors were now preparing the screenplay.[3] I was also explicitly prohibited from entering the studio.'

Brecht's suspicion about a stylistically inappropriate adaptation was only fuelled when he learned that the film was to be distributed exclusively to cinemas agreeing to also take the Otto Ernst film *Flachsmann als Erzieher*, (Flachsmann the Teacher), which was to be produced later.[4] In other words *The Threepenny Opera* is to be doctored up so that it can please the fans of *Flachsmann als Erzieher* too.

The film producer fears the over-exaggerated power of the censor and the pre-release critiques of the film distributors who are willing to accept only what has earned them a good box-office income in the previous weeks. Their misdirected dominance is seriously underrated even in professional circles.

'Since no one ever spoke with me about the style of *The Threepenny Opera*, the public will most likely find something completely different from what it expects,' Brecht said. His case will soon be one among many – our authors must learn to protect themselves from being violated by those who have unartistic views.

[GBFA 21/445–6. Hand-corrected typescript of November/December 1930. Apparently the text was written for the lawsuit proceedings in conjunction with the *Threepenny* film. Originally written in the first person, it was later changed by Brecht and Elisabeth Hauptmann into a third-person narrative. For further details, see 'The *Threepenny* Lawsuit'.]

The Experiment is Dead, Long Live the Experiment!

No snob doubts that artistic experiment is dead. It is true that art had made its peace with the powers that be, long before they armed themselves for their war. As usual it was a series of separate peaces. *The Loyal Opposition of Her Majesty the Market sensed its responsibility and could no longer shut its pockets to the knowledge* that elsewhere it's the same the whole world over, lest loyalty is not to be a blind delusion. *The film studios stocked up with literature's most illustrious names at exactly the time when the box-office theologians insulted the man they would not touch with a barge pole as a 'Rembrandt'.* And yet it is not the last we've heard of it, for *the avant-garde is surrendering but it will not die.* Whoever has seen a prize-winning Hollywood film will no longer think a pebble in the brook is so dead . . .

[GBFA 21/446–7. Typescript written around 1930, probably originally for 'The *Threepenny* Lawsuit' but not included. The text continues after the last sentence as follows (crossed out by Elisabeth Hauptmann):

> Joking aside: the real experiments were not wilful escapades but arduous attempts to adapt to the new demands of the time. New subject matter and new classes of audience made them necessary. These problems are pushed aside today. And here the real limits of the usefulness of our experiences become visible . . .]

The *Threepenny* Lawsuit

A Sociological Experiment

[GBFA 21/448–514. The film version of *The Threepenny Opera*, which was shot by Georg Wilhelm Pabst from 19 September through mid-November 1930, was not based on Brecht's screenplay 'The Bruise' (see above), although it did incorporate significant elements from it. On the grounds that the production had not fulfilled its contractual obligation of 'protecting' the integrity of the artists' original play, Brecht and Weill threatened the entire investment of the production company by filing suit against Nero-Film (Brecht on 30 September, Weill on 1 October, 1930). Their lawsuits were filed ostensibly not because the company had rejected the screenplay but in order to regain the film adaptation rights to the play. The trial lasted four days, from 17 to 20 October 1930, and generated an unusually large press response. This owed both to Brecht's own notoriety and to the fact that the case had a signal function, for it touched on the sensitive question of competition between the cinema and the theatre and on the speculative issue of artists' rights to control their ideas in the mass media. The judgment was delivered on 4 November, with the court deciding against Brecht that Nero-Film had neither breached the contract nor infringed his copyright, since Brecht himself had changed the original play. In Weill's parallel suit, however, the court found in his favour and granted an injunction against the film's release because Weill, contrary to Brecht, had fulfilled his contract as specified, whereas Nero-Film had introduced additional music without Weill's permission. Brecht reached an out-of-court settlement with Nero on 19 December 1930, before his appeal was scheduled to begin on 23 December, and Weill settled for damages on 9 February 1931. The film opened in Berlin on 19 February 1931 and undoubtedly contributed to the play's international fame as well as to Brecht's, although there is no record that he ever actually saw it.

Based on this court experience, Brecht wrote 'The *Threepenny* Lawsuit' in 1931 (published in 1932 in his book series called *Versuche*) in order to develop a far-reaching critique of 'bourgeois ideas' about art under capitalism. Not intended as a documentary record, his commentary on the lawsuit in the essay is sometimes inaccurate (e.g., he quotes selectively from the trial proceedings and maintains a one-sided, flawed understanding of 'co-determination'). Rather it presents Brecht's analysis of how the capitalist system functions, unmasking the justice of the bourgeois state as the justice of the ruling class that is willing to violate its own legal system in order to protect its financial interests. Brecht plays the role of the naive artist who goes to court to defend the inviolability of intellectual property guaranteed by the liberal, democratic constitution. There he discovers that in fact the validity of individual ownership is measured against economic consequences, for in the case of the cinema the economic risk is so great that the profit motive in producing the commodity (the film) is considered more important than the right of the poet to his immaterial property (the ideas). In short, Brecht shows that, contrary to what many artists would like to believe, the work of art, like other commodities, is subject to market forces.]

Contradictions are our hope!

This past winter the film adaptation of the stage play *The Threepenny Opera* provided us with an opportunity to confront several *ideas* that are characteristic of the current state of bourgeois ideology.[5] These ideas, stripped of the behaviour of public institutions (the press, the film industry, the justice system), are a small part of the enormous ideological complex constituting culture, and the latter can be judged only if this complex is observed and made accessible to observation in its practices, i.e., functioning, in full operation, constantly produced by reality and constantly producing it. Once these ideas are grasped in their entirety – those that intervene in reality and those that do not – our image of culture will be complete and there is no other way to complete it. Everything said about culture from a more remote, general point of view that does not take account of practice can only be an idea and therefore must be tested in practice.

We must take care to seek the large, abstract things like justice or personality not only where we happen to find them – in some mediocre heads or mouths; one must also search for them in common reality, in the film industry's deals and in the deals of those who earn their bread by maintaining the justice system. To have noble ideas is not the same as to have culture. When the question arises whether there is justice *or* legal process (should the two not happen to coincide), then the answer must be: legal process. And confronted with the choice: legal process or the law (should both not be granted together), we would have to choose legal process. In any case we should speak of justice only to the extent that it exists at all in the legal process. Now, to tease out the ideas from an always functioning reality, from the continually adjudicating courts, from the press which expresses and manufactures public opinion, from the industry which unceasingly and freely produces art, methods are needed other than 'objective, disinterested', passive contemplation. This other, 'non-objective' etc. method will be demonstrated in what follows and is called a 'sociological experiment'. A full evaluation of the experiment will not be presented, the experiment itself being rather deficient because it has been inadequately planned and was undertaken by too few people who are themselves insufficiently specialized. Since such large institutions like the press, the courts, etc. are subject to them, these experiments would need a society that proceeds systematically and shares the work in order to make visible what must be seen. Indeed, the whole of literature, such as it is produced by individuals, is becoming more and more questionable.

I. The Legal Suit

When we had our publisher draw up a contract for the filming of *The Threepenny Opera* last summer, we saw an opportunity to earn money as well as an opportunity to make a film. The film company committed itself to making the film according to our plans and granted us the right to co-determination for the shooting script. Apparently the company had not really understood the entire scope and the real consequences of this latter, more unusual, part of the contract, as would soon become evident. When it learned that we had completed the script version, it showed all the symptoms of deep disappointment. In the company's view it had become a bitter necessity to dig once more into the purse in order to get us to abandon our efforts. Against all prudence and financial temptations, however, we insisted stubbornly on this script. Greatly irritated, the company now declared the contract invalid owing to some not very plausible excuses concerning the inconvenient clauses and took steps to produce without us a film that would be (only in this form) as commercially viable as possible. So we had to appeal to the court.

To protect the intention and artistic form the following agreements were included in the contract for the film adaptation:

'The producer grants the authors a right of co-determination in adapting subject matter for a shooting script.'

'The composition of new music and the adaptation of the existing music may be undertaken only by the composer Kurt Weill, who will be separately remunerated for it. Similarly, new song texts for the existing music as well as for possible new compositions may only be written by the poet Bert Brecht, who is also to be commissioned by the producer to collaborate on the shooting script. The producer will remunerate separately the author Brecht for this activity.'

They were supplemented by the following special agreements:

'a) Mr Brecht will deliver the basic material for the screenplay.[6] For this purpose Nero-Film will assign him Mr Neher and Mr Dudow as collaborators. In consultation with Mr Brecht, who will preserve the characteristic style and content of *The Threepenny Opera* for the sound film, Mr Lania will prepare the final screenplay with the assistance of Mr Vajda.

b) Mr Brecht will write the texts for the screenplay.

c) Mr Brecht is entitled to demand changes in the shooting script that do not alter the basic material and are feasible from a practical viewpoint.

d) Mr Brecht will deliver to Mr Lania today approximately one-third of the screenplay's basic material. He agrees to deliver a second section on the 12th day of the month and the final section by the 15th day of the month. His work will be undertaken wherever he is residing, but within Germany.'

In reference to the arrangement, it was agreed that Lania could receive the basic material *orally* and would later write the script with Brecht at the latter's place of residence. It is apparent that the author had organized the work so that the company was able to register its wishes for changes only after completion of the script. When Brecht delivered the basic material to Lania, and Lania reported on it to the company emphasizing that, in the manner provided for in the contract, that is, in consultation with Brecht, he could now produce the script, the company declared Brecht in breach of contract without further hesitation because he had delivered the material in a form that made his further involvement (i.e., further consultation with him) necessary. The court agreed with this judgment and said:

'The plaintiff must give the defendant the opportunity to look at the material in order to allow his representative to determine which parts of the script are deemed unsuitable. Only if the refusal of the defendant exceeds the limits of his right of co-determination and especially if it is not justified by objective reasons such as the expenditure of large sums or the fear of censorship problems has the defendant violated the contract.'

In other words, the company had not demanded in the contract any right of co-determination, yet the court granted it anyway. Beyond the binding contract the court declared:

'. . . admissible changes to the work for which the entitled may not withhold his agreement in good faith.'
'The cinematic adaptation of a stage play demands considerable changes to the original work.'
'Moreover, the author's right protecting against changes of the stage play is also limited by the common knowledge that fundamental changes are necessary for the purposes of film adaptation. The statutory grounding of §9, that changes affecting the essence of the work and modifying its impact are not permissible, is void therefore when adapting a stage work insofar as one can assume that the author of the stage work will not generally be held responsible for the film's deficiencies, but rather only the author of the screenplay. For this reason too the author of the stage work who has assigned the rights of film adaptation must permit extensive changes in good faith.'

The court rejected Brecht's suit.

The court named the main reason for its rejection of the author's suit his determined refusal in the court to make any recommendations for changes to the film that had already been completed without him.

'The defendant is currently no longer bound by the contract, since the plaintiff turned over to the court the material without recognizing any legal obligation towards the defendant and also refuses to exercise the right of co-determination in a reasonable way. Despite the court's request to explain in detail what he objects to in the screenplay, or, should his claim be correct that he does not know this screenplay, to list his objections based on an inspection, as suggested by the court, he declared that he could approve of no work by the defendant that was not based on a screenplay adapted by him.
Since the court determined through a comparison of the script and the basic material that extensive parts of the script by Lania approved by the plaintiff and a series of scenes from the stage

play were adapted only with changes necessary for the cinematic impact, the plaintiff's position of total rejection appears unjustified according to the contract between the parties. On the contrary, the defendant must have the right to produce the film without the plaintiff in view of his refusal to exercise his right of co-determination in a reasonable way.'

'Therefore it did not suffice if the plaintiff was prepared to continue his collaboration even after the defendant had declared his withdrawal from the contract, which at that time may not have been justified because the plaintiff's final refusal to hand over the material was not yet certain.'

The company, itself shocked at such a complete victory, returned to the author the film rights in a settlement and paid for the court costs – a shocking act of mistrust towards the administration of justice, which does not appear to be well-founded in the judgment of the original jurisdiction!

The press's position emerges from the following newspaper clippings:

It is a legal issue.

Is the film author a supplier or an equal partner? (*Magdeburgische Zeitung*)

Until now there has been almost no precedent for authors who secure such rights in contracts with film companies. (*B.Z. am Mittag*)

Whatever the judgment will be, one thing is already clear today, no one has the right to change, alter or transform into its opposite the work of intellectuals for whatever reason and no matter what the amount of money paid. It is an ancient, guaranteed right that the productive work, the achievement of creative people must remain inviolable. (*Neue Berliner 12 Uhr Zeitung*)

It is to be welcomed that finally a court will determine in this way that theatre directors and film makers have no right – except that of epigones – to distort a stage play in any way they please. For the primacy of art . . . must unconditionally . . . be preserved. (*Deutsche Allgemeine Zeitung*)

There is hardly any decency and backbone left in matters of art and art deals . . . There is no trust and no consideration for the work itself. There is only immodest promotion, especially on the part of the director, or resentment on both sides . . . In this sense Brecht's appearance in the case of *The Threepenny Opera* was a commendable signal. (*Kölnische Zeitung*)

What does it cost?

When it came to negotiating the value of the litigation, the following dialogue ensued: Attorney Dr Frankfurter: 'Are you willing to accept 25,000 Marks for signing over all rights, or what amount would allow us to lay aside this complaint?' Bert Brecht: 'It is not an issue of material value.' (*Berliner Börsen-Courier*)

The right of the author

And therefore we must thank Bert Brecht that he refused during the proceedings *the settlement offer of 25,000 Marks* from the other side. Brecht explained that it was more important for him to learn what his rights are. (*Neue Berliner 12 Uhr Zeitung*)

He is not for sale: what did he steal?

First the judge insisted on raising the question of plagiarism with which Brecht had been charged . . .[7]

Attorney Dr Fischer explains that *The Threepenny Opera* is not an original work at all. Brecht had 'inserted' in his work Ammer's translations of Villon's poems without violating the style. When he was questioned about this, he declared the entire copyright law medieval and outmoded . . .

Brecht refused to discuss ownership and property rights. The plaintiff wished to defend his ownership of this work for purely legal reasons only, and otherwise he viewed it as the property of the audience to whom he transferred it. In his opinion the question here is: 'Can industry do with art as it pleases?' (*Neue Zeit des Westens*)

The world of facts

From a legal perspective, Dr Frankfurter's elaborations were especially interesting. He stated that here an artist was coming up against the world of facts. Brecht assigned the film rights to *The Threepenny Opera* to Nero-Film in return for financial compensation. What the company does with its rights is not his concern. They have the right to make the film in twenty years or today. They may have a new script produced to their taste without letting Brecht say a word against it.

There was much talking and arguing during this lawsuit and the auditorium full of writers listened attentively to the lawyers' words. (*Berliner Tageblatt*)

A denunciation

The constellation in this suit about the sound-film adaptation of *The Threepenny Opera* is, then, 800,000 Marks vs. justified public interests. Naive as their behaviour may seem at first sight, the authors are subjecting themselves to an obligation to the general public when they litigate, for only they have the opportunity to uphold the established interests of the public and of art. Obviously the court cannot ignore the 800,000 Marks, as if they were nothing. Yet, opposed to them is a weighty value, hardly to be measured in numbers, that concerns the security of contractual agreements, even if they at first appear unusual. (*B.Z. am Mittag*)

Reason enters

In any case, by now the financial investment already comes to 800,000 Marks, so that a prohibition of the film could have *enormous consequences*. On the other hand, probably an additional 800,000 Marks would need to be sacrificed, if today one were to repair *The Threepenny Opera* (insofar as it is completed) according to the exact intentions of its creator, as a lawyer for the defendant explained.

On the one hand 800,000 Marks, on the other an artist who is simply fighting for the idea of his work: the judgment in this case will perhaps become a historical document. (*Der Film*)

Subtle but important differences

The production company claims that Brecht wanted to introduce a tendentious political theme into the film.

Considering the writer's general attitude, that is probably the case.

In the theatre this is the guaranteed right of any creative artist. In the cinema, however, we cannot tolerate such a specialized world view without serious financial loss.

But film-illiterate writers should cease to create complications in which the scribe doubtless is ninety to one hundred per cent in the wrong.

Anyone who enters into work or commercial relations with the cinema must be aware that this is an industry consisting of people who bet their money on one card and then must earn the applause of several thousand theatres or simply lose their money. The film appeals to a large audience that does not seek and understand deep philosophical thought processes.

If the matter is such, we urgently wish the court to place itself unambiguously on the side of the film industry.

There are nasty tongues claiming that this is in general more of a financial than a literary question.

Even the gentlemen who are especially gifted and talented in this domain must be made to understand that they will not always succeed with what are called 'trivialities' among those who frequent the 'Romanisches Café'.[8] (*Kinematograph*)

These are not opposed world views but only opposed interests. Otherwise it is a matter of an absolutely transparent struggle for the all-too-famous ego, for the preservation of stylistic aspects, not for the declaration of an opinion. Opposed to this cult of the ego is an obvious commercial interest.

Aesthetic nihilism fights a windmill battle against international capital. *Egomania vs. egomania.* What does it have to do with us? (*Tägliche Rundschau*)

And yet this much seems certain, that even Mr Brecht, despite the reverential estimation of his own work, did not prohibit the film adaptation but expressly permitted it. He who loves his child so dearly, as Brecht apparently does his *Threepenny Opera*, perhaps should not expose it in the first place to the dangers of film adaptation. (*Vossische Zeitung*)

Honour the writer who on principle does not allow his work to be filmed. (*Frankfurter Zeitung*, the film company lawyer, Dr R. Frankfurter)

In a word

In a word we see that the German cinema is on the move . . . even if sometimes confusion emerges . . . (*Berliner Tageblatt*)

As the final straw, several journalists chimed in who had not supported our suit but now complained that we had ended our idealistic suit for vulgar, materialistic reasons and that we may even have been motivated by them from the outset. In the interest of the experiment's clarity we think it is right to mention them as well.

The 'financial side' of the Threepenny lawsuit

On the part of the film company that produced The Threepenny Opera, the financial side of the case against the company was pushed into the limelight by means of a detour through several popular scribes who to some extent enjoy financial relations with the company. As far as money is concerned, it is the custom among idealists in this country in this period of high capitalism to speak of it with nothing but contempt. I must confess that I instructed my lawyer at the outset of the suit (which was not conducted for money) to calculate my costs very carefully (also as far as the risk was concerned). I do not have too much money, and it is the only means at my disposal for protecting my work – which for the most part demonstrably does not earn any money, (*He Said Yes, The Decision, The Baden-Baden Lesson on Consent, A Reader for Those who Live in Cities, The Mr Keuner Stories*, etc.) – from the damaging influence of large financial institutions. This money also allows me to reject certain idealistic journalists who, despite their meddling, would like to spend it for their ideals.

When Nero-Film Company last summer deduced from the purchase price the right to treat *The Threepenny Opera* as they pleased, ignoring all contractual conditions, I decided to appeal to the court in protest, despite the financial considerations. The lawsuit had the goal of exposing publicly the impossibility of working with the film industry even under contractual guarantees. This goal was reached when I lost the suit. Everyone can see that the lawsuit demonstrated the deficiencies of the film industry *and* of the administration of law. It would have made sense to appeal to the higher courts, if it had been possible to prevent the film's distribution. My attorneys advised me that this possibility did not exist. Under these circumstances, not being in the right, but rather being wealthy would have been necessary. A positive judgment (hardly to be expected) by the High Court, for example, would not have affected the film, which would already have been released long before, but only showed that an author's legally sanctioned right can never prevent the release of a film not produced according to contractual conditions. Hence, at this point I broke off the suit, which had served its purpose by clarifying the legal situation (insofar as it was a reality).

After I had brought this precarious thing to an acceptable conclusion by the skin of my teeth – something that lay in the public interest and yet was abandoned by everyone – all sorts of people came forward who until then had paid no attention to the struggle and continued to regard the incident 'from an objective point of view'. To this purpose they informed themselves upon the film's release about the 800,000 Marks and trumpeted now 'in the public interest' with great flourish what the connoisseur Karl Kraus has called a deception of intonation. This consisted of linking the commentaries they could have 'made' if, after having won the lawsuit, I had let my silence about the film be bought with a financial award, to the actual fact that I had *lost* the suit, received *no* award and *made no promise at all to remain silent*. The film company never succeeded in silencing me through open or concealed financial rewards – for example, my opinion that its film was a botched piece of work and a shameless distortion of *The Threepenny Opera*. Without my guidance it did not succeed in making this film into a work that was even halfway equal to the stage play. It did not succeed in preventing in principle the release of a *Threepenny* film. It did not even succeed (to note with satisfaction the financial side) in cheating me out of a part of my remuneration or in plunging me into lawsuit debts. It will also not succeed in casting the slightest suspicion on my corruptibility; if I couldn't be bought off, what was there in it for me? It has only succeeded in producing the film with the help of a court judgment that serves my purposes by allowing me to clarify the current legal situation . . . (*Der Scheinwerfer*)

II. From Speculation to the Experiment

Our position in this lawsuit revealed from the outset important contradictions: in turning to the court, we were forced to seek justice in a legal system that we in no way wished to recognize as a seat of justice because its laws put at our disposal only the right to private property. Moreover, we saw quite soon that even in this form we would not get justice.

The public had the right to our pursuit of justice: we were obliged to transfer the intellectual attitude of our work, an oppositional one, into every form that our work assumed. In fact the public had not made this claim for quite some time. They gladly permitted writers to accept money for pale copies of their works in any form. But we, enemies of the Pope, had the responsibility to be more papal than the Pope himself.[9] We had to furnish the public with a claim which they were no longer in a position to make themselves but yet to which they were still indebted. The speculative quality of our suit soon receded behind these possibilities of bringing into view social attitudes (the press, the cinema and the courts), that is, of staging an experiment in collaboration with players who otherwise are difficult to engage. This short-lived speculation would have consisted in using our legal rights to get our hands on the means of production for the film. We had guaranteed rights, contracts. But the time for contracts was past. They had been sacred in barbaric times. Who could have missed their passing? By now the social order was running so smoothly that everything is self-regulated. Are there contracts in nature? Does nature need contracts? Large financial interests operate with the force of nature. Where contracts still exist (they do where profits are distributed), their validity need only be appraised from financial perspectives. The balancing game among these players was far more interesting and to show it was far more useful than making a film. Here there was much to see, much to make visible. For there was still some hesitation on the part of the collaborating institutions, at least among the press and courts, who still suffered under the after-effects of the nursery, a charming embarrassment about subjecting themselves unquestioningly to the logic of facts. The instructors were also learners. In the wake of traditional legal sentiment, there were ideas connected to important and still potent social prejudices of the most profitable kind. Newer institutions like the cinema assume responsibilities much too hastily in what appear to be insignificant secondary areas, proceed downright anarchistically, not knowing that they too must rely on something like morality, even though in other areas. Space has to be found for them without this morality deteriorating. A hard bit of work!

The anticipated attempts of the justice system to accept logic were not going to be frustrated by us. We had to abandon whatever fell by the wayside but carefully orchestrate the process so that it was clearly perceptible in a quick enough and public enough way. We had to free ourselves completely from the wish to be right, something completely different from the wish to get justice. We had to establish (acquire by purchase) the existing right, just being issued, and insist on it only until it had justified or compromised itself. The suit had to become an image of reality, had to say something about it. Reality was to be constructed in the lawsuit.

For this we had only limited means at our disposal, only so much time and so much money. We instructed our lawyers to use our money as carefully as possible because money provides us the opportunity to work without patronage and because our trust in the courts was not much greater than that in the industry. Our risk was over 15,000 Marks. The victory of the logic of facts was only a question of time. It was better to lose the first lawsuit than the third. This determined our behaviour after we lost the first lawsuit. Of course, the worst-case scenario would have been to win in the first instance (as happened to Weill), because then sheer lack of money would have prevented us from clarifying the real legal situation, which would have consisted in losing further up the line. The film would have been released after the court allowed us to prevent the release by depositing in escrow a sum we did not possess. A victory in the appeal would have proved that even in this case of proven illegality the industry risks at most minor damages. But at least the law would have remained the law. And it would have been our fault! Luck saved us from proving that in capitalism there are still judges. After losing the suit in the first instance and quickly giving up, we abandoned the 100 per cent completion of the experiment (we would have achieved a wider and deeper result with appeals), not only out of financial considerations but also because the anticipated results would not have changed anything in principle. The insights gained up to this point would not have been devalued by possible future ones. It is insignificant whether this or that judge would have betrayed a few more traditional views. He could have done so in any case only because in a *practical* sense these views would have had no consequences (the destruction of the film)! We had to be pleased that already the court of first instance and not the third executed this act of reason that we expected and that we had to make possible. We could not have afforded financially to get to the real facts in losing only in the second appeal. Already in this phase the lawsuit had become a full-fledged experiment. We had definitely not planned it only as an experiment, but even if we had, we would not have been able to conduct it any other way. Conducted in order to reach something *specific* – for instance the film's prohibition – or a *specific* insight – for instance the court's bankruptcy – it would hardly have revealed anything useful in this sense. The case could not have been argued from beginning to end with the goal of winning or losing; that would have resulted in nothing. We had to trust the lawsuit and at most figure that it would somehow offer some insight into the way intellectual property is treated financially today. In other words, we had to rely on society's deep antagonisms. We could not foresee whether the courts would judge us in the wrong. It would only have been cynical to assume this from the start. We were certain only about one thing: even if the courts judged us in the right, it would only prove that our laws were completely outdated. In this case we could reckon with an enormous public outcry (winning would have meant that the film, an object worth a million, would have ended up in the court bailiff's small furnace because of a writer's claims to intellectual property). Both the artists' and the courts' other-worldliness would have been proven, and to the applause of the public the cinema would have abandoned all art owing to the fact that it no longer was supposed to be able to violate it.* All the newspapers would have advised us not to go 'too far' and to let the film be released after we would have been proven 'right', and they even would have been prepared to concede us financial damages in any amount. When the court decided against us in the suit, it proved the flexibility of the laws,

---

* 'If the courts had decided that under existing laws the creator of the original idea has the right of co-determination for the film, it would not have served well the authors' goal. Currently their advice and suggestions are sought after, if their work is to be transformed and adapted for the film; under this other interpretation all film producers would explicitly exclude the author by contract arrangement from any collaboration.' (*Frankfurter Zeitung*, Dr R. Frankfurter)

admitted the rights of hard reality, demonstrated worldliness and the unstoppable disintegration of bourgeois ideas about property (that can only be sanctified by the owner) and art (whose 'organic' unities are increasingly being destroyed).

The lawsuit was to be viewed as a sociological experiment, organized for the purpose of seeing certain ideas at work. For this purpose we emphasized explicitly to the public that our struggle was aimed against one million Marks. We freely disclosed our concern as to whether we could expect justice under these conditions. We used the curious residue of discomfort that the bourgeoisie still feels towards an all-too-obvious confirmation of capital's power. The 800,000 Marks can do a lot, we said, no one doubts that. There is, then, perhaps only one thing left that it cannot do: prevent us from showing what it can do. Those who regard the litigation only as a moral act (an even higher morality because it was not for financial gain) can hardly understand the experimental character of a lawsuit that focuses on morality itself as the problem. Those, too, who regard an experiment only as a systematically planned undertaking, geared from the beginning only to experimentation, cannot comprehend (i.e., evaluate) an undertaking like the *Threepenny* lawsuit. For these people it is an incomprehensible, fluid event which out of a moral act gradually becomes an experiment about morality as such. An initial act of simply reacting to an intolerable injustice becomes a systematic process which chooses a general injustice as its object or, better, it chooses a social condition which excludes acts of justice and morality. In the course of this development the court becomes the defendant, whose defence is the social order, which then also becomes a defendant. For the court, which in the beginning was permitted to apply the law, is soon forced to state something about the law. The legal case becomes unimportant and the case of law becomes acute. Now all sorts of ideas are suddenly freed up, such as those that are produced by the constantly changing reality (and themselves have the quality of reality) and those that are dismissed by reality (become ideologies). Since the law is corrected by reality, reality comes into view, when one corrects the law.

III. The Critique of Ideas

1. 'Art does not need the cinema.'

Honour the writer who on principle does not allow his works to be filmed ... He must decide whether he will not permit his work to be filmed, which would be his free, artistically very respectable will or, if he wants to have the financial earnings, he

1. Brecht saw *The Gold Rush* in March 1926 (see 'Less Certainty!!!'); in 'Effects of Chaplin' (1936) he specifically mentions this sequence.

2. Lotte Reiniger's *Abenteuer des Prinzen Achmed.* See Brecht's comment 'Mutilated Films'(1928) on the mistreatment of films by the cinema exhibitors.

3. In 'On Film Music' (1942) Brecht lists a number of Soviet films, including *Youth of Maxim* (by Kosintzev and Trauberg), that develop 'real' individuals in contrast to American films that lack individuals.

4. In 'The *Threepenny* Lawsuit' Part III section 6, Brecht refers to the 'rotting meat' sequence in Eisenstein's film *Battleship Potemkin*.

5. Lars Hanson in Mauritz Stiller's *Saga of Gösta Berling*. In 'The German Chamber Film' (1924), Brecht cites Lars Hanson and Charlie Chaplin as models of alternative acting styles to the German histrionics familiar from Expressionist films.

6. (l to r) Berlin theatre critic Alfred Kerr, Bertolt Brecht, and manager of Radio Berlin Ernst Wiechert broadcasting a conversation on 'The Crisis in the Theatres' in April 1928.

7. (l to r) Actor Erik Wirl, Brecht and composer Hanns Eisler at a gramophone recording session in 1931.

8. Georg Wilhelm Pabst's 1930 adaptation of the Brecht/Weill musical led to Brecht's lengthy essay 'The *Threepenny* Lawsuit'. Cover page of *Illustrierter Film-Kurier*.

9. *Right:* The first page of the contract between Brecht's publisher Bloch-Erben and Nero-Film for the *Threepenny Opera* film.

FELIX BLOCH ERBEN
BERLIN-WILMERSDORF 1
NIKOLSBURGER PLATZ 3

VERLAG UND VERTRIEB
DRAMATISCHER UND
MUSIKALISCHER WERKE
FÜR BÜHNE, FILM UND RUNDFUNK

REDAKTION UND VERLAG
DES „CHARIVARI"

FERNSPRECHER: AMT OLIVA 1176 UND 1177
TELEGRAMM-ADRESSE: „CHARIVARI" BERLIN

RM ... Pf.
RM ... Pf.
... .Wilmersdorf, d. 27. Mai 1930

Vertrag

zwischen

dem Verlage Felix Bloch Erben, Berlin-Wilmersdorf 1, Nikolsburgerplatz 3
und der Universal-Edition, A.G., Wien I, Karlsplatz 6, (Musikverlag)
(beide im folgenden kurz "Verlag" genannt)

einerseits

und

Nero Film A.G.
Berlin W.8. Unter den Linden 21

(im folgenden kurz "Produktion" genannt)

andererseits.

§ 1

Der Verlag hat an dem Theaterstück mit Musik "Die Dreigroschen-
oper" (The Beggar's Opera), Ein Stück mit Musik in einem Vorspiel und
acht Bildern nach dem Englischen des John Gay, übersetzt von Elisabeth
Hauptmann, deutsche Bearbeitung von Bert Brecht, Musik von Kurt Weill,
das alleinige unbeschränkte Verfilmungsrecht für die ganze Welt, das
hiermit der Produktion im Einverständnis und in Vollmacht des Text-
dichters und der Komponisten übertragen wird.

Dieses Recht umfasst die kinematographische Verwertung von Text
und Musik des Theaterstückes für alle Länder und alle Sprachen und nach
jeder Hinsicht, für stumme, Tonfilme (Plattenfilme und sonstige Systeme),
Farbfilme, plastische Filme oder sonstige eventuell noch durch techni-
sche oder sonstige Neuerungen entstehenden Arten für die ganze Welt, und
zwar zur alleinigen und ausschliesslichen Benutzung.

§ 2

Die Produktion ist verpflichtet, in allen üblichen Ankündigungen
darauf hinzuweisen, dass das Originalwerk von Bert Brecht und Kurt Weill
stammt.

./.

10. On the set of *Kuhle Wampe* with Adolf Fischer, Bertolt Brecht, and Martha Wolter.

11. Poster for *Kuhle Wampe*.

The first page of the [scor]e for 'Solidarity Song' [by H]anns Eisler for *Kuhle* [Wa]*mpe*.

Right: Outdoor location [sho]t of *Kuhle Wampe*, with [Ber]tolt Brecht in coat and

14. Brecht met Soviet film maker Sergei Eisenstein in 1932.

15. *Left:* Fritz Lang in the mid-1940s.

must once and for all make do with what he gets . . . (*Frankfurter Zeitung*, the lawyer for the film company, Dr Frankfurter)

We have often been told, and the court held the same opinion, that when we sold our work to the film industry, we gave up all our rights; the buyers acquired through purchase the right also to destroy what they had bought; the money satisfied all further claims. These people felt that, by agreeing to deal with the film industry, we put ourselves in the position of someone who brings his laundry to a dirty ditch for washing and later complains that it is ruined. Those who advise us against using these new apparatuses concede to them the right to work badly and out of sheer objectivity forget themselves, for they accept that only dirt is produced for them.[10] Yet from the outset they deprive us of the apparatuses which we need in order to produce, because more and more this kind of producing will supersede the present one. We will be forced to speak through increasingly complex media, to express what we have to say with increasingly inadequate means. The old forms of transmission are not unaffected by the newly emerging ones nor do they survive alongside them. The film viewer reads stories differently. But the storywriter views films too. The technological advance in literary production is irreversible. The use of technological instruments compels even the novelist who makes no use of them to wish that he could do what the instruments can, to include what they show (or could show) as part of the reality that constitutes his subject matter, but above all to lend to his own attitude towards writing the character of using instruments.

There is, for example, a major difference according to whether the writer approaches things as if using instruments or whether he produces things 'from within himself'. What the cinema itself does, that is, the extent to which it maintains its identity against 'art', is not unimportant in this connection. It is conceivable that other kinds of writers, dramatists or novelists, can for the moment work more cinematically than the film people. To some extent the former depend less on the means of production. But they nonetheless depend on the cinema, on its progress and regress, and the scriptwriters' means of production are saturated by capitalism. Today the bourgeois novel still projects 'a world'. It does so in a purely idealistic way from within a world view: the more or less personal, certainly individualistic view of its 'creator'. Of course, inside this world each detail fits exactly, though if removed from its context, it would never for a moment seem authentic in relation to the 'details' of reality. We learn about the real world only as much as we learn about the author, the creator of the unreal world; in other words we learn something only about the author and nothing about the world. The cinema cannot depict the world (its 'setting' is something else entirely) and allows no one to express himself (or anything else) in a work, and allows no work to express a person. It provides (or could provide) useful conclusions about the details of human actions. The splendid, inductive method it at least facilitates can be of unforeseeable significance for the novel, in so far as novels can still signify anything at all. For the theatre, for instance, the cinema's treatment of the person performing the action is interesting. To give life to the persons, who are introduced purely according to their functions, the cinema simply uses available types who encounter specific situations and assume in them particular attitudes. All motivation from within a character is excluded; the person's inner life never provides the principal cause of action and seldom its principal result; the person is seen from the outside. Literature needs the cinema not only indirectly but also directly. In the decisive extension of literature's social obligations, which follows from the refunctioning of art into a pedagogical discipline, the means of representation must be multiplied or frequently changed. (Not to mention the *Lehrstück* proper, which would demand the transfer of the cinema apparatuses to all those involved!) These apparatuses can be used better than almost anything else to supersede the traditionally untechnical, anti-technical, 'transcendent' 'art' associated with religion. The socialization of these means of production is vital for art. To say to the intellectual worker that he is free to renounce the new work tools is to assign him a freedom outside the production process.* Similarly, the owners of the means of production say to the labourer that they do not force him to work for the wages they set for him, he is 'free' to go. The armed and the unarmed, the murderers and the victims face off as equals, both are permitted to fight. The migration of the means of production away from the producers signals the proletarianization of the producers. Like the manual labourer, the intellectual worker has only his naked labour power to offer, yet he is his labour power and nothing more than that. And, just like the manual labourer, he needs these means of production more and more to exploit his labour power (because production is becoming ever more 'technical'): the horrible vicious circle of exploitation has begun here too!

To understand the situation we must free ourselves from the

*See No. 12, where it is shown that no rights exist outside the production process.

widespread idea that only one part of art needs to be concerned with the battles for the modern institutions and apparatuses. According to this idea there is a part of art, true art, that – completely untouched by these new possibilities of transmission (radio, cinema, book clubs, etc.) – uses the old ones (the freely marketed, printed book, the stage, etc.). In other words this true art remains completely free from all influence of modern industry. According to this idea the other part, the technological art, is something else altogether, creations precisely of these apparatuses, something completely new, whose very existence, however, is in the first place beholden to certain financial expectations and therefore bound to them for ever. If works of the former sort are handed over to the apparatuses, they immediately become *commodities*. This idea, leading as it does to utter fatalism, is wrong because it excludes that so-called 'untouchable art' from all processes and influences of our time, treating it as untouchable only because it is impervious to the progress of transmission. In reality the whole of art without exception is placed in this new situation; art must confront it as a whole and not split into parts; it will become a commodity as a whole or not at all. The changes wrought by time leave nothing untouched but rather always encompass the whole.

The (widespread) idea discussed here is therefore harmful.

2. *'The cinema needs art.'*
The revitalization of the sound film by means of the truly poetic script would be an infinite gain. (*Kölnische Zeitung*)
I find that the position of the producers and their followers is totally unproductive. As far as I am concerned, they need to understand nothing about art but they must be able to calculate its use value and for purely practical reasons proceed like a progressive industrialist who entrusts tasks to real artists. (*Frankfurter Zeitung*)

The demand for art in the cinema encountered no resistance. It came just as strongly from the newspaper columns as from the film factory offices. Films could only be sold as a means of pleasure, so the producers from the beginning shared with art the same market. The general idea that a means of pleasure had to be refined and that this was the domain of art, art being generally the most refined of all means of pleasure, led to the further engagement of artists for the cinema. We do not want to broach the familiar discussion about the subtle distinction between real and false art in order to prove, for example, that the cinema had instinctively seized upon false art (to be marketable, art must first be purchasable). Already the definition as a means of pleasure lends both types of art quotation marks. In any case 'art' has established itself against the apparatuses with a vengeance. Almost everything we see on screen today is 'art'. It must be 'art': as 'art' this kind of thing was already integrated into the market, thus accommodated by it, even if in a slightly different, now somewhat antiquated form as novel, drama, travelogue, critique. The cinematic form introduced greater distribution possibilities (as well as an enormous turnover of capital) and added to the old charms those of the new technology. Only in this way can the director impose his 'art' against the new apparatuses with the supportive pressure of the sales office: he imposes what he, as any run-of-the-mill spectator, understands by art and can do himself. He does not know what art is supposed to be. He probably believes it should produce common emotions, coordinate impressions, or 'all such things'. In the domain of art he has the reasoning power of an oyster, nothing more in the domain of technology. He is unable to comprehend anything about the apparatuses: he violates them with his 'art'. In order to grasp reality with the new apparatuses, he would have to be an artist, in the worst case a connoisseur of reality, but under no circumstances a connoisseur of art. So he produces with them the familiar, tried and true 'art', which is simpler: a commodity. He has the reputation of a tasteful arranger, it is said: he 'understands something about art'! As if one could understand something about art without understanding something about reality! And here the apparatus together with the subject matter functions as reality. This situation did not provide the new apparatuses with the possibilities available to them. No matter whether their main task was to generate the social phenomenon of art – this too they would have taken more easily in their stride if they could have avoided from the start the necessity of producing something like old 'art'. Applied to the sciences, for example, in medicine, biology, statistics, etc., in order to document visible behaviour or to show simultaneous events, they would have learned more quickly to document human interactions. The latter is difficult enough, and it is unsolvable without a very substantial, specific function among the tasks of the entire society. The situation has become so complicated because the simple 'reproduction of reality' says less than ever about that reality. A photograph of the Krupp works or the AEG reveals almost nothing about these institutions.[11] Reality as such has slipped into the domain of the functional. The reification of human relations, the factory, for example, no longer discloses those relations. So there is indeed 'something to construct', something 'artificial', 'invented'. Hence, there is in fact a need for art. But the old concept of art, derived from experience, is obsolete. For those who show only the experiential aspect of reality do not reproduce reality itself. It is simply no longer experienced as a totality. Those who show the dark associations, the anonymous feelings that reality produces, do not depict reality, itself. You shall no longer recognize the fruits by their taste. But speaking in this way, we speak about an art with a completely different function in social life – that of depicting reality and we do that simply to liberate all that 'art' achieves hereabouts from whatever demands do not stem from its function.

It is not right that the cinema needs art, unless we create a new idea of art.

3. *'The public's taste can be improved.'*
Whereas all the better industrial companies today know that quality goods raise profits and therefore they hire professionals who can enhance quality, the film industry scorns professional advice at every turn and invests its energy instead in playing the role of judging taste itself. *Film distributors*, for instance, claim responsibility for functions for which they notoriously have none of the prerequisites ... they maintain that they know public needs and, on the basis of this presumed knowledge, influence the entire film production branch. There would be nothing wrong with such dilettante ambitions, if they produced great successes. Experience teaches, however, that – other than those film productions which speculate in misguided instincts like *The True Jacob* or *Three Days in Confinement*[12] – these ambitions are at home in the lowest spheres and can succeed in barren provincial towns only because there are no other distractions there. Thus experience teaches that the distributor who believes he should decide the type and quality of films in truth acts *against* his own commercial interest and stumbles from one mistake to another. Many difficulties in the film industry can be traced simply to the illusion of agents and buyers that they are art experts and public opinion researchers. That they are not, dishonours them in no way; that they nonetheless want to be, demonstrates their commercial incompetence. In reality they usually migrate towards the lowest level of public taste – innumerable films substantiate this thesis – and yet the philosopher Georg Simmel has made clear the fact that the average always lies somewhat above the lowest threshold. From a practical point of view one should not treat philosophers with

such contempt. (*Frankfurter Zeitung*)

If we add physics to the metaphysical commentaries on the cinema that already fill the newspaper pages not devoted to advertisements, that is, if we concern ourselves with the actual mechanism, the cinema's why and wherefore, since it cannot possibly be just charity on the part of a few financiers to convey to the public the latest technological developments and the writers' most beautiful thoughts, if then – overlooking the broad 'rear' offered in the foreground and turning to the anxiously hidden 'front' in the background – if we consider the cinema as the (poorly performing) business of pumping rather rigid, hardly varying, but from the perspective of impact quickly exhausted types of entertainment into a huge, amorphous, unimaginable public, then we will hardly avoid this last absolute obstacle to all progress called public taste, just as when we follow virtuously the familiar metaphysical method. This complicated, costly and lucrative thing, public taste, hinders progress. There is no doubt about the customers' growing influence on the product's 'how', and its reactionary impact. Our progressives must fight this influence. It is represented by the film buyers, the market's provincial organizers. More precisely, these are really people who have assumed the office to which the press itself is entitled, to our metaphysicians of the culture pages: choosing the right thing for the consumer. We have to fight them, then, because they are reactionary. Now, our metaphysicians can find them without any trouble: they occupy the back rooms of the daily journals, the advertising offices! There the physicists sit together and discuss public taste. They understand it just as little as the metaphysicians in the front room, but it is not so important to understand something in order to exploit it. For them this costly and lucrative thing, public taste, is the true expression of the movie masses' real needs. It is empirically detectable, and in their sharpened instincts these people, who *depend financially on the accuracy of their analysis*, act as if the roots of this taste lay in the social and economic situation of these masses, as if the customers purchased correctly, as if the purchase were demanded by the customer's situation. In other words, this taste could not be changed by aesthetic instruction or the so ably and vigorously modelled ruminations of our Kerrs and Diebolds, but only by real, fundamental changes in the situation.[13] Our metaphysicians consider the organization of the world, however, to be a matter of taste. They would never investigate, say, the social value of sentimentality. Should they want to, they would lack the methodology and the necessary knowledge. A certain humour, and even its special clumsiness, is not only a product of material conditions but also a means of production. Recently Ihering did something along these lines for the theatre when he insisted on the occasion of *The Captain of Köpenick* that a parade march can still have an explosive impact even as a caricature and why it is so.[14] As long as we only fight against the consequences of causes unknown to us and only criticize symptoms in a purely conceptual world, our demands can at best be regarded as harmless in the practical realm, where what we fight for has a solid social function and is a real commodity with a value for both the customer and the merchant. The struggle on the part of progressive intellectuals against the influence of merchants is based on the assumption that the masses do not know their interests as well as the intellectuals. But these masses have fewer aesthetic and more political interests and at no time was Schiller's suggestion to make political education a matter of aesthetics so obviously hopeless as it is today.[15] Those who fight under this banner appeal to those who finance the films with the request that they educate the consumers. They propose the capitalists as the pedagogues of the masses! Practically they imagine (although they are on no account obliged to imagine anything practical) the great process of education as if their fellow intellectuals, who share similar tastes and are commissioned by the financiers to produce the films – the directors, scriptwriters, etc. – would use the capital 'put at their disposal' to educate the consumers. Basically they want to incite them to sabotage. No wonder the latter almost always express a strange, deep moral indignation at such suggestions. The director of the *Threepenny* film refused *out of decency* to endanger the capital 'entrusted' to him, and it is just as impossible to undermine this decency as it is to undermine the decency of the supportive critics. At most concessions to good taste can be extorted, but is there more at stake? Should we demand more than the simple refinement of the means of pleasure? Public taste does not improve by removing bad taste from the movies, but the movies will become weaker. Do we know what we remove with the bad taste? The masses' bad taste is rooted more deeply in reality than the intellectuals' good taste. Under certain social conditions the refinement of the means of pleasure weakens it. The concept 'means of pleasure' perhaps implies too much luxury in itself to be applied to the cinema. Perhaps the cinema plays a much more important role? Perhaps it is better to say that it serves recreation? In any case, it is absolutely necessary to examine carefully public taste precisely where it refers to the expression of social interests that the public wishes to satisfy in the cinemas. One would have to proceed, however, experimentally, that is, in cooperation with specific cinemas that serve in particular middle-brow audiences and among them well-defined or working-class strata, that screen specific films, and that survey the reactions with the proper instruments. The collected results would further have to satisfy the demands of predictability, that is, they would have to be prepared in a way that the industry could use them, in other words, without absolute judgment.

The idea of the cultural columnists is, then, inadequate: the public's public taste will not be changed by better films but only by changing its circumstances.

4. 'Film is a commodity.'

... According to this one cannot say that there is no reason to consider the scriptwriter in a different or lesser light than the stage dramatist ... The former fabricates a mass commodity that enters the international market. In this sense and through the related financial risk he carries a greater economic weight; therefore the financial investments must be evaluated differently ... Yet, the entire production of a marketable commodity that defines the commercial activity of the film producer is also from another perspective of a different nature. He must work according to supply and demand and depends much more than the stage director in his city on fashions, public taste, the subject matter's topicality, the competition of the world markets. (Judgment of the High Court, see No. 13)

Anyone who enters into work or commercial relations with the cinema must be aware that this is an industry consisting of people who bet their money on one card and then must earn the applause of several thousand theatres or else simply lose their money. (*Kinematograph*)

Everyone agrees that film, even of the most artistic kind, is a commodity. Some believe that this does not harm it, that it is only incidentally a commodity, that the commodity form is only the form in which it circulates in the market and on no account must necessarily define it entirely. They say that art's function is precisely to liberate the cinema from this enslavement. Those who believe this have no idea about the modificatory power of the commodity form. The fact that in capitalism the world is transformed into production *in the form of exploitation and corruption* is not as important as the fact of this *transformation*. Others say that the film differs from a work of art because it is more a commodity than the latter can be, that is, the nature of the film is defined by its commodity character. Almost without exception they lament this fact. No one apparently can imagine that this means of entering the market could be beneficial for a work of art. Yet they defeat with a gesture of 'heroic realism' (seeing things as they are) something which never escapes the businessman: the fact that a thing is marketable. There remain works of art in other genres which are not commodities, or only in small measure, so that their commodity character barely affects them, so to speak. Only those who blind themselves to the enormous power of the revolutionary process that drags everything in this world into the circulation of commodities, without exception and without delay, can assume that works of art in any genre could be excluded. For the deeper sense of this process consists in leaving nothing without relation to something, but rather in linking everything, just as all people are linked to each other (in the form of commodities). It is the process of communication itself.

We have, then, two false ideas before us:

1. The ('bad') commodity character of the film is cancelled out by art.

2. The artistic character of other art genres is not affected by the ('bad') process in the cinema.

5. *'The cinema serves recreation.'*

Producers cannot act otherwise. A film is such a major economic undertaking, represents such an aggregate of daring, capital and film labour, that it must not be endangered by the moods of prima donnas, lack of knowledge about the needs of the cinema, or – in the case of Brecht – even political tendentiousness. (*Frankfurter Zeitung*, the lawyer for the film company, Dr Frankfurter)

As long as cinema's social function is not criticized, film criticism remains a critique of the symptoms and has itself only symptomatic character. It exhausts itself with issues of taste and is limited by class-given prejudices. It cannot recognize taste as a commodity or the weapon of a particular class but rather accepts it as an absolute (what everyone is able to buy is accessible to everyone, even if not everyone can buy something). Now, *within* a certain class (here the one with purchasing power) taste could be productive by creating something like a 'lifestyle'. (Immediately after the bourgeois revolution of 1918 such tendencies became visible in the cinema. Wide sectors of employees, who saw inflation as an opportunity to ascend into the dominant class, learned a remarkably stylized behaviour from Bruno Kastner etc., which could be studied in any coffee house.[16]) But mainly the sharp distinction between work and recreation characteristic of the capitalist mode of production divides all intellectual activities into those serving labour and those serving recreation and makes of the latter a system for the reproduction of labour power. Recreation is dedicated to non-production in the interest of production. This is, of course, not the way to create a unified lifestyle. The mistake is not that art is dragged into the circle of production but that it happens so partially and is supposed to create an island of 'non-production'. Those who buy tickets transform themselves in front of the screen into idlers and exploiters. Since the object of exploitation is put inside them, they are, so to speak, victims of 'imploitation'.

6. *'In the cinema human interest must play a role.'*
   The human interest aspect must be deepened. (The director)
   The story may even be to a large extent foolish, if – as is today almost always the case – the foolishness or sentimentality of its inventive structure is embedded in an invented detail which is scenically-mimetically authentic and realistic and by which the human interest in hundreds of individual moments triumphs over the primitive falsity of the whole. (Thomas Mann)

This idea coincides with the notion that films must be philistine. The general applicability of this eminently rational thesis (rational because who should make any other kind of films or look at them, once made?) is produced by the inexorable demand for 'profundity' on the part of the metaphysicians of the press, the partisans of 'art'. They are the ones who wish to see the 'element of fate' emphasized in human relations. Fate, once a grand concept, has long since become a mediocre one, where accommodating oneself to circumstances has produced the desired 'transfiguration' and 'inwardness', and one exclusively of class struggle, where one class 'determines' the fate of another. As usual our metaphysicians' demands are not hard to satisfy. It is simple to imagine everything they reject presented in such a way that they would accept it with enthusiasm. Obviously if one were to trace certain love stories back to *Romeo and Juliet,* or crime stories to *Macbeth,* in other words to famous plays that need contain nothing else (need show no other kind of human behaviour, have no other kind of causes determine the course of the world), then they would at once exclaim that philistinism is the province of the How and not the What. But this 'it all depends on How' is itself philistine. This beloved 'human interest' of theirs, this How (usually dignified by the word 'eternal', like some indelible dye) applied to the Othellos (my wife belongs to me!), the Hamlets (better sleep on it!), the Macbeths (I'm destined for higher things!) etc., today occurs on a mass scale as philistinism and nothing more. If one insists on having it, this is the only form in which it can be had; to insist is itself philistine. The grandeur of such passions, their non-philistinism, was once determined by the role they were meant to play in society, which was a revolutionizing one. Even the impact that *Potemkin* made on these people springs from the sense of outrage they would feel if their wives were to try to serve rotting meat to them (enough is enough!).[17] Similarly Chaplin knows perfectly well that he must be 'human', that is, philistine, if he is to be permitted to do anything different and to this end changes his style in a pretty unscrupulous way (viz. the famous close-up of the hangdog look which concludes *City Lights*!).[18]

In fact the film demands external action and not introspective psychology. Capitalism has an impact on this by provoking, organizing and mechanizing certain needs on a mass scale, revolutionizing everything. It destroys great areas of ideology by concentrating only on 'external' action, by dissolving everything into processes, by abandoning the hero as the medium and mankind as the measure of all things, and smashes the introspective psychology of the bourgeois novel. The external point of view is proper to the cinema and makes it important. For the cinema the principles of non-Aristotelian drama (a type of drama not depending on empathy, mimesis) are immediately acceptable. Non-Aristotelian effects can be seen, for instance, in the Russian film *The Road to Life*, simply because the theme (the education of neglected children by means of certain socialist methods) prompts the spectator to establish causal links between the teacher's behaviour and that of his pupils.[19] By means of the key (educational) scenes the analysis of the causes becomes so gripping for the spectators that they 'instinctively' dismiss any motives for the children's neglect borrowed from the old empathy-type of drama (domestic unhappiness plus psychic pain instead of world war or civil war)!* Even the use of work as a method of education arouses the spectators' scepticism, for the simple reason that it is never made clear that in the Soviet Union, in total contrast to all other countries, work actually does determine morality. As soon as the human being appears as an object, the causal connections become decisive. Similarly the great American comedies depict the

---

* See Herbert Ihering's review of *The Road to Life* (*Berliner Börsen-Courier*, [28 May 1931]).

human being as an object and could have an audience entirely made up of reflexologists. Behaviourism is a psychology that, based on the needs of commodity production, seeks to develop methods to influence the customer, an active psychology, therefore, quintessentially progressive and revolutionary.[20] Its limits are those that correspond to its function in capitalism (the reflexes are biological; only in certain films of Chaplin are they already social). Here again the road leads only over capitalism's dead body, but here again this is a good road.

7. *'A film must be the work of a collective.'*
I could imagine that it would be quite meaningful for those involved, both the artists and the producers, *to consult with one another about the question of forming a collective and its mode of working. (Reichsfilmblatt)*

This idea is progressive. Indeed, a film should do nothing that a collective cannot do. This limitation alone would be a fruitful law, 'art' would be excluded. In contrast to an individual a collective cannot work without a clear point of reference and evening entertainment is no such clear point. If the collective, for instance, had certain didactic intentions, it would immediately form an organic body. It is the essence of capitalism and not something generally valid that 'unique' and 'special' artefacts can only be produced by individuals and collectives bring forth only standardized mass commodities. What kind of collective exists today in the cinema? The collective consists of the financier, the merchants (public taste researchers), the director, the technicians and the writers. A director is necessary because the financier wants nothing to do with art, the merchant because the director must be corrupted, the technician not because the apparatus is complicated (it is unbelievably primitive) but rather because the director has not even the slightest inkling about technical things, the writer finally because the audience itself is too lazy to write. Who would not wish under these conditions that the individual contribution to the production should remain unrecognizable? At no time during the work on the *Threepenny* film, including that during the lawsuit, did those involved share a common notion of the subject matter, the purpose of the film, the audience, the apparatus, etc. Indeed, a collective can only create works which are able to make 'collectives' out of the audience.

8. *'A film can be regressive in content and progressive in form.'*
The film is essentially the art form in which the material weight of the artistic means imposes the greatest limitations on the

creative mind; the mind is not the master of the cinematic means of expression, they are always cumbersome, complicated, unreasonably expensive tools. (*Reichsfilmblatt*)

The Threepenny Opera *offers us an unheard-of wealth of technical perfection.* As much as this technical perfection charms us on the one hand, we are disheartened on the other to ascertain that its use is not merited. (*Der Jungdeutsche*)

What we have is a cinematic spectacle, certainly not unified but magnificent, worked with such technical and artistic perfection that the substance almost disappears. (*8-Uhr-Abendblatt*)

A fascinating cinematic impression, no matter what was intended. (*Filmkurier*)

What ends does this perspective serve? Is it supposed to separate the wheat from the chaff? Then the wheat would be the form, since the 'form' functions as the form of presentation. In practice the formula serves to find a market for the most wretched trash. Never could one write in a film review that the content of this or that film is good and the form bad. In reality the reference to quality (a quality free of meaning and content) is regressive, short and simple. In reality there is no difference between form and content, and what Marx said about form is valid here too: it is good only in so far as it is the form of the content. An edit and a sequence that aim principally to please correspond to a dramaturgy with the same primary goal. Our intellectuals regard the form of *Love Parade* or *The Brothers Karamasov* as good because it is the form of its (reactionary) content.[21] There is not the slightest difference between the content of the ideas in, say, *Old Heidelberg* and *The Brothers Karamasov*.[22] The technique of the presentation takes care precisely of that. Our critics are all too quick to confuse this ability to present things appetizingly with the improvement of the apparatuses. An example of technical progress, which is actually a digression, is the perfecting of the photographic apparatus. They are much more light-sensitive than the old boxes used for daguerreotypes. It is possible to work with them almost without taking into consideration the light conditions. They have a series of additional qualities, above all for shooting close-up, but the likenesses they produce are undoubtedly much worse. With the old, less sensitive apparatuses several expressions ended up on the plate that was exposed for a relatively long time. As a result the final image had a more universal, lively expression, so something of the functional. Yet it would certainly be quite wrong to declare the new apparatuses to be worse than the old ones. Perhaps they still lack something that will be discovered tomorrow, or one can do something with them other than shoot faces. But why not faces? They no longer capture the faces, but must the faces be captured? Perhaps there is a way of making photographs with the newer apparatuses that would dismantle the faces? This way of using the apparatuses, which are undergoing change, will most certainly not be found without a new function for such photography. The intellectuals are uncertain about technology. Its brutal but powerful intervention in intellectual matters fills them with a mixture of contempt and admiration: it becomes a fetish for them. In art this relationship to technology expresses itself in the following way: everything can be forgiven, if it is 'well executed'. Hence, this technology profits from the shimmer of its separability ('it can be directed towards better, more meaningful functions!'). What it makes possible could also be something other than nonsense. This is how the nonsense gets its shimmer in reality and in the marketplace. Obviously the whole lot of accomplishments can be thrown on the junk pile when cinema's social function changes. The use of the apparatuses can be learned in three weeks: they are unbelievably primitive. The typical director – who tries to work as true to nature as possible, whereby nature is what he has seen on stage, in other words, who tries to deliver the most perfect imitation possible of an art-work – attempts to conceal all the shortcomings of his apparatuses, whereby for him the short-comings are any features that prevent the apparatus from making a copy true to nature. He regards as the proof of his professionalism the skill with which he elicits the true imitation of a real stage set by means of such a deficient apparatus. The good man, who must fight as well a bitter battle for his art with some people from the marketing division who understand nothing about the business and who keep trying to trip him up, this good man lets no one touch his apparatus who may not possess this skill. So close to the business, he is miles away from any inkling that these deficiencies of the apparatus could be its qualities, because this would presume the refunctioning of the cinema. Cinema technology is a technology that makes something out of nothing. (The film *Karamasov* is indeed something, an assemblage of various charms.) This some-thing is made from nothing, that is, from a pile of trivial ideas, imprecise observations, inexact statements, undemonstrable asser-tions. This nothing came forth from something, from the novel *The Brothers Karamasov*, that is, from a series of precise observations, exact statements and demonstrable assertions. The cinema tech-nology that was necessary to make something out of nothing had first been forced to make nothing out of something. This is a practice from which it cannot be removed. It is not usable for making something out of something. This is, then, the technology that performs the tricks, for it is not art but a trick to make out of a portion of filth a tasty dessert.

9. *'Political censorship is to be rejected on artistic grounds.'*

[Sources available]

The intellectuals' battle for an improved cinema is especially unfortunate where it confronts the state and censorship. Here they must struggle not against the public's condescension towards the cinema but against the censor's condescension towards the public. Yet here finally the viewing masses' real interests become visible, those about which even they don't know much, but which the censor knows. Here and nowhere else the education takes place that the 'progressives' and pathbreakers would like to control. The mass of petty-bourgeois consumers are to be educated in a morality that, rigorously applied, is suitable for ensuring the satisfaction of their entertainment *and other* needs. The social class which sets store by the sentimental and humoristic treasures of the cinematic army barracks and student bars is not always sure about choosing the correct political and cultural perspectives that ensure these charms. This class must hire professionals who can enlighten them. Interestingly it is not even necessary to draw on the wishes of the upper middle classes to understand the censorship process. It can be viewed and understood as a schizophrenic process within the petty bourgeoisie, based on the structure: *I* tell *myself* that *I* must restrain *myself*. The petty-bourgeois knows that he could not digest everything he might eat. An 'unimaginative', straightforward, pessimistically oriented filming of whatever can be photographed in a student's life, that is, in the life of a type who in the briefest amount of time must hoard a maximum of expensive and hard-to-market specialized knowledge while sacrificing a large part of his energy, or in the life of the worker type who is drafted and drilled for war against his class brothers, this simple filming would attack the basic situation of these ticket buyers who could still imagine themselves even worse off than they are now. For there are people who can buy no movie ticket at all! In a world with humour people would have no need for humour! These people have an obscure intuition that the untouched filming of the act of birth signifies a political act. The search for an answer to the 'why' would lead to the *ABC*s of sociology because one would have to consider the influence of the political situation on the senses, which appear to be only biologically determined. Everyone knows that the physical pains felt by the birth-mother are not the truth of the birth.[23] The truth is something more totalizing. But into what kind of world do these uteruses expel their creatures? Where does the heroism of the partial truth come from, if it is not that of the total truth? What do our enemies of censorship fight for when they are fighting for the right to see the birth act? They would get sick. They are fighting for the right to get sick. They will not succeed. They will not be allowed to vomit, even if they make threats. The priceless comedy is that they wish to reject the filmed birth act on artistic grounds, while the censor rejects it on political grounds. Hence the struggle of the two 'powers'! For artistic reasons they request that the class struggle be interrupted! In terms of taste a real abyss separates them from the cinema masses (since they would be the ideologues of the upper middle class, as far as taste goes, which oddly is the same as culture in this case) and in terms of political savvy an abyss separates them from the upper middle class (that is, a dependency which pays off). They do not understand that their own economic and social position depends on the sanctity of marriage (possibly with the exception of their own) and motherhood. Once again – where do they belong? To those strata that do not know their political interests. And what must they do? They must be educated. And once again – what constitutes their impossible situation? *They would have to be able to desire political art not for artistic but for political reasons.* There are no valid aesthetic arguments against political censorship. At the very least they would have to be in a position to apprehend critically the political-cultural situation of the art consumers (which is their own) instead of criticizing only the symptomatic taste of these people. They themselves find it difficult to lift themselves above the petty-bourgeois class, for whom essentially films are made, the only class in which the concept of 'humanity' is still relevant (*humanity is petty-bourgeois*) and the only class which owing to its situation thinks on principle in a retrograde way. Yet the self-limitation of this sort of thinking is not retrograde. We are approaching the era of mass politics. What may sound comical for the individual ('I shall not grant myself freedom of thought') does not for the masses. The masses do not think freely as individuals. For the individual continuity is a condition of thinking; and for a long time this continuity was only possible for the individual. Our intellectuals, who do not constitute a mass but rather dispersed individuals, understand thinking precisely as an inconsequential reflex because it has no continuity backwards, forwards or sideways. Anyone who really belongs to the masses knows that he is able to advance only as far as the masses can. Our

intellectuals, who – each on his own – advance by separating themselves from the masses, do not really move ahead but rather hang
on to their brief head start. The uniformly functioning masses of
our age, who are steered by common interests constantly geared
towards them, move according to clearly defined rules of thought,
which are not generalizations of individual thinking. These rules
have as yet been insufficiently investigated. To some extent they
can be derived from the thinking behaviour of individuals where
these think as representatives or agents of mass units. Thinking in
the next phase of capitalism will not have the same sort of freedom
that laws of competition have forced on the capitalists. But it will
have a different one.

10. *'A work of art is the expression of a personality.'*
     A work of art is a living creature and the creator who will not
     tolerate its mutilation is right ten times over. (*Frankfurter
     Zeitung*, the lawyer for the film company, Dr Frankfurter)

It would have been possible to transform *The Threepenny Opera*
into a *Threepenny* film while maintaining the status quo in the
utilization of the film apparatuses if its social thesis were the basis
of the adaptation. The assault on bourgeois ideology would have
had to be staged in the film as well. Intrigue, settings, figures were
to be treated with complete freedom. The approach of breaking up
the work while maintaining its social function within a new
apparatus was rejected by the film company. Nevertheless, the
work was of course broken up, but according to commercial
criteria. To reach the market, an art-work, which is in terms of
bourgeois ideology the adequate expression of a personality, must
be subjected to a very specific operation that splits it into its
components. To a certain extent the components enter the marketplace separately. The process to which the art-work – this
'adequate expression of a personality' – is subjected in order to
reach the market can be clarified in the accompanying chart
showing its dismantling [see 'Chart of the Dismantling Process'].
    It is a chart of the disintegration of the literary product, of the
unity of creator and work, meaning and story, etc. The work can
be given a new or several new authors (who are personalities)
without eliminating the original author for the purpose of market
exploitation. His name can be used for the altered work, that is,
without the work. Even the rumour of his radical convictions can
be used without their fruit, the very work itself. The work can be
used as literature without its meaning, i.e., with another or with no
meaning at all. The thesis is dismantled into a sanctioned, socially

Chart of the Dismantling Process

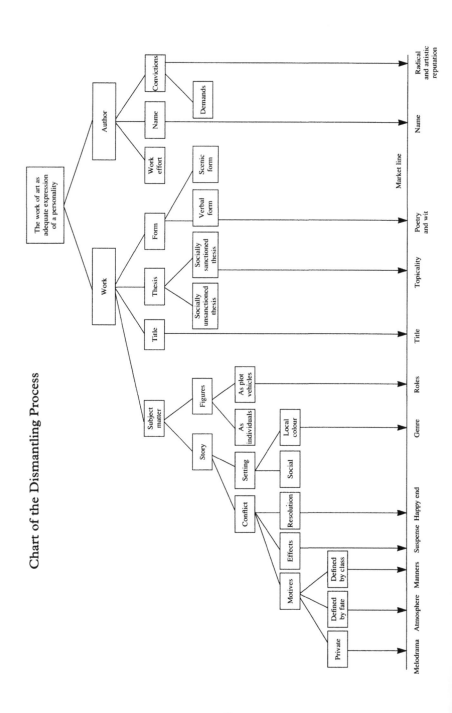

acceptable one and into one that reaches the market only as a rumour. The work's subject matter can assume a different form, or the form can be given a different (or partly different) subject matter. Moreover, the verbal and scenic form may appear without one another. The subject matter's story can be presented by other figures, the figures can be introduced into a different story, etc. This demontage of art-works seems at first to follow the same market laws as cars that can no longer be driven and are therefore dismantled so that the component parts can be sold (iron, leather upholstery, lights, etc.). We witness the ineluctable and hence permissible disintegration of the individualistic work of art. It can no longer reach the market as a unity. The strained condition of its contradictory unity must be destroyed. Art is a form of human communication and therefore dependent on the factors that generally determine human communication. These factors revolutionize the old concept. Some examples:

1. A work of art is an invention that, once invented, immediately assumes commodity form, that is, it appears separately from its inventor in a form determined by the commercial possibilities in the market. (a) Court judgment according to which the author must allow changes to a work that qualify its impact because someone else puts his name to them – the scriptwriter. (b) Authors such as Heinrich Mann, Döblin, Hauptmann do not ask for the right of co-determination.[24]
2. A work of art can be reduced to the invention of a story, which is invented according to market needs. It has no innate intellectual thesis incorporated into it. (The film companies' practice, uncontested by the authors.)
3. A work of art can be dismantled into its components and individual components can be removed. It can be mechanically dismantled, in other words according to economic and police criteria. (Court judgment according to which the author must permit the company to decide which parts of the manuscript are not usable.)
4. Language is unimportant. It is to be separated from the important dimensions of gesture and mime. (The court found our complaint concerning the modifications of the text unworthy of an answer.)

Nonetheless this butchered work enters the market as a unity. The chart can be read not only from top to bottom but also in reverse. In this case it is no longer a matter of how a particular art-work (like *The Threepenny Opera*) can be made marketable, but rather of the way in which an art-work must be constructed from the commercial perspective. The dismantling process is, in other words, a production process. The sentence 'the whole is more than the sum of its parts' applies not only to the chart's upper part but also to the lower.

The idea that the work of art is the expression of a personality is no longer valid for films.

11. 'Capitalism's contradictions are like the snow of yesteryear.'
The press reports are presented by and large chronologically,* but the sequence derives its humour from the fact that the excerpts from various newspapers look as if they could have been from only one of them, without the readers having been especially surprised. If you admit the latter, you will find the sequence justified. Indeed the distribution of opinions is only the dramatic development of one and the same fundamental attitude, the bourgeois one. Only together do they provide the whole. The individual journalist himself shares the opinions of all the other journalists and participates in the development of the full opinion. Here too a collective is at work that makes the individual's contribution unrecognizable. How is it formed? It is formed by the class struggle. By the shared work of proletarianization and the shared fate of becoming the proletariat. The ideological schizophrenia of the petty-bourgeois journalist manifests itself in the cohabitation in his consciousness of different realms of ideas, in their gradual shifting towards one another. At one and the same time he has at least two ideas about the same thing: he derives one from upper-class idealism, which will impose Individuality, Justice, Freedom, etc. on reality and the other from reality itself, which prevails in all its tendencies against the idealism, deflects it, domesticates it, *but also lets it exist*. The contradiction cannot be liquidated until the entire bourgeois system is liquidated. In a comical fashion the fiction of a certain intellectual freedom ensues for the journalist. He can choose, i.e. defend one or the other idea since both must be defended. The battle report reads then: first I had the upper hand, then he did. The whole comedy of the situation comes into perspective in the exclamation of two boneheads when we broke off the lawsuit: we should never have begun the lawsuit or never have broken it off. They considered the opening of the suit idealistic and its liquidation rational and for them there is an enormous difference between idealistic and rational thinking. Those who think rationally have no right to be regarded as idealists and

* See Part I.

idealists have no right to be reasonable (according to our two champions of utmost consistency, either we were unreasonable enough to begin the suit or idealistic enough to lose it to the point of self-destruction). Even our leftist friends regarded the lawsuit as superfluous. (The importance of proving that in a lawsuit against industry the individual is in the wrong! Doesn't everyone know that already? Indeed, everyone knew it.) For us it was interesting to see how far the disintegration of trust in justice had advanced in all circles: everyone who spoke with us, without exception, warned us before they learned of our case and even after they had seen our contracts about conducting a lawsuit against a million Marks. But wasn't it also interesting to know where everyone's knowledge leads them? The truth is: it is not enough to know that capitalism has become increasingly incapable of ordering its affairs as long as it is still capable of holding the masses in disorder. It is also not enough to say this, because the knowledge about its failure provokes calm rather than disquiet; we must constantly prompt it to fail. Capitalism cannot die, it must be killed. When enough facts about class struggle have penetrated our consciousness, then class struggle may appear as a natural category and the actions of individuals as well as groups strike even themselves as determined from the outset by class struggle, which leads to a dangerous passivity. Then class struggle is no longer a human issue, but rather humanity becomes the object of class struggle. For many leftist writers the world is boarded off with barricades. The barricade conceals the adversary and protects him more than it does them. The world then consists of two worlds that are detached from one another, not attached. From this perspective a large number of people are petty-bourgeois and petty-bourgeois people are nothing more than petty-bourgeois, belonging to an immutable and natural category. A certain way of eating fish is petty-bourgeois, certain social tasks are performed by petty-bourgeois people and those who perform them are petty-bourgeois. Contempt protects them from any demands. Similarly, industry is unintellectual and the courts are unjust, just as the trees are green and it is more reasonable for industry to be unintellectual than for us to attack it for that. The concept 'snow of yesteryear' plays a special role here. If this or that is so and so, it is snow of yesteryear. Pity the person who is caught in the snow of yesteryear, especially when shovelling it! It must be new snow. Nothing gets protected like the snow of yesteryear. Literature is increasingly assuming a commodity character and the laws of competition force our literature to invent new things, what is not familiar or has been already forgotten. In this way an injustice, having become old, is no longer offensive, a serious insult after two weeks is only a minor irregularity and capitalism, which is just another 'subject-matter', is a bad subject, snow of yesteryear.

12. *'The rights of the individual must be protected.'*

[Source: Civil Code]

The court declared the author's right to protection against changes to a stage play to be limited also by the general knowledge that, for the purposes of filming, changes are necessary that touch the work's essence and affect its impact, but that the author of the screenplay rather than the author of the stage play is to be held responsible. Such changes must be accepted. But a suit would not be rejected, if it could be proved that the changes exceed this standard ... According to the contract, the author, who was guaranteed his right of co-determination, expressly contested the company's competence in matters of taste. Dismissed by the company, the author can only argue that the court *itself* should intervene. Thus, he is forced to acknowledge the competence in matters of taste on the part of some judge or another. Two second-rate scribes, Béla Balász and L. Vajda, attempted to 'preserve the style' and the judge decides intuitively, without having seen the film, that they succeeded in imitating the author's way of writing, in other words, in forging his signature. The judge himself declared the forgery a success! Don't the rights of the individual count for something? Let's put it this way: he has no rights outside the production process. *There are no rights outside the production process.* The only right the court explicitly allows the individual is the one he needs in order to assume responsibility towards the general public, which is then recognized as his obligation. (The author must answer to the public for the damage done to his work.) When someone else assumes this responsibility (with his agreement or without), the subsidiary rights also disappear. In a form of production that makes unrecognizable the contribution of the individual to the production, it is difficult to protect the right of the individual. Yet it resurfaces in discussion of the production's revenue.

13. *'Incorporeal rights must be protected.'*

The idea that incorporeal rights must be protected is as general and secure as the idea that Law transcends economic and social processes and expresses humanity's innate sense of justice. This Law is independent of everything material, criticizing and clarifying it. This idea of the Law would, for instance, ensure that contemporary human relationships emerging from economic developments – a natural process – take their bearings from a stable, unshakeable sense of justice. Contradicting this idea are, however, the courts' very weighty judgments. It is useful to read carefully the following decision of the High Court:[25]

Does the film contract provide the screenplay writer grounds for a claim against the film producer to duplicate and distribute the film? 1st Civil Senate. Judgment of 16 June 1923 in the case of D. & Co. (defendant) vs. W. (plaintiff). I 185/22. 1st Regional Court of Berlin I – 2nd Superior Court of the same.

The plaintiff is the author of the screenplay *Only a Dancer*;[26] the defendant acquired it from him for a film but has not yet produced it. The lawsuit wishes to arrive at a judgment that forces the defendant to produce the film, duplicate it and distribute it for screening under the name of the author. Both previous jurisdictions granted the plaintiff's suit. The defendant's appeal was successful.

Reasons:

Concerning the litigious question whether there exists an obligation to film on the part of the defendant, the Superior Court considers that the expressed acceptance of such an obligation is not demonstrated; witness N.'s declarations and the content of the letter of confirmation show nothing conclusive about it. Lacking the formal promise of the defendant, the Court must examine whether even without a special agreement such an obligation is justified. There is no legal stipulation; commercial conventions cannot be accepted as binding. Yet an examination of the legal nature of the contract would lead to the conclusion of the existence of such an obligation to film. The contract is, granted, not a publisher's contract; thus, ¶1 of the Publishers' Code would not be directly applicable. Nonetheless, an application corresponding to the obligation of the publication law would appear to be in order concerning the duplication and distribution of the work. *This obligation is based on the idea that the publisher is for the author only the means to communicate to the general public the products of the intellect. The payment does not usually represent the author's main goal, rather the goal is primarily to communicate the work to the public. There is no reason to place the scriptwriter in a lesser position than the author of other intellectual products. The higher costs of the film producer in comparison to those of a publisher cannot be the deciding factor.* To this extent the issue is no different from that of the first production of a stage play. In specific instances the disproportion of the means needed for the

apparatus might lead to the negation of the obligation to produce. But the defendant here has not provided adequate
evidence for this. What distinguishes the film entrepreneur from
the theatre entrepreneur is essentially that the latter is personally
involved in the stage production, whereas the former duplicates
and distributes the reels of film. This distinction, however, does
not offer a basis for differentiation in the jurisdiction of the
litigation.

It is impossible to follow this line of argument; it derives more
from a judicial construction than from a consideration of the
legal facts at hand.

The presiding judge assumed correctly that the film contract is
not a publisher's contract and that the opinion applicable to
literature is in this case wrong (see Goldbaum, *Urheberrecht*, p.
93).[27] Similarly the analogous application of ¶1 of the Publishers'
Code cannot be approved. Certain similarities between a
publisher's contract and a film contract and between the latter
and the Superior Court's comparison to a stage production
contract are not substantial enough. On the other hand, the
differences in both of these instruments are so significant that it
is unacceptable to transpose principles of publication law to
cinema law. For publishing the already practised law, as it
emerged through jurisprudence and scholarship based on the
customs of the highly reputable German printing industry, led to
regulations in law codes in accordance with the needs of the
book and musical score trade. That the needs of the film industry
and cinema market are quite different from those of the book
trade is evident. Thus, they necessarily have a different effect on
the legal relations between scriptwriter and film producer.
Altered economic circumstances provide therefore the opportunity for
an especially careful consideration of the legal exigencies and the
general application by analogy of legal principles in more or less related
domains.

In view of the differences in the domain under investigation, the
following details must be considered:

1. The object of the publisher's contract are written works and,
since there exists no law for art publications, it extends as well in
general application by analogy – by common law – in part to
products of the fine arts and photography. The duplication of the
original work takes place fundamentally without a personal,
intellectual contribution on the part of the publisher, more in a
mechanical form. On the other hand the duplication is restricted
to the same artistic medium. The circumstances are no different

in the case of translations (see Goldbaum, *Urheberrecht,* p. 93), when books translated from one language into another do not fall within the framework of a mechanical but of an intellectual achievement, or in the case of engravers, who are not on the same level as printers. For the decisive factor is first of all that in both cases it is a matter of remaining in the same artistic domain (the literary work or the image) and that, despite all the investments of intellectual activity, it is a question of scrupulously respecting the original work down to the utmost detail. The dramatization of a book, however, is no longer covered by the publishing law. *It is, moreover, characteristic that the publisher himself is supposed to bring to the public the duplicated, true reproduction of the original work as a commodity in larger or smaller quantity and conforming to the intention of the publisher's contract in order to introduce to the public the author and his work.*

2. The situation is different for so-called stage performance contracts in the case of written dramatic works. Here there is no duplication. The distribution is also different. A play is put on stage as defined and carried out according to the production contract only for this particular theatre. The distribution of the work as a commodity in the sense of the publisher's contract is eliminated. The number of performances is usually contractually defined and limited. The transposition of the work into another artistic domain is not a consideration in the case of the stage play since it is written by the author ready for use. The director is here only the author's assistant. The latter can be and is frequently himself involved in the stage production.

This perspective must be somewhat modified in the case of stage performance contracts for ballets, mimes, etc., that are only based on a scenario. For here the dramatization must be created, that is, the transposition from verbal language into gestural language. Here the director, stage producer or ballet master contributes something essential, so that the artistic structure comes to life. But even in these circumstances there is no distribution beyond the framework of the theatre that signed the performance contract. There is no commodity trade involved. Whether there obtains any kind of performance obligation in the acquisition of such scenarios will not be considered here. For it is characteristic of the stage performance contract that the performance obligation is limited (according to number and days, etc.) and therefore is mentioned expressly in words.

3. The film production contract is once again different. It contains isolated elements from the publisher's and performance

contracts and adds new ones as well. It is a specially conceived contract that must be appreciated on its own legal merits. Like the publisher's contract, its object is an original text. But this is not the object of duplication and distribution, rather from this object something is produced. As with the scenario of the ballet or mime, first it is dramatized, that is, the situations only described by the original text must be transformed into actions and performance. Gestures take the place of words as the means of expression. Simultaneously there is a transposition into another artistic genre; the work first transformed into a dramatic mime must be transposed at the same time into a work of images. Even if this happens by means of photography, that is, in a more mechanical way, it is nonetheless not simply a matter of filming mechanically a ballet or a mime that has been performed on a theatre stage. The cinema has its own rules that are not only of a visual nature but rather determine and affect the essence and content of what is represented. The essence is the dissolution of the dramatic process into single shots that results from the disappearance of the word and compression into short, independent scenes. Their sequencing and combination, arrangement and plausibility are contained only implicitly in the original film text. They obey their own principles, which are different from those of the verbal drama and distinct as well from those of pure stage mime. It is the responsibility of the film director not only formally to stage this but also, in a certain sense, to transpose all of these indispensable things into reality. He is not the scriptwriter's assistant but at the very least his collaborator. This is valid as well for the so-called shooting script, for only during the filming itself does the director, who is literally constrained to look through the lens of the camera operator, recognize what is necessary for a good film. Hence the many technical modifications and the frequently divergent opinions of author and director which, however, the latter can or should not necessarily always accommodate. For he is if not principally then partially responsible for the film's creation as a visual work in its own right. Only then is the strip of film duplicated and distributed as a mass commodity; but even here usually not directly by the film producer but rather through the intervention of commercial film distributors. What the film reel contains, however, is not – as in the case of the book – the intellectual product of only the original text's author, but his and the director's cooperative work. The latter also plays a role vis-à-vis the public, a circumstance usually reflected in the importance and reputation of the company that has engaged and secured his intellectual skills. *As a result it cannot be stated, as is the case in the contested judgment, that there are no grounds for considering the scriptwriter differently or in a lesser role than the writer of stage plays.* The screenplay prepared for the shoot is not the same as nor similar to the stage drama. The film entrepreneur is also not a theatre entrepreneur. The latter produces on his stage one or more performances, as agreed, of the play. *The former produces a mass commodity that is intended for distribution around the world. In this case, and owing to the commercial risk involved, he is under greater economic pressure. Therefore the financial costs must be weighed differently.* Once a film is produced, if it is unusable or not readily usable, then the film's mass circulation as a commodity by the distributor is obstructed. In contrast, the stage manager simply cancels the next performance in his theatre without causing a major setback in his commercial undertaking. *Yet, in still other respects the film producer's entire business policy, aiming at the fabrication of a distributable commodity, is different. He must work according to supply and demand and depends much more than the stage director in his city on fashions, public taste, the subject matter's topicality, the competition of the world market.* For it is not enough to produce at great expense negatives and copies of a film; they must also circulate as commodities. In this area the film producer no longer has an exclusive, determining influence on the decisions of the commercial film distributors. For the distribution, and especially for screenings in the cinemas, new costs are generated (like electricity, depreciation of apparatuses, etc.), which the buyers in the large film market can only recoup if the film is successful. Once again the distribution is different here from the case of a book, which is produced just once and sold by the publisher himself. Finally it is more difficult to anticipate the quality of a usable film script than that of a published drama; for the former remains still – as explained – in a certain sense unfinished.

The relationship between playwright and theatre or writer and publisher does not therefore provide a basis for ascertaining a reasonable mutuality of interests – the source of a healthy economy – between scriptwriter and film producer. On the one hand there is the scriptwriter's legitimate wish not only to obtain his remuneration for which he transferred the exclusive rights of performance but also to reach the public and film audience with his intellectual product; on the other there is the interest of the film producer, who helps create the work with his director and carries the enormous economic risk of production and exploitation. Even in publication law there are indications that in the case of cooperative work no obligation obtains for duplication (¶47 of the Publishers' Code), just as special rules are provided in ¶6 of the Literary Copyright Law in the case of collaborative work. For this reason we declare that a general application by analogy of ¶1 of the Publishers' Code is not justified. The entire legal nature of the film contract as a specialized contract has not yet gone through an evolution corresponding to the economic development (as did the publication law before its judicial regulation) that would permit us to consider the author's legal right to insist on production as appropriate and compatible in good faith, if it is not contractually stipulated.

We have not investigated or decided whether the scriptwriters' interests in the future development of their legal relationship to the film producers will not be served in another way than by the rejected obligation to produce the film, for example, by the return of the original text if the work is not produced within a certain time limit, be it with or without a claim for compensation according to the specific situation.

Consequently the suit is rejected as ungrounded.

The third section, which treats the specificity of film production, gives – as we see – an excellent dialectical explanation of the crucially expanded sector of technology in the cinema and concludes that 'it cannot be stated that there are no grounds for considering the scriptwriter differently or in a lesser role than the writer of stage plays'. He must be viewed as part of the apparatus. This apparatus includes, however, the commercial organization as well. The opposition between author and production technology is resolved dialectically and at the same time it characteristically includes technology's dependence on the market. The author is pulled into the technical process, viewed as commodity production. The protection of the author's incorporeal rights is eliminated because the producer 'is under too great an economic pressure'. Intellectual interests can be protected only as long as they are not too expensive. Any longer and one cannot do them justice. For 'altered economic circumstances provide the opportunity for an especially careful consideration of the legal exigencies and the general application by analogy of legal principles' (such as the protection of incorporeal rights). The whole thing is called 'a reasonable mutuality of interests – the "source" of a healthy economy – between scriptwriter and film producer' and constitutes a document of the most decisive materialism. If the opposition between material and incorporeal interests were not unresolved –

the rape of the former is not a completely satisfactory solution –
then the entire apparatus, here so artfully unified and rationalized,
would have intellectual, incorporeal interests as well. In short, if
everything were not directed only at the protection of profits, we
would not have much to oppose to it from our side.

Yet it is most certainly not the case that the obsolete, generally
widespread ideas about an ideal and absolute Law mentioned at
the beginning have been abandoned by the courts in favour of the
newly emerging ideas in decisions such as those by the High Court
discussed above. On the contrary, it seems that for very vital
reasons the capitalist social system cannot relinquish its old ideas.
Dominant ideologies are just as conflated as dominant classes.
Every idea is beholden not only to one but to several others; it also
holds more than one destiny in its hand. It should not be retained
or rejected according to its immediate utility which is, as already
stated, multiple, because even the fact of rejection can be harmful.
Ideas must be tested again and again in practice, and frequently in
isolation from one another. Practice remains young, while the
ideologies age, and they are no stronger than their weakest link, the
single idea. Chained together as they are for better or worse, they
drop an absolutely compromised idea only with the greatest
hesitation, after it has changed its name more than once . . . But at
the cradle and coffin of every ideology sits practice.

It is useful to return to our particular legal case for a moment.
We tried in a specific, real case to get 'justice', to take a specific
bourgeois ideology at its word and to let it be proven wrong by the
bourgeois practice of the court. We pleaded our lawsuit by insisting
on ideas which were not our own but which we had to assume were
those of the court. In losing the suit, we discovered their new ideas,
which do not contradict general bourgeois practice: they only
contradict the old ideas (which constitute in their entirety that
classical upper-class ideology). Do bourgeois institutions, then,
relinquish completely their old ideas? They relinquish them
practically, but not ideologically. Practically they withdraw their
ideologies from circulation but 'in other respects' they retain them.
The joke is that they (especially they) can carry out their practices
neither if they abandon their ideologies nor if they put them into
effect.

The composer Weill received a judgment that looked as follows:
based on our contract he, too, could not object to the film. ('The
contractual agreements concerning his collaboration only give him
the right to demand compensation if his collaboration is rejected
unjustly.') He could have objected if the film company had been

guilty of gross textual modifications. But it was guilty of such alterations in a still acceptable proportion (see Brecht's judgment). Even if the company had undertaken alterations affecting the music, Weill would have had the opportunity to do several things. But the company had already assured the court during the lawsuit that this was not the case. Nevertheless, the court found in Weill's favour. Could he then object? Yes, just as long as it had not been *ascertained* that the deviations from the manuscript were acceptable. Unfortunately (see above) this had been ascertained! Neither with the Weill judgment nor the Brecht judgment could anything happen to the film. But Weill was in the right and Brecht was in the wrong with his complaint. How objective the court's attitude must seem when it so carefully separates the wheat from the chaff!

Weigert's judgments were in their end-result (the production was made possible!) irreproachable from the perspective of the highest authority.[28] Yet this justice does not look as presentable as, say, that delivered by the High Court. The difference between the logical effort of the High Court and that of Mr Weigert is quite striking.

The desire to protect the apparently still indispensable *belief* in the ideal and individual right beyond the production process, where *justice* itself can no longer be protected, generates really grotesque distortions, as illustrated in the following case reported to me. An architect sued a hotel company because it had engaged another architect to alter its façade. He claimed the façade to be his intellectual property. The court found in his favour. What were his rights here? Obviously there was no question of having the new façade demolished. The issue was that the architect was to have his loss – an ideal loss – appropriately compensated. The architect, however, had to demonstrate the material loss he suffered. Since the man cannot do this, he receives no compensation. Nonetheless, he was in the right and it is still forbidden to assail the intellectual property of another. Just as forbidden as it is customary. Comical as it may seem, in this legal decision there is the indication of a way out. Incorporeal claims are protected and – incorporeally fulfilled. The State recognizes the offended sense of justice as *justified*.

14. 'The court must make production possible.'

Extraordinarily decisive because it revolutionizes all behaviour and all ideas is the role that production plays or, more exactly, the constant growth of this role. Justice, freedom, character have all become functions of production, thus variables. No longer is a cognitive act possible outside the general production process. One must produce in order to know and production means to be in the production process. Even the place of the revolutionary and of the revolution is the production process. There is a simple but little noticed example: the surprisingly small role for the unemployed in the revolution. Out of this minor role will emerge immediately a major role when unemployment begins to threaten production seriously.

The machinery of justice works as one component in the general machinery of production. The court's behaviour manifested in every point of the proceedings the willingness to make possible in a practical way the production of the film, and film production was understood as the routine fabrication of routine films. In this willingness, the judge merely made the effort to ascertain the role played by the various parties in the production process. For example, it was simply ascertained whether the author facilitated or hindered the production. To facilitate meant that the author contributed to a film such as the company routinely fabricated based on commercial calculations, to hinder if the author demanded a different kind of film. Out of the author's right to maintain control over the screenplay from the outset, an author's obligation was constructed via the lawsuit (in the local court), a duty to make recommendations to an already completed film based on a screenplay by another. The contracts played a subordinate role. They were likewise evaluated according to their role in the production process. If they contained (and they did contain) demands by the author for the right of co-determination in the way the film was to be produced, then they were regarded as part of the author's sabotage of the production and placed the author's entire behaviour, which was the main object under consideration, in an unfavourable light. The author was Shylock, insisting on his piece of paper in order to strangle the company. Unable to comprehend the conditions under which a work of art is produced, the court refrained from expecting that the company produce a work of art. But able to comprehend the conditions under which a film (as mass commodity) is produced, the court refrained from expecting that the company fulfil its contracts. Our standpoint was not tenable. We insisted stubbornly on contracts to which we were entitled because the competition would otherwise have signed (and broken) them, which would have meant the company's ruin. For the film was acquired from us with the advance from the money that its sale was to earn. It had to be sold before it could be bought. These contracts hindered the production of the film, hence they had to be changed. It had been agreed that before the completion of the screenplay the company was not supposed to be permitted to intervene; Mr Weigert cancelled this agreement. It had been agreed that the material for the screenplay would be communicated orally to L. Lania, the scriptwriter. Mr Weigert demanded it in writing. It had been agreed that only a screenplay written by Lania and accepted by the author would be filmed. Mr Weigert condemned the author, who would have accepted such a screenplay, because he did not accept the one produced by the company . . . etc.

In short, Mr Weigert held the company not to the contracts that it had signed but rather to those that it should have signed. Thus, the court's worldly knowledge triumphed over that of the industry and bad contracts were improved in an ideal way. It was in other words unimportant that the company had not engaged Mr Weigert to write its contracts. In a parallel suit by the composer against the film company he was found in the right and the film was banned. The company had fired him out of nervousness and the court found in his favour on the grounds that he had put himself sufficiently at the disposal of the production. In his (musical) recommendations, which he continued to make up to the end, the court could recognize no hindrance at all to the production; those that were not only musical did not have to be considered . . . By means of this judgment the court demonstrated its indifference to the fate of the millions that were at stake. It was merely a question of production. But if justice 'diminishes' proportionately to its distance from production, it nonetheless does not play a very brilliant role in proximity to production. In order to be the purely calculable factor that is needed for financial estimates, justice must become much more primitive. The more dynamic and complicated economic life becomes, the more static and primitive will justice be. That makes it, however, less calculable as well.

IV. Summary

The ideas used in this work were not gained from observing the film produced by the Nero Company based on *The Threepenny Opera*, nor from reflecting on the ideas of art, cinema, business, etc. that are necessary to produce such trash. On principle the film was not considered, and the reader of this work would be well advised simply to ignore the sorry result of the director's diligent efforts. Otherwise, in reference to this result he can no longer recognize what is progressive in a certain sense in some of these ideas, which was precisely the goal of our little investigation. For there are progressive tendencies which lead to results that are in themselves retrograde. One of the reasons for this is that such tendencies can have several results at the same time (in our case, for example, more than just the film), and another reason is that these tendencies can be thwarted by others. In practice we have before us an extremely complicated field of contradictory tendencies and ideas. Whether the director in question is especially unintelligent can be ignored because the director's intelligence is unimportant for the industry. Much more interesting for us is the fact that the film critics, in agreement with the industry, simply ignore the idiocy of the plot and the base conviction of the entire film and grant the 'artist' Pabst a right to stupidity, which is generally granted to poets, painters, musicians, etc., and which is in fact more of an obligation. The function of these artists is not usually sought in the sphere of intelligence, a certain lack of reason is reckoned as innocence. Nonetheless the stupidity is more an accompanying trait than a driving force of this production. The wonderment that someone speaks at all when he has nothing to say gives way to understanding when one hears that he is paid for speaking. Speaking can have several functions, at one time to direct attention to something specific and at another to divert attention from something specific. Many people contend that a sensible text distracts them more from music than an illogical one. Stupidity would immediately disappear from film production if it or stupidity assumed a new function. This, however, depends entirely on the social system. And the evaluation of ideas (this is the main point) depends principally on the function that they could have not only in the given social systems but also in the imagined ones, i.e., in those social systems that are in the path of our development.

We have drawn ideas from practice, actually we have subjected them to practice. They are working theses that must be pursued beyond their result (the film). The theses partially contradict certain other ideas that do not come from practice but rather are situated far from it, before it, if not to say, above it: elements of upper-class ideology, of idealistic origin.

Underpinning many of these ideas is the idea of an inviolable phenomenon called 'art' that is directly fed by humanity but is able also to do without it. It is the idea of art as an independent phenomenon of a social nature, which can impose itself on society, which can and must manifest itself everywhere and under all circumstances, making use of the entire external world only as a medium. When the people die who bring it forth, it does not die along with them. Even the drying up of the consumers does not lead to its disappearance.* Its utility is considered to be great, but

---

* 'When people no longer wear pearls, oysters will continue to produce them' (Hebbel, cited from memory).

no one dares to name it because one of its most valued predicates is supposed to be a certain uselessness. Its utility is supposed to reside in the claim that there is something in it that escapes common usage and is loved with indifference. Indifferent love rates as the height of the human spirit. The making of art is attributed to humanity's innate drive to express itself. This need is an inborn one, it is said. Humanity expresses itself like fish swim. This is a purely predicative assertion and for its further application in larger systems it needs Aristotelian logic, which can operate with such assertions. The tautological character of such conceptual definitions bothers no one there, and it would not have to bother us if it did not conceal the view of the function of art and so make the implementation of art difficult. Now practice, which must implement art, finds itself, as already mentioned, in an increasingly strong opposition to this idea of 'art'. It is therefore not necessary to dissolve this idea – which corresponds to many others that constitute the Aristotelian-medieval world view – or to destroy it by means of its own concepts. It is more correct to let the evolution of reality take care of this, not simply by waiting but by provoking reality with experiments in order to formulate the process more visibly through acceleration and concentration. One should also be open to the flow of new concepts, thus increasing the conceptual material, just as Bacon suggested, admittedly without much success in the humanities but with all the more in the sciences, because the obstinate insistence on preserving the old conceptual material that can no longer apprehend reality is very significant. However the art-work is conceived and whatever the reason for its existence, it is sold and this selling plays a new role of great importance in the global system of human relations. The selling, which has become quantitatively so powerful, regulates not only the old relations through indifferent customs adapted to the time (they have just 'followed suit') but it also introduces completely new goals for the exploitation and thus also for the production of the art-work. If the concept of the art-work is no longer applicable to the thing that is created after the art-work has been transformed into a commodity, then we must prudently and delicately but fearlessly let go of this concept, if we do not want to liquidate the function of this thing itself along with it. It must go through this phase without any surreptitious purpose. This is no inconsequential detour from the proper path but rather a change from the bottom up that eliminates its past to an extent that, when the old concept resurfaces – and it will, why shouldn't it? – no more memory of the thing that it once described will be awakened. The commodity phase will relinquish its current specificity but it will have charged the work of art with another, inherent specificity. The sentence 'The work of art is a commodity' would also be just a predicative, tautological assertion if it did not indicate something more of the art-work's function, something of what constitutes its principal value.

In this sense the conversion of intellectual values into commodities (art-works, contracts, processes are commodities) is a progressive process, which can be affirmed on the condition that the progress is conceived as the act of advancing and not as the result of being advanced, in other words the commodity phase must also be seen as surmountable in its turn by the ongoing advance. The capitalist mode of production smashes bourgeois ideology. A few working theses that can be observed in the production of any routine film, in the execution of any routine process, suffice already to illuminate the unstoppable victory of capitalism, which long ago transformed itself into the mad run its ideologues can no longer keep up with. Their lunch is now provided only by corruption, a roof over their heads serves only to cover a bad conscience. What disappears with them is the type of petty-bourgeois that originally created the ideological construction called '*Humanity*'. The technology that triumphs here, and appears to be condemned to nothing more than guaranteeing the profits of some dinosaurs and thus of barbarism, can achieve very different things in proper hands. It is our task to get it into the proper hands. In practice the justice system makes production possible. How is it supposed to protect, then, an ideology ('intellectual property is untouchable'!) that endangers production? In practice the critics encourage impersonal works, ideologically they demand personal ones. And although everyone can see that works whose value derives from the unique expression of an individual personality are no longer produced today and, even if produced, they would no longer find their way to the consumer, the concept of the value of a personality is still measured by the way it expresses itself in a work and the concept of a work's success by how much of the personal is expressed in it. Capitalism is consistent in its practices out of necessity. But if it is consistent in its practices, then it is inconsistent in its ideology. Whatever its usefulness, it is for capitalism itself, but it is not therefore useful only for capitalism. Reality arrives at a point where the only obstacle to capitalism's progress is capitalism itself.

V. On the Organizing of Sociological Experiments

We spoke of a 'sociological experiment' when society's immanent contradictions are provoked and made perceptible by appropriate measures (appropriate behaviour). Such a sociological experiment is simultaneously the attempt to comprehend the functioning of 'culture'. Public thinking is unleashed and takes place with distributed roles. It is almost literally a matter of a thought process. The material is alive, it functions, it is not only an object of contemplation. The viewer himself is alive as well and not outside but inside the processes.

The sociological experiment is a process that allows us to show the 'public situation' as it *develops*. The driving tendencies that appear in practice appear as inconsistencies in ideology. For example, in practice a film is produced collectively and perceived as a work of art, before the concept of art allows for collective work. Or a certain planned economy – the dictatorship of demand over supply – establishes itself in the production of art without the concept of art relinquishing the value it places on the personality, etc. These ideological inconsistencies must be grasped. Bourgeois culture is not what it thinks about bourgeois practices. It is not a question of recognizing some kind of dualism here. Not a hair separates this culture from its practices. Facing any bourgeois behaviour, one must constantly hold on to reality and rise into theory only as far as the last step allows and the next demands. There are enormous dangers in any deductive process. Even induction resists freeing itself from the facts and above all these facts must be themselves actively formed and constantly able to criticize theory. For actually we need from all knowledge only hints for our own behaviour and information about the adversary's likely behaviour.

For the revelation of forgeries, which the bourgeois press photographers have on their conscience, the most appropriate method would be to write descriptions as if the reader were simply put in a position to learn such falsification. The forger's character would only appear where he reveals traits that are necessary for the falsification. The longer morality is kept out of the investigation, the more powerfully it assumes its rights in the end. Thus a work on nationalism would gain immensely if it not only concerned itself with an investigation of nationalism as a form of expression or with the analysis of nationalists, but also observed nationalism as a proposition and therefore only admitted to the investigation of this idea the practices it develops. If its practicability were actually investigated, if the question were raised whether today a nation can be constructed of the type needed by the nationalists for their plans, that is, one with the most effective means of mobilization, then all the economic and ideological factors begin to appear in their proper and unsuspicious position, ideas like blood relations etc., for example, as specialists' propaganda material. This is so because apparently national groups that actually lend themselves to effective operations in the foreign policy domain can be created only with great difficulty.

An example of an unusable definition is Thomas Mann's definition of the cinema as a 'spectacle for the eye spiced with music'.* Mann describes the phenomenon from a perspective that makes it seem unchangeable. Reading these kinds of descriptions is like reading definitions and one holds on to the custom of accepting such definitions as long as they contain nothing that is obviously false, i.e., refutable. That is very dangerous because definitions are operations by which things are placed into certain systems. If these systems are ignored or assumed, they are reinforced in absentia by the definition. In this way every new thing (that must be defined) helps the old by defining itself on the basis of the latter. Mann's definition of the cinema, for instance, helps the novel, from which it is taken. But the cinema has nothing to do with this pseudo-definition, where it does have something at all to do. The failure of cinematic adaptations of famous novels shows how the film actually serves very different functions. It destroys and unmasks the novels. Not the film but the novel produces its debacle. Working with old concepts, one works with highly impractical concepts. The concept of art, for example, includes something like hostility towards the apparatus. Pure humanity (= artistic) is thought of without the apparatuses, in other words in a form that does not exist at all. If man is the tool-producing animal – and he is not in every irrefutable definition – then pure humanity certainly can include the apparatus. All definitions that include the concept of art hostile to the apparatus do not make the subject matter easy to manage but rather push 'art' out of reach and admit their own ineffectiveness. Yet the point is to establish definitions that make possible the management of the material in question.

Even if someone organized an experiment like ours or applied the lessons from such an experiment only to make a routine film, i.e., a film that 'serves recreation', uses 'art', is a commodity, tries to be thematically regressive and formally progressive, is an 'art-work' in

---

* [Thomas Mann, 'Über den Film',] *Schünemanns Monatshefte*, [Berlin, August] 1928.

which 'human interest' plays a role and, by means of a few gestures to the sociological experiment, puts under the court's protection all practices that contribute to such a production, thereby acting in complete agreement with the public, even then it would be more useful to have undertaken such an experiment than to show how to reach the conclusion that the German cinema is situated quantitatively far below the level of the Russian or for that matter the American, or to express simply the indignation that in the cinema good and useful apparatuses are misused. There is absolutely no hope for success in projecting a certain 'culture' and trying to convince 'reality' of it. By means of such deductions one simply forfeits the opportunity to understand how reality functions and so to figure out what are the revolutionary and what are the reactionary tendencies in what has already happened. The experiment mobilizes contradictions of this sort in the things and the processes and maintains the movement of the process itself during the investigation.

The sociological experiment shows social antagonisms *without resolving them*. The organizers themselves must assume the position of an interested party in the force field of opposing interests, a thoroughly subjective, absolutely partisan perspective. In this way the sociological experiment differs fundamentally from other investigative methods that assume the most objective, disinterested perspective possible on the part of the investigator. Without pursuing these methods further, it can be stated that they have little prospect of even modest success precisely because they assume something no longer assumable, that an objective perspective is possible in a radically antagonistic social system. Only the participating, active subject is capable of 'understanding' here. Assuming this subjectivity, one could organize sociological experiments in any dimension, one could even imagine something that the status of current technology would not permit, just as one can conceive of operations beyond the current reach of surgery. Above all, many apparently private occasions must be developed for these undertakings by changing their function, as the *Threepenny* lawsuit did. *The courts, and with them the press, must be involved systematically and on a grand scale in organizing sociological experiments.* Since the public prosecutor in the bourgeois state in no way represents the interests of the entirety, the interests of the individual injured party being also those of the masses, court lawsuits can be used precisely to bring into the public consciousness the deeper, less noticeable social processes that constantly transpire and constitute bourgeois practices. To comprehend the sociological experiment is to 'find a handle' on reality. It does not come about in an act of observation, it does not end when an observation has been made. Here experience is supposed to provide the foundation of control. Most public events, and the most important among them, are far from developing a scientific consciousness. In comparison, science itself works, of course, more consistently and methodically, but even science will not be able to depend much longer on the primitive organization of congresses at which the results of the division of labour are exchanged. Discussion methods are needed that resemble more closely collective thinking processes. The materialist dialectic will elaborate these methods. But it will be of the utmost importance that the objects come forth alive, at their most complete level of functioning and not dead or excluded from the production process (say, for the purpose of observation).

Part V
The *Kuhle Wampe* Film
(1932)

[The film *Kuhle Wampe* was planned and produced over the period of almost a year in 1931. The credits as well as the original film poster list the Bulgarian film maker Slatan Dudow (or Dudov in English) as director and Brecht and Ernst Ottwalt as scriptwriters. The censorship card, however, lists Brecht as director, assisted by Dudow. The film today is often screened under both Dudow's and Brecht's names and in its post-1960s reception it has frequently been attributed – incorrectly – to Brecht alone.

According to regulations governing film distribution in the Weimar Republic, *Kuhle Wampe* was submitted to the Film Inspection Board in Berlin in March 1932. On 31 March the Board announced its decision to prohibit the film's release because of its emphatic propagandistic tendencies. Two board members, as well as the production company Praesens Film, appealed this decision and on 9 April the board met once again (see below, 'Short Contribution on the Theme of Realism' and the translator's notes to it), only to confirm its original judgment. Owing to massive public protests and Praesens Film's willingness to cut scenes considered by the Board to be inappropriate, the Berlin Film Inspection Board met for a third time to consider the film on 21 April and agreed to its release (with several additional cuts and limited to screenings for adults only). *Kuhle Wampe* had its first screening in Moscow in mid-May 1932, with Brecht and Dudow present, and opened in Berlin in the Atrium Cinema on 30 May 1932. It ran successfully but briefly, falling victim to the elimination of left-wing films with the accession to power by the National-Socialists in March 1933. It was screened later in 1932 in Amsterdam, Paris (Cinéma Falguière) and London (Film Society) and opened in New York City in February 1934 (Gayety Theatre) under the title *Whither Germany?* and in September 1936 in Zurich.]

Film without Commercial Value

1. A Communist film no longer has commercial value because Communism is no longer a threat for the bourgeois public. It no longer arouses interest. It would be different for a National-Socialist film.

2. Artistically valuable films are commercially damaging because they ruin the public's taste by improving it. They are themselves, however, not commercial. (If they were, then the capitalist would risk this dangerous improvement of taste for reasons of competition, just as he would risk Communist propaganda.)

3. To earn their money, they are willing nevertheless to enable us to produce a (damaging) film. To punish us for our opposition to capitalism and for the essay 'The *Threepenny* Lawsuit', they disregard our financial claims, thus exploiting our serious difficulties.

Conversation on 22 January in the offices of Tobis.

[GBFA 21/544. Typescript written in January 1932. Brecht's comments here indicate that, after the collapse of the Communist Prometheus Film Company when the film *Kuhle Wampe* had almost been completed, it was offered first to Tobis Film, but finally was taken on by Praesens Film. See explanatory notes to the article 'The Sound Film *Kuhle Wampe*'.]

The Sound Film *Kuhle Wampe or Who Owns the World?*[1]

1.

Owing to a series of especially favourable circumstances (the dissolution of a film company, the willingness of a private individual to invest not too large a sum of money as well as his acting talent in a film, etc.) we were able in summer 1931 to use the opportunity to produce a small film.[2] Fresh from our experiences of the *Threepenny* lawsuit, we insisted on a contract – for the first time in cinema history, we were told – that made us, the film makers, the holders of the copyright in a legal sense. This cost us our right to the usual remuneration, but we gained for our work otherwise unobtainable liberties. Our small team consisted of two scenarists, a director, a composer, a production manager and – last but not least – a lawyer.[3] Obviously the organization of the work caused us a lot more trouble than the (artistic) work itself, that is, we gradually came to see the organization as an essential part of the artistic work. This was possible only because the work as a whole was political. Just as we were completing our work, which at all times faced the possibility of interruption, after nineteen-twentieths of the film had been shot and large sums of money spent as well as loans taken out, one of our creditors, who held a monopoly on the apparatuses we needed, told us that the company had lost all interest in the release of our film and preferred to write off the debt rather than to allow us to continue working.[4] It believed that qualitatively better films increased the expectations on the part of the press, which did not necessarily coincide with those of the paying audience,* and that the film would not be commercial because Communism no longer posed a threat in Germany. On the other hand, other companies would not give us credit because they feared the film would be censored, indeed less by the state than by the cinema owners themselves. The former is, of course, only the expression of the latter, since the state in any case is not the impartial third party beyond the fray but rather the executor of big business and, as such, one of the parties.

2. *Description of the film*

The sound film *Kuhle Wampe or Who Owns the World?* consists of four independent parts that are separated by self-contained musical compositions accompanied by images of apartment buildings, factories and natural landscapes. The first part refers to a real incident, showing the suicide of an unemployed youth in those summer months when the destitution of the lower classes increased because of emergency decrees: unemployment pay for young people was discontinued. Before jumping out of the window, said young man took off his watch so as not to damage it. The beginning of this part shows the search for work as – work. The second part shows the eviction of a family owing to the decision of a judge (who uses the phrase 'their own fault' for the misfortunes of a family that can no longer pay the rent).† The family moves outside the city to a campsite called Kuhle Wampe where they take up residence in the tent of the daughter's boyfriend.[5] (The film for a while had the working title 'Ante portas'.) There the young girl gets pregnant. Subject to the pressure of the lumpen petty-bourgeois conditions in the tent colony (the combination of a sense of owning a piece of property and receiving a small government dole creates odd forms of social behaviour), the young couple becomes engaged. On her own initiative the girl breaks off the engagement. The third part shows workers' athletic competitions. They take place on a mass scale and are brilliantly organized. They have a political character, and the recreation of the masses has the mark of militancy. Over

---

* [Although a footnote is marked here in the typescript, no note is provided; the reference is probably to 'The *Threepenny* Lawsuit'.]

† This formulation 'their own fault' in eviction judgments is one of the already shattered pillars that shamefully exposes past glory. Don't those who use this infamous phrase notice that, by applying to themselves the concept 'without fault' and to those whom they rob of their roofs the concept 'at fault', they forever eliminate the concept of guilt. In fact, this is exactly what is happening here! [Although no footnote number is marked, this note in the typescript most probably refers to this sentence.]

3,000 working-class athletes from the 'Fichte Hikers' participated in this part.[6] The two young people from the second part are among the athletes. The girl has had an abortion with the money her girlfriends helped collect and the couple have dropped the idea of marriage. The fourth part shows the people returning home by rail as they discuss a newspaper article that reports on the destruction of Brazilian coffee beans to support the commodity market price.

3. Five poems from the film
1) Song of the Homeless (Constitution of the Reich)[7]
2) On Nature in Springtime[8]
3) Song for the Athletic Competitions[9]
4) Solidarity Song[10]
5) The Appeal[11]

On the poems
The 'Song of the Homeless' was dropped for fear of a general prohibition, 'The Appeal' for technical reasons.

The 'Solidarity Song' was sung by approximately 3,000 working-class athletes. The 'Song for the Athletic Competitions' is sung by a solo voice during the motorbike and rowing races.[12]

The poem 'On Nature in Springtime', spoken by a solo voice, connects the lovers' three walks. This part of the film was screened during the production for proletarian athletes and was criticized for the nudity in it.[13]

[GBFA 21/544–7. Unpublished typescript from 1932, signed by 'Brecht. Dudow. Höllering. Kaspar. Ottwalt. Eisler. Scharfenberg.' Brecht's secretary Elisabeth Hauptmann added the name of composer (Hanns) Eisler, and Kaspar probably refers to the stage designer Caspar Neher, whom Brecht often consulted.]

The Film *Kuhle Wampe*

The film *Kuhle Wampe* was made under great financial pressure by the young director S[latan] Th[eodor] Dudow. Most of the scenes had to be shot at the utmost speed, for example, a quarter of the entire film in two days.[14] The only support we obtained came from the Communist athletics groups who organized for us as many as 4000 working-class athletes on certain days. Owing to the difficulties of constantly raising money the film production lasted for over a year,, and in the meantime developments in Germany raced ahead (spread of fascism, increasing unemployment, etc.).[15] When the film was finished, it was immediately prohibited by the censor.[16] The film's content and purpose are best summarized by presenting the reasons for the censor's decision to prohibit it.

We showed how certain working-class groups accommodate themselves in a tired and passive way to the 'swamp'. The Interior Ministry declared: this is an attack on Social Democracy. Such an attack is prohibited just as an attack on the church, etc., that is, on any institution which supports the state.

We showed: the fate of an unemployed youth who never finds his way to the workers' militant struggle and who is driven to death by the cutbacks in unemployment assistance for young people, undertaken in the name of Brüning's emergency decrees.[17] The Interior Ministry declared: this is an attack on the President who signed the emergency decrees and who is here being accused of insufficient concern for the welfare of suffering workers.

We showed the activity of the large Communist workers' athletics groups that comprise in Germany about 200,000 workers and place athletics in the service of the class struggle. The Interior Ministry declared: this is a show.

[GBFA 21/547–8. Unpublished fragmentary manuscript, written in April/May 1932 for the film's first preview in Moscow in mid-May.]

Short Contribution on the Theme of Realism

One seldom succeeds in testing the actual impact of artistic methods. At the most one usually hears approval ('Yes, you showed it just like we know it') or that it was 'provocative' in some way. Here is a little test that succeeded.

With S[latan] Dudow and H[anns] Eisler, I made the film *Kuhle Wampe* that depicts the desperate conditions of the unemployed in Berlin. It consisted of a montage of several relatively self-contained, short pieces. The first one showed the suicide of a young unemployed worker. The censor raised questions about it, and there was a meeting between the censor and the company's lawyers.

The censor proved to be an intelligent man. He said: No one disputes your right to depict a suicide. Suicides happen. Moreover, you can depict the suicide of an unemployed worker. That also happens. I see no reason to hide that, gentlemen. But I object to the way you have depicted the suicide of your unemployed worker. It does not accord with the general interest, which I must defend. I am sorry I must make an *artistic* reproach.

We said (irritated): ?

He continued: Yes, you will be astonished that I reproach your depiction for not being sufficiently *human*. You have not depicted a person but, well, let's admit it, a type. Your unemployed worker is not a real individual, not a flesh-and-blood person, distinct from every other person, with his particular worries, particular joys and finally his particular fate. He is drawn very superficially. As artists you must forgive me for the strong expression that *we learn too little about him*, but the consequences are of a *political* nature and force me to object to the film's release. Your film proposes that suicide is typical, that it is not simply the act of this or that (pathologically disposed) individual but rather the fate of an entire social class! Your standpoint is that society induces young people to commit suicide by denying them the possibility to work. And you do not even shrink from indicating what one might advise the unemployed to do in order to change the situation. No, gentlemen, you have not behaved as artists, not here. You were not interested in showing the shocking fate of an individual, which no one would prevent you from doing.

We sat there disconcerted. We had the unpleasant impression of being caught red-handed. Eisler cleaned his spectacles with a gloomy expression, Dudow was bent over in pain. I stood up and – despite my dislike of speeches – made a speech. I rigidly upheld the untruth. I mentioned individual traits that we had given our young unemployed worker. For example, that he laid his watch aside before jumping out the window. I argued that this purely human trait alone had inspired the entire scene. That we had shown other unemployed workers who did not commit suicide, 4000 of them, because we had shot a large workers' athletics group. I objected to the shocking reproach that we had not behaved artistically and suggested the possibility of a press campaign against such a charge. I was not ashamed to declare that my honour as an artist was at stake.

The censor was not shy about going into details of the presentation. Our lawyers watched with dismay as a real debate about art ensued. The censor stressed that we had lent the suicide act an explicitly demonstrative character. He used the expression 'something mechanical'. Dudow stood up and excitedly demanded that medical opinions be sought from specialists. They would testify to the fact that acts of this kind often evoke something mechanical. The censor shook his head. That may be, he said obstinately. But you must admit that your suicide avoids anything that seems impulsive. The audience will not even want to stop him, so to speak, which would be the expected reaction to an artistic, humane, warm-hearted presentation. Good God, the actor does it as if he were showing how to peel cucumbers!

We had a hard time getting our film through. Leaving the building, we did not conceal our admiration for the astute censor. He had penetrated far deeper into the essence of our artistic intentions than our most supportive critics. He had taught a short course on realism. From the perspective of the police.

[GBFA 21/548–50. Unpublished typescript written in spring 1932, after the Film Inspection Board's decision on 9 April. The 'censor' refers to Interior Ministry expert Kurt Haentzschel. Other parties at the meeting included four members of the Inspection Board, two lawyers of the film company Praesens Film (Otto Landsberg and Paul Dienstag), their independent expert Harry Graf Kessler, two company representatives, Bertolt Brecht, Ernst Ottwalt, Slatan Dudow, a board stenographer and a photographer. The meeting was chaired by the director of the Film Inspection Board, Ernst Seeger. Contrary to Brecht's report here, Hanns Eisler is not documented as having been present at the meeting. See *Protokoll der Film-Oberprüfstelle*, No. 4636, Berlin, 9 April 1932.]

Kuhle Wampe or Who Owns the World?

Scene segmentation

[Although the film's original screenplay, entitled *Weekend – Kuhle Wampe*, is extant and was published in the appendix to volume 19 of GBFA (pp. 441–571), that text represents no more than the working basis for the completed film. Indeed, Brecht's contribution to this first version of the screenplay was minor, probably consisting of the dialogues, whereas he was involved both on the set and during the final editing of the film. Thus, what follows is a translation adapted from the 'scene protocol' or segmentation prepared in the late 1960s by Wolfgang Gersch and Werner Hecht (Frankfurt am Main: Suhrkamp, 1969), using a 35mm copy of the film owned by the State Film Archive in the German Democratic Republic (East Germany), now held in the Federal Film Archive in Berlin. The shot-length given in metres was measured at the speed of 0.456 metres/second, or five metres corresponds to 11 seconds' running time.]

[*Reel I*]
Kuhle Wampe or Who Owns the World?

Screenplay:	Bertolt Brecht, Ernst Ottwald[18]
Music:	Hanns Eisler
Director:	S. Th. Dudow
Producer:	George M. Höllering, Robert Scharfenberg
Cinematography:	Günther Krampf
Sound system:	Tobis Melofilm System, Tobis-Klangfilm
Sound technician:	Kroschke, Michelis
Sound editor:	Peter Meyrowitz
Sets:	Robert Scharfenberg, C. P. Haacker
Musical director:	Josef Schmid
Orchestra:	Lewis Ruth
Cast:	Hertha Thiele [Anni Bönike], Martha Wolter [Gerda], Lilli Schönborn [Mrs Bönike], Ernst Busch [Fritz], Adolf Fischer [Kurt], Max Sablotzki [Mr Bönike], Gerhard Bienert [man with a goatee], Alfred Schäfer [Franz Bönike]. [Others not listed in the credits include: Willi Schur (Otto, a guest at the engagement party), Martha Burchardi, Karl Heinz Carell, Karl Dahmen, Fritz Erpenbeck, Josef Hanoszek, Richard Hilgert, Hermann Krehan, Paul Kretzburg, Anna Müller-Lincke, Rudolf Nehls, Erich Peters, Olly Rummel, Martha Seemann, Hans Stern, Karl Wagner, Hugo Werner-Kahle and the agit-prop theatre group 'Das rote Sprachrohr' (Red Megaphone).]
˙Ballads:	Helene Weigel, Ernst Busch

World distribution and rental: Praesens Film GmbH, Berlin SW 48

Shot	Length	Editing / Sound	Description	Title / Dialogue
1	1.6 m	fast montage shots 1–30 accompanied by rapid, staccato music		[Title I]: One unemployed worker less
2	2 m	fade-in	Brandenburg Gate (Berlin)	
3	1.7 m	dissolve	factory yard, 4 smokestacks in foreground	
4	1.6 m	long shot	factory buildings on right and left sides of street, connected by a closed bridge; the Spree River in the background.	
5	4.5 m	camera pans right	a train moves into the frame from the left towards the camera; the smoke envelops the windows of a nearby apartment building	
6–13	6.5 m		brief shots of large apartment buildings and back courtyards in Berlin working-class district	
14–30	13.7 m	montage of front-page newspaper headlines	'20 instead of 26 Weeks' (*Vossische Zeitung*, 2 October 1931) 'Westfalia South splits off' (*Deutsche Allgemeine Zeitung*, 5 March) 'Spy war of the Iron Front . . . against the officials' (*Völkischer Beobachter*) 'Against the Bötz-Pension' (*Lokal-Anzeiger*, 24 October 1930) 'Japan accepts' (*Germania*, 1 March) 'Unity London–Paris' (*Vorwärts, Berliner Volksblatt*, 24 January 1931) 'One Billion and 800 Million' (*Die Rote Fahne*, 5 June 1931) '. . . urtius on his foreign policy' (*Berliner Tageblatt und Handelszeitung*, 11 February 1931)	
		rapid shots of entire front	'2.5 million without work, the result of Mr Schacht's policies'	

Shot	Length	Editing / Sound	Description	Title / Dialogue
		pages that roll upward out of the image frame music ends	'3/4 million unemployed!' 'Four million! Increase of unemployed under pressure of young' 'Unemployment increases! 2,700,000 seeking jobs in June' '4.1 million unemployed. Rapid increase in unemployment in August' 'Almost 4.5 million unemployed / Increase of 180,000 in second half of December' 'Almost 5 million unemployed / On 15 November 4,844,000 / Increase since 1 November is 220,000' 'Over 5 million unemployed & part-time workers / Unemployment increases again' '315,000 unemployed in Berlin 100,000 unemployed without support'	
31	4 m	fade-in fade-out	newspaper title: 'Employment Classifieds', *Berliner Lokal-Anzeiger* (free)	
32	33.9 m	fade-in, long shot, music begins	street with pillar covered in advertising posters, street workers in the background; pedestrians and bikers enter from both sides, park their bikes, greet one another, wait or walk away; the young Bönike is the third to enter; he stands with his bike to the right of the column	
33	6.5 m	medium shot	unemployed workers waiting with their bikes; people on foot join them and build a group	
34	2.5 m	see 32	the entire street is now filled with unemployed people waiting	
35	8 m	medium shot	a biker enters from the right with newspapers, gets off the bike and distributes the papers; the unemployed push to grab a copy from his hands and try to get out of the crowd	

Shot	Length	Editing / Sound	Description	Title / Dialogue
36	4.9 m	close-up	the unemployed push up to the newspaper seller	
37	3.6 m	close-up	young Bönike scans the classifieds quickly but carefully; others read in the background	
38	4.9 m	close-up	the distributor gives away the last copy and waves away the others; the unemployed move off, among them a helpless, heavy woman	
39	3.6 m	medium	unemployed sit on their bikes and read the classifieds; young Bönike puts the paper in his pocket and takes off on his bike	
40	3.1 m	full shot	several men from the group follow Bönike on their bikes	
41	2.6 m	full shot	the bikers go from right to left past houses, cars, streetcars	
42	3.9 m	medium shot camera in front of bikes	bikes going from right to left, framed so that only the feet pumping the pedals are seen	
43	2.2 m	medium shot	the bikers pass apartment buildings; the first three pass by, with Bönike in the middle	
44	2 m	see 42	downhill the bikers do not have to pump so much	
45	1.6 m	full shot

camera pans left | bikers enter back right, a horse-drawn wagon passes in the foreground; the approaching bikers pass through a building entry | |
| 46. | 4 m | full shot | in a building courtyard, on a window the sign 'gatekeeper'; pushing his bike, Bönike goes to the window where we see the gatekeeper's face; apparently he gives a negative answer; Bönike exits the frame, the next biker enters, gets off and after hearing 'no', drives off again; gatekeeper hangs a sign in the window; the third biker hardly pauses and the fourth rides right by | |

Shot	Length	Editing / Sound	Description	Title / Dialogue
47	2.1 m	close-up	the sign in the window written in chalk	[Sign]: 'Workers will not be hired'
48	1.8 m	see 46	two bikers ride right by the window	
49	2.9 m	close-up	travelling shot with bikers from left to right	
50	1.9 m	medium, travelling shot	Bönike in foreground on bike, in the background buildings and street traffic	
51	2.4 m	close-up, travelling shot	bikers as in 49; front wheel and handlebars of bike	
52	9.4 m	full shot slow pan up, pause at top, quick pan down	factory yard; six unemployed bikers with Bönike in the lead ride in quickly from the left through an arch in the background; rows of windows on the six-floor building; bikers race out of the yard, Bönike now in third position	
53	2.2 m	close-up	shot in front of the fast-moving bike wheels; feet pumping fast	
54	1.8 m	extreme close-up	Bönike's head, its movements suggest the fast rhythm of the bikers; he looks back at his 'pursuers'	
55	2 m	see 53		
56	16.5 m	long shot pan right	a street leads from background into the foreground, on the right a building with the half-covered sign 'Glass . . .'; the six bikers ride towards the camera and turn into a factory yard where a truck cab and trailer are standing; in the background an outdoor elevator; another biker with a piece of glass under his arm crosses in the opposite direction the path of the group of six; shortly thereafter the bikers return, pushing their bikes; young Bönike crushes the newspaper into a wad and tosses it; in the background they meet up with others who	

Shot	Length	Editing / Sound	Description	Title / Dialogue
		music ends	are pushing a wheelbarrow with crates in it	

[*Reel II*]

Shot	Length	Editing / Sound	Description	Title / Dialogue
57	5.5 m	full shot music from far away – polka medley	the bikers enter from the right, pushing their bikes along the street; young Bönike nods to an older unemployed worker and enters an apartment building	
58	3.1 m	low angle; music louder	courtyard façade of a back wing of the building	
59	13.3 m	full shot	in the small back court two street musicians (harmonium and saw) play with their backs to the camera; in the background a crumbling façade and a basement apartment entry; Bönike enters right, pushing his bike, pauses to watch and listen to the musicians, then exits left	
60	18.9 m	medium shot	Bönike family's living-room; Mr Bönike lies on the sofa covered with lace, reading a newspaper; a certain article interests him, he sits up, puts the paper on the table, takes his pencil stub from a jacket pocket and writes a note on it; a plate is placed on the table; he looks up at the mother, who is setting the table; she doesn't answer; he puts the pencil away and continues reading	Mr Bönike: The boy won't get support at all any more. Mr Bönike: You don't care about anything any more do you.
61	2.7 m	medium shot	in the foreground a bicycle hangs from the ceiling; young Bönike is tying the pulley rope to a nail; the music outside breaks off; he takes off his cap and exits right	
62	9.5 m	medium shot pan to table	young Bönike enters the living-room and goes to the table, sitting down across from his father; he looks at his father and then looks away blankly;	

Shot	Length	Editing / Sound	Description	Title / Dialogue
			his father looks him over and then turns away, playing with his spoon; a soup terrine is put on the table, the cover raised, soup is ladled into the father's bowl	
63	5.8 m	medium shot	the mother, only half in the frame, serves the soup; the door to the kitchen in the background opens and Anni enters; she removes her hat, takes a comb out of her purse and combs her hair	Anni: Hello! Anni: The welfare office is going to pay the back rent for the Schulzes next door.
64	9.4 m	full shot	father and son eat while the mother puts another plate on the table; she closes the soup terrine and sits down; Anni enters from left and sits down with her back to the camera	Mrs Bönike [*to Anni*]: They won't pay a penny for us. Mr Bönike: You never know. At the welfare office they take it as it comes.
65	5 m	close-up	frontal shot of the mother eating soup	Mrs Bönike: 'The early bird gets the worm.' If you don't try anything, how can you be surprised things go to pot.
66	2.1 m	long shot	unemployed workers riding their bikes at high speed on a street, following the camera	
67	1.4 m	medium shot	over-the-shoulder of the son to the father	Mr Bönike: And the boy doesn't even bother to greet the building manager.
68	4.4 m	medium shot	over-the-shoulder of the mother to Anni and the father; Anni continues to eat	Anni: Greeting won't help when you haven't paid the rent in six months. Mr Bönike [*angry*]: He can damn well say hello. Unemployed and impolite to boot, no one can afford that.
69	1.4 m	medium shot	over-the-shoulder of the son to the mother	Mrs Bönike [*sternly to her son*]: That's not the way to get a job.

Shot	Length	Editing / Sound	Description	Title / Dialogue
70	3.1 m	see 68		Mr Bönike [*to son on the right*]: Not that way, not when impolite. Anni: Not when polite either!
71	0.9 m	medium	over-the-shoulder of the mother to Anni	Anni: There are no jobs.
72	2.3 m	see 42	the unemployed on their bikes, pumping the pedals	
73	4.6 m	medium shot	between mother and son to Anni and the father, who gesticulates wildly with his spoon	Mr Bönike [*to Anni*]: You can be poor, you can have bad luck. But there are also people who don't have bad luck seven months in a row. Anni: You think the boy is especially lazy. Mr Bönike: Yes, that's what I think.
74	6.8 m	full shot	the mother from behind, the son on the left, Anni on the right, the father frontal Mr Bönike stands up, rests his hands on the table and shouts at Anni Mr Bönike exits right	Anni [*provocatively*]: And you? How far did you get? You've got no more than the dole in your pocket too. Mr Bönike: You don't have to waste your time at the unemployment office the whole day and then come home with your lip. Hard-working people get on. Mrs Bönike [*to her husband*]: Good God, what will the neighbours think?
75	1 m	medium shot	Mr Bönike agitatedly pulls on his jacket in front of the kitchen door and looks angrily at his family	
76	1.4 m	medium shot	the young Bönike sits and stares blankly at the table and the empty plates	
77	1 m	see 75	Mr Bönike goes to the kitchen and exits left	
78	5.3 m	close-up; pan to Mrs Bönike's face	Mrs Bönike scrapes the leftovers onto a plate	Mrs Bönike: Every day the same fight.

Shot	Length	Editing / Sound	Description	Title / Dialogue
79	3.2 m	full shot, sound of steps	Mr Bönike in the stairwell descending	
80	8.9 m	full shot	Anni and her brother, who still stares blankly, sit silently at the table; the mother cleans up, folds the tablecloth and places a bowl on the table	
81	1.6 m	close-up	Anni looks up and smiles at her brother	
82	3.7 m	close-up	over-the-shoulder of Anni to her brother, who stares impenetrably into the void	
83	2.9 m	close-up	Anni smiles and then looks serious	
84	9 m	full shot	Mrs Bönike cleans up in the kitchen, removes her apron and exits left	
85	10.1 m	full shot pan left pan right	young Bönike sits at the table in the foreground; Anni stands at the mirror in the background and puts on make-up; someone whistles, Anni turns, moves off left and bends out of the window; she returns to the mirror, finishes her make-up, puts the lipstick in her purse and exits right	Anni: Coming!
86	3.3 m	full shot	a wall-hanging above the kitchen table with a proverb and embroidered flowers	'Don't blame the morn that brings hardship and work. It's wonderful to care for those one loves.'
87	27.7 m	medium shot camera pans and follows Bönike camera dollies in on watch (close-up)	sitting at the table, young Bönike listens to the receding footsteps of his sister; when he hears no more, he rises, goes to the window, opens both casements abruptly, and grips them with both his hands; he looks at his left arm with the watch, turns to the left, removes it slowly and carefully puts it on the chest of drawers; he turns to the window again, places the flower pot to the side, and climbs onto the sill	

Shot	Length	Editing / Sound	Description	Title / Dialogue
88	6.5 m	see 79	Mrs Bönike slowly climbs the steps, carrying a heavy bag	
89	3 m	close-up	young Bönike's left hand holds onto to the upper window frame; as he jumps, his head and left shoulder appear in the image; the hand lets go and a horrible scream is heard from below	
90	3.1 m	close-up	the window sill with the displaced flower pot	
91	3.1 m	extreme close-up	the wristwatch, showing six o'clock	
92	2.1 m	see 42 and 72	the unemployed on their bikes, pumping the pedals	
93	3.1 m	medium shot	the bike suspended from the ceiling, over a metal bedframe	
94	4.3 m	long shot, high angle from window	excited people gathered round Bönike's body, which is covered with a tarpaulin	
95	3.7 m	full shot voices of playing children	part of the group (a woman, a worker, a child, a cop); in the background a woman and two children look out of the window; Anni and her boyfriend Fritz push through the crowd from the left; he looks at the covered body, then at the cop	
96	5.3 m	medium shot, children's voices	Fritz and Anni look down, at each other and then at the covered body	Fritz [*to the cop*]: What have you done now? Woman: Jumped from the window.
97	4.8 m	full shot, low angle	two women on a stairwell landing; a third goes up to join them	1st woman: And he put the wristwatch on the table first. 2nd woman: Of course, it would have been ruined, from the fourth floor.
98	4 m	medium shot, extreme low angle, children's voices from afar	three children (silhouettes against the sky) look up, a corner of the building in the upper right corner of the image	Child [*left*]: Which window was it? Child [*right, pointing*]: That one! Child [*middle, pointing*]: Nah, not that one, There.

Shot	Length	Editing / Sound	Description	Title / Dialogue
99	1.3 m	close-up	a woman on the stairwell landing	Woman: One unemployed worker less.
100	2.6 m	full shot, high angle	five women in the stairwell	1st woman: Such a young man. 2nd woman: And the father doesn't know a thing yet.
101	16.6 m	medium shot	Mr Bönike standing with another man at a bar, each with a half-full glass of beer; they drink chasers and smoke	Mr Bönike: They've got 7 million unemployed in America too. Man: Well, before they used to drive to work in a car and now they're demonstrating because of unemployment. Mr Bönike: But on foot! Man [*nods in agreement*]
102	1.5 m	close-up	over-the-shoulder of a police officer to the cop, behind are heads of the crowd	Officer: Motive for the deed? Cop: Unknown!
103	1.7 m	close-up	stairwell	Old woman: Such a young man. He had his best years still to come.
104	4.3 m	full shot; camera pans with driver; noise of the car	a police ambulance on the street; the driver noisily slams the door and moves left to get in the car; the ambulance drives off and turns right	

[*Reel III*]

Shot	Length	Editing / Sound	Description	Title / Dialogue
105	2.6 m			[Title II]: The best years of a young man
106–121	50.2 m	dissolves between short takes; music grows more agitated with the wind	forest paths, forest in sunshine, grasses and trees waving in the wind; the wind increases, shaking the grass and making waves on the lake	
122	6.3 m	medium shot	a judge sits behind his bench covered with files at his right; he takes one, pages through it and reads the judgment;	Judge [*slowly*]: In the matter of the building owner [*fast, monotone*] Gustav Stephan, plaintiff, against 1. Franz Bönike, 2. his wife Greta, née Mohr, accused, due to

Shot	Length	Editing / Sound	Description	Title / Dialogue
				non-payment of rent, the court has decided . . .
123	6.4 m	full shot	Mrs Bönike is standing on a ladder in the empty living-room, removing the hanging light from the ceiling; she descends and exits left with the lamp; sun shines through the window in the background	(off-voice of judge): . . . the accused are sentenced to abandon apartment to the plaintiff. Although the accused has been unemployed for a long period, the Bönike couple could have paid the overdue rent with a bit of good will. Their current difficulties must be seen as their own fault.
124	1.3 m	see 122	the judge takes another file from the pile	Judge: In the name of the people.
125	2 m	close-up	On a door a white sign printed in black letters, with the numbers pasted on	[Sign]: Court 234, Division: Rental Issues
126	3.6 m	medium shot	over-the-shoulder of Anni to an official, sitting at a desk, behind him a file case full of files; he reads, looks up at Anni and makes gestures regretfully with his hand	
127	2.3 m	long shot	the courthouse corridor, Anni shuts the door where the sign of 125 is hanging, exits right	
128	5.6 m	full shot, parallel travelling shot; street noise	Anni is walking quickly on the sidewalk, often masked by parked cars; in the background are storefronts and other pedestrians	
129	2 m	close-up		[Sign]: Welfare Office Room 15
130	2.1 m	medium shot	Anni sitting on a bench; on the left a door opens, an official enters halfway and hands Anni a piece of paper with a regretful gesture	
131	4.3 m	see 128	a different street	
132	3.4 m	medium shot	over-the-shoulder shot of Anni to the fat building manager who looks out of his door with	

Shot	Length	Editing / Sound	Description	Title / Dialogue
			an unfriendly mien; closes the door with the sign . . .	[Sign]: To the Building Manager
133	3.2 m	close-up, parallel travelling shot	Anni is walking along a street with store fronts	
134	1.4 m	close-up		[Doorbell sign]: Braun, Bailiff, 5–7 p.m.
135	2.7 m	close-up	the head of an older man framed in a door; has a look of regret on his face	
136	3.5 m	see 133	other pedestrians in the background	
137	2.1 m	medium shot	a telephone booth; Anni enters from right and opens the door of the booth	
138	4.7 m	medium shot loud workshop noise	a car repair shop; Fritz is in the pit under a car spray-washing the motor; he puts aside the hose and exits	Voice: Fritz, telephone!
139	2.3 m	full shot	in the repair shop, with gas tanks, ads for Shell Oil on the wall; Fritz, dressed in work clothes, walks towards the back of the shop to a door with a shelf on which the telephone sits; takes off his cap and lifts the receiver	
140	1.8 m	close-up	Anni's head through a glass pane of the telephone booth, the receiver pressed to her ear	
141	13.1 m	medium shot	Fritz leans on his left elbow while talking on the phone	Anni's voice: It's come to the eviction now. The bailiff was just there. The furniture is out on the street. Fritz [*matter-of-factly*]: Yes, and now what? Anni's voice: Yes, and now what? Fritz: Then you'll just have to come out to my place at Kuhle Wampe. Anni's voice: Is that possible? Fritz [*laughing*]:

Shot	Length	Editing / Sound	Description	Title / Dialogue
		fade-out		Naturally. I'll bring a car for the furniture.
142	3.4 m	fade-in extreme close-up see 104 slight pan dissolve	spare tyre on the back hood of an open convertible that drives away from the camera; the Bönike's street; the open car – loaded with furniture and household appliances – turns right at the corner	Off-voice of commentator during shots 142–48: About one hour by bus from metropolitan Berlin, set among the grass and woods on . . .
143	1.1 m	close-up dissolve	Fritz, in a black suit with white shirt and tie, sits at the steering wheel, Anni is next to him, holding a coffee grinder	. . . the inviting shores of the Müggel Lake, not far from the Müggel hills, is the tent colony . . .
144	2.2 m	full shot travelling shot front of car dissolve	busy city street; the open car looks like a hay wagon overflowing with an entire household	. . . Kuhle Wampe, Germany's oldest weekend colony. It was established in 1913 with ten or twenty tents. After the War it . . .
145	1.6 m	medium shot dissolve	shot over the car's radiator through the windshield, Fritz and Anni with furniture piled behind them	. . . expanded to such an extent that it now comprises ninety-three tents in which three . . .
146	3.9 m	full shot travelling shot in front of car dissolve	the car turns right; street traffic with cars and bicycles	. . . hundred persons are housed. The pedantic cleanliness within the colony and in its surroundings is remarkable. The . . .
47	4.8 m	medium shot dissolve	the car is driving on a road through a forest	. . . colony 'Kuhle Wampe Club Supporters' is a member of the Central Organization of . . .
148	4.4 m	long shot	in the background the car turns into a sandy forest path and drives towards the camera	. . . Beach Clubs Inc. The Club's relationship with the authorities is currently a good one.
149	2.5 m	travelling shot music starts: 'Schwarzen-berg March'	an oval sign hanging between two trees	[Sign]: Kuhle Wampe Club Supporters
150	6 m	high angle full shot	a descending path seen through branches from high angle; Fritz, Anni, Mr and Mrs	

Shot	Length	Editing / Sound	Description	Title / Dialogue
			Bönike carry furniture and household goods	
151	5.5 m	medium shot pan	Mrs Bönike comes with a chair under her left arm towards the camera; Mrs Bönike from behind carrying a washbowl stand and folding stool with the right arm	
152	3.6 m	close-up music from shot 149 ends	on a table next to two cups and flowers is a radio with a large, horn-shaped loudspeaker, on the right a seated woman	Radio voice: You just heard the ' Schwarzenberg March', written in 1814, in our programme of 'Army Marches Old and New'
153	9 m	full shot music starts	on the right a row of large, neat living tents with sun shades and flower pots in front of the windows; Fritz enters from the right with the Bönike family; they place furniture next to a tent; Fritz helps Mr Bönike move a chest of drawers and they go back on the same path, leaving Mrs Bönike behind	Radio voice: Now you will hear the march 'Deutsche Kaiserklänge' German Imperial Tune].
154	2.8 m	long shot	large tents in the forest; a man with a backpack pushes his bike, following him a woman in long trousers	
155	2.8 m	full shot	images of the tent colony: people working on their tents, sitting down, running by, etc.	
156	2.8 m	medium shot	two men and a woman carry a boat	
157	2.8 m	full shot	people on reclining chairs, strollers in bathing suits	
158	3.3 m	see 153	Fritz and Mr Bönike come with a sofa; Mrs Bönike and Anni carry a small table into the tent	
159	1.5 m	full shot	between the tents is a sign pointing the way	
160	2.7 m	medium shot	a gravestone in the sand with a wreath in front of it	[Inscription]: Here rests our last hope for work: 'Kuhle Wampe'

Shot	Length	Editing / Sound	Description	Title / Dialogue
161	1.4	full shot	a bicycle, folding table and kitchen utensils at the entry to a tent	
162	1.3 m	medium shot	a shirtless man in a reclining chair smokes a cigar	
163	1.4 m	close-up	the head of a young man reading the paper	
164	1.4 m	medium shot	group playing cards	
165	1.4 m	medium shot	two chess players, a third man watches	
166	1.3 m	medium shot music from 153 ends	a woman sitting next to a tent is embroidering	Radio voice: Attention, Berlin! You just heard the march 'Deutsche . . .'
167	1.4 m	medium shot	a man sitting in a tent and cleaning mushrooms	Radio voice: . . . Kaiserklänge'. That completes today's morning programme . . .
168	1.3 m	full shot	a man sits near a tent and peels potatoes	Radio voice: . . . from the Berlin Broadcast Hour.
169	1.4 m	medium shot	seen through the entry to a tent a woman is busy cooking	
170	1.4 m	close-up	three hotplates with pots	
171	1.6 m	close-up fade-out	over-the-shoulder of a man who lifts a spoon to his mouth, he blows it and shakes his head	
172	10.6 m	fade-in, full shot	a second tent has been added in front of Fritz's tent; he pounds at a stake for the new tent, grabs a new rope and pounds that stake into the ground; Anni hands him the third rope; Fritz looks at Anni, pounds some more and then stops to look at her again	
173	7.7 m	medium shot orchestral music starts: 'Das Frühjahr' [The Spring]	Anni stands in front of the mirror in a slip and combs her hair; she takes a pencil from her purse, leans towards the mirror and darkens her eyebrows	
174	7.1 m	full shot	Fritz paces back and forth in front of his tent; after a while Anni comes out in a dress with	

Shot	Length	Editing / Sound	Description	Title / Dialogue
			a cap on her head and a purse under her arm; Fritz takes her arm and they exit right	
175	9.6 m	long shot Helene Weigel sings the ballad 'The Spring,' accompanied by orchestra	forest bathed in sunshine; Anni and Fritz enter from left, walking on a path which they then leave; at first Fritz has his hands in his pockets, then he puts his arm round Anni's waist; they disappear behind some trees	Off-voice: [1] The play of the sexes renews itself / Each spring. That's when the lovers / Come together. The gently caressing hand / Of her lover brings a tingle to the girl's breast. / Her fleeting glance seduces him. [2] The countryside in spring / Appears to the lovers in a new light. / The air is already warm. / The days are getting long and the fields / Stay light for a long time
176–186	43.1 m	montage of images	nature shots: leaves and grass moving in the wind, the forest, a meadow, a tall birch, a tree silhouette against the sky	[3] Boundless is the growth of trees and grasses / In spring. / Incessantly fruitful / Is the forest, are the meadows, the fields. / And the earth gives birth to the new / Heedless of caution.[19]
187	8.2 m	see 175	Fritz and Anni come out of the forest and go back, he with his hands in his pockets, she following at some distance; he looks back over his shoulder at her; they exit left	

[*Reel IV*]

Shot	Length	Editing / Sound	Description	Title / Dialogue
188	10.3 m	fade-in; medium shot	Mr and Mrs Bönike are sitting in the tent, nearby the petroleum lamp is on a small table; Mr Bönike holds a cigar in his right hand and a newspaper in the left from which he reads aloud slowly, sometimes spelling out words; across from him on the right Mrs Bönike is sitting on a metal-	Mr Bönike: I am a courtesan but not a spy, a courtesan who was paid well for her love, who demanded and got five thousand, even thirty thousand as the just price for her favours. That was the refrain of Mata Hari's defence . . .

Shot	Length	Editing / Sound	Description	Title / Dialogue
			frame bed with a pencil in her hand, unnoticed by her husband	[inhales his cigar].
189	1.2 m	extreme close-up	the worried face of Mrs Bönike	Mr Bönike's voice: . . . Among her favourites were . . .
190	1.7 m	close-up	Mrs Bönike is calculating her household expenses in a notebook: bread 45, potatoes 15, margarine 30, cheese 15, liverwurst 20, onions 15, cabbage 38, herring 25, cigars 30, salt 15, fat 45; she draws a line	Mr Bönike's voice: . . . also, as it was put, the one-time . . .
191	1.2 m	close-up	liverwurst with a price-tag '¼ lb. liverwurst 20 pfennigs	Mr Bönike's voice: . . . police president of Berlin, Jagow . . .'
192	1.4 m	medium shot	potatoes with a price-tag '10 lbs. 20 pfennigs'	Mr Bönike's voice: . . . the Prince of Braunschweig . . .
193	1.4 m	medium shot	Mrs Bönike's hand writes	Mr Bönike's voice: . . . Mr von Jagow got to know Mata Hari when . . .
194	4.7 m	medium shot	Mr Bönike, who is now sitting upright, holds the paper in front of his eyes	Mr Bönike: . . . she performed at the Winter Garden. He visited her backstage to see how the nude dance . . . Mata Hari . . . and whether everything . . .
195	2 m	extreme close-up	Mrs Bönike's head	Mr Bönike's voice: . . . was legal. She was called the Queen of Dance . . .
196	1.3 m	close-up	package of rendered fat with price-tag ½ lb. excellent veal fat, home-style 45'	Mr Bönike's voice: . . . but known as the Queen of Sensual Pleasures . . .
197	2.6 m	close-up	herring with price-tag 'special sale! best German herring, 12 pieces 50 pfennigs, about 2 lbs.'	Mr Bönike's voice: . . . The rich connoisseurs admired her as a delicacy of the rarest kind . . .
198	7.7 m	medium shot	Mr Bönike holds the news-	Mr Bönike: . . . The effect

Shot	Length	Editing / Sound	Description	Title / Dialogue
			paper comfortably again; Mrs Bönike continues to write her accounts in the notebook; in the background the wall-hanging from the previous apartment can be seen (shot 86)	of her dances came especially from the veils and nudity, from the snake-like and lustful movements, in short, from the [*phonetic sounding out*] symbolism of love or-gies, as seen indeed . . .
199	1.9 m	extreme close-up	Mrs Bönike's handwriting	Mr Bönike's voice: . . . in the expressive dances of the most primitive . . .
200	1.2 m	close-up	onions with the price-tag 'onions 15/lb.'	Mr Bönike's voice: . . . and oriental peoples . . .
201	15.4 m	medium shot	over-the-shoulder from the father to the mother, who writes while sunk in thought	Mr Bönike: . . . Only her small breasts were covered by small, chiselled copper plaques. The upper arms and ankles were decorated with bracelets set with gleaming jewels. Otherwise she was naked, from her fingertips to her toes . . . [*he puffs smoke*]
202	1.1 m	close-up	bread with price-tag 'bread 45'	Mr Bönike's voice: . . . The dance revealed her flexible and firm structure in its an-androgenous agility. Between the arching lines reaching from her open under . . .
203	1 m	close-up	margarine with price-tag 'margarine ½ lb. 30 pfennigs'	Mr Bönike's voice: . . . arm below her raised hands . . .
204	1.1 m	close-up	cheese with price-tag 'best farmer's mountain cheese ½ lb. 30 pfennigs'	Mr Bönike's voice: . . . to the depression at her waist . . .
205	21 m	medium shot	from behind Mr Bönike to Mrs Bönike	Mr Bönike: . . . The legs were an ideal shape and were raised like two fine columns of a pagoda. The knee caps were like two round lily buds. Everything had a

Shot	Length	Editing / Sound	Description	Title / Dialogue
		pan to right pan to Anni slow fade-out	Anni enters, takes off her cap and sits down next to her mother, dejected; Anni looks at Mrs Bönike and then turns away	delicate am-amber colour. Everywhere gold and pink lights played. Born on the column's capital of long, softly arched thighs the narrow ivory-coloured stomach . . . Anni: Hi!
206	7.7 m	fade-in, full shot	in front of the tent Fritz and Anni are leaning on a table, silently standing next to each other; Mrs Bönike comes out and goes round the two to the back of the tent; both watch her, then lower their heads again	Fritz [*mutters – incomprehensible*]
207	7 m	extreme close-up fade-out	the serious faces of Fritz and Anni	Fritz: Were you there? Anni: It's too dirty there. [*pause*] I'm not going to ruin my life.
208	11.1 m	fade-in, full shot fade-out	Anni and Mr Bönike are sitting in the tent at the table in front of the window; both are eating; Anni jumps up, throws something on the floor, grabs her cap and purse and exits right; Mr Bönike watches her and pushes his chair angrily to the side.	Mr Bönike [*threatening*]: If anything happens, [*very loud*] I'll beat you to a pulp.
209– 211	15.9 m	fade-in, full shot medium shot factory noise begins	women workers are sitting near each other at an assembly line; they take a part, do their task rapidly, and place it back on the conveyor belt; an intercut shot shows a single woman who is working at the line on an electrical unit; then the working line again with the women's rapid movements	
212	2.9 m	pan medium shot	electrical testing device serviced by women and girls; Anni in a work apron behind a protective grille, back-to-back with her colleague Gerda; the space between their two work tables is closed off by a rope	[Sign]: High voltage!

Shot	Length	Editing / Sound	Description	Title / Dialogue
			with a sign hanging from it	Danger! Life-threatening!
213	5.2 m	close-up	Anni tests various contacts of object with two wired poles; in the background there are other women	
214	5.2 m	see 212	both continue working on the assembly line	Gerda [*turned towards Anni*]: Don't lie, something is the matter with you. Anni [*to Gerda*]: Don't make trouble here at work, otherwise I'll be fired tomorrow.
215	3.5 m	close-up	Gerda tests an object, reading off the measurement; Anni in the background	
216	3 m	see 212		Anni [*to Gerda*]: I can't stand it any more. If it goes on, I'm moving away from out there.
217	5 m	see 209		
218	4 m	see 210 factory noise stops (see 211)		
219	7.5 m	medium shot, pan down	a car radiator over a pit; Fritz sprays the engine, another repairman is busy greasing it	
220	1.9 m	extreme close-up	the car's radiator	
221	6.1 m	medium shot	continues 219 Fritz continues his work	Worker [*turned to Fritz*]: Paying alimony and single taxes, you might as well get married. Fritz [*looking at him briefly*]: Nonsense. Fritz [*after a pause*]: I want my freedom.
222	3.9 m	medium shot fade-out	Fritz working, silently	
223	9.5 m	fade-in	in Fritz's tent; Anni is sitting at the coffee table, Fritz is standing next to it, he takes his jacket; finishes his cup of coffee;	Anni: Where are you going? Fritz: I still have to wash a car tonight. Anni [*reproachfully*]: You

Shot	Length	Editing / Sound	Description	Title / Dialogue
			he exits quickly left, followed by Anni	wanted to talk with Father tonight. Fritz: But I can do it tomorrow too.
224	6.1 m	medium shot	Anni and Fritz walk along a path, followed by the camera; a group of children comes their way	
225	0.9 m	extreme close-up	Anni looks down at the children	
226	1.1 m	long shot	children passing by	
227	1.1 m	extreme close-up	Anni's face	
228–256	34.9	simultaneous dissolves image montage accompanied by increasingly rapid music (motifs from the film and children's songs)	Anni's visions: children's faces circle round her; her head gradually fades out; children's faces, a baby, children's faces; poster ad with nursing mother; the children passing by; cod liver oil ad with a man carrying a fish on his back; pre-printed pink slip filled in with reason for layoff 'no work'; children's faces; a baby basket with 'heaven'; ad for Nivea baby soap; shop window with baby shoes; waving baby with pacifier in a carriage; ad for Nestle children's pap; decorated coffins in a shop; identity card from the employment office with the following information: Anna Bönike, born 28 June 1911, in Berlin; residence in Berlin, 27 Trift St, single, occupation – worker, group 52, date 11 January 1932, form no. 4879, payday – Wednesday; house façade (see 58); group of people surrounding the covered body of Anni's brother with ambulance next to it; the driver closes the ambulance door (see 104); coffins in a shop window with a sign; from inside the coffin shop looking at the street; dolls; baby dolls; dolls;	[Sign]: 'Dr med. Dohmeyer, Gynaecology 4–6' [Ad]: 'Nestle's sweetened milk and children's pap' [Sign]: 'Free office consultation and advising for pregnant mothers, hours Monday, Tuesday, Thursday 9–10' [Ad]: 'Scott's emulsion for our children' [Sign]: 'Strieber, midwife' [Sign]: 'No waiting! No medical exam! Under state control WORRY-FREE Funeral Insurance Group Inc., Cremation' [Sign]: 'Entire burial costs 99.50 Marks'

Shot	Length	Editing / Sound	Description	Title / Dialogue
			children's toys	
257	1.1 m	extreme close-up	frontal shot of Anni walking along the path with a very worried expression	
258	3.8 m	medium shot, parallel travelling shot	Anni and Fritz walking next to each other on the forest path	
259	4.3 m	full shot streetcar bell	forest area; in the foreground end-of-the-line for the street-car; two men get on; Fritz takes leave from the streetcar door – shakes Anni's hand; another man jumps on the moving streetcar; Anni exits left, another streetcar pulls in	
260	6.6 m	long shot	a forest path; Anni enters from the side and disappears along the path	
261	3.9 m	full shot pan; pop song 'Life without Love' from loudspeaker; street noise	movie posters; a young man passes by; Fritz and his friend Kurt enter, look at movie posters	[Poster]: 'Nie wieder Liebe'[21]
262	5.1 m	medium shot	Fritz and Kurt are standing in front of a showcase with film stills; Fritz looks at the photos	Kurt: What are you going to do with Anni? Fritz: Marriage is out of the question. I'm not going to ruin my life. Kurt: What will happen to the girl? Fritz [*turning away*]: Very unfortunate.
263	2.8 m	full shot fade-out	in front of the cinema; Fritz goes to the cashier and pays; they exit left	
264	17.7 m	fade-in, full	Fritz and Mr Bönike are sitting at the table in the tent; it is evening; both are smoking heavily; they avoid looking at each other	Mr Bönike: Now you're in a spot! Fritz: Why? It happens in the best of families. Mr Bönike [*after a moment's pause*]: Are you going to marry the girl? Fritz: I guess I don't have much choice.

Shot	Length	Editing / Sound	Description	Title / Dialogue
				Mr Bönike [*after a pause*]: When do you want the engagement party? Fritz: Pretty soon, I guess.

[*Reel V*]

Shot	Length	Editing / Sound	Description	Title / Dialogue
265	6.5 m	fade-in; close-up, pan to table; undistinguish-able sound of voices starts	an oval sign partially covered by fir tree branches, a festive table with flowers, Mr Bönike in a black suit with white bow tie; sitting on his right is bald Uncle Otto and his wife and other guests	[Sign]: Congratulations
266	2.1 m	medium shot	Anni is standing at the table, she looks down and laughs, plays with her hands; in the background a white porcelain clock and furniture	
267	1.4 m	close-up	Mr Bönike, seated next to a man with a dark bow tie, looks over his guests and smokes	
268	1.8 m	see 266	Anni notices his look and, embarrassed, plays with a fake flower on her belt; she laughs bashfully and looks away	
269	1.4 m	close-up	a girl with a pearl necklace, seated between two young men, smiles at Anni	
270	1.6 m	see 266	Anni takes something from the table and looks at it	
271	1.1 m	medium shot	Uncle Otto, his wife, a young man and the girl with the pearl necklace in conversation	
272	1.9 m	medium shot	Anni smiles at Kurt and Gerda who are sitting next to each other; they also smile, then turn away and start talking	
273	2.3 m	full shot	the entire long table with the seated guests, Mr Bönike in the background; on the left Kurt who takes something from the table and puts it in	

Shot	Length	Editing / Sound	Description	Title / Dialogue
			Gerda's mouth	
274	1.7 m	medium shot	Mrs Bönike is standing in a separate room and handing in stacks of plates	
275	2.2 m	full shot	over-the-shoulder of Mr Bönike to the table; in the background Anni takes the plates from Mrs Bönike and puts them on the table	
276	2.5 m	see 274	Mrs Bönike hands in a cake	
277	5.1 m	close-up	hands grab for the cake slices until the plate is empty	
278	2 m	see 275	the guests are drinking coffee, Mrs Bönike as well; only Anni is standing in the background	
279	1.5 m	medium shot	Anni is standing next to Kurt with cake and a coffee cup in her hand, both are eating	
280	2.4 m	medium shot	Kurt and Gerda are drinking coffee, eating cake and smiling at one another	
281	1.2 m	see 274	Mrs Bönike hands in another pot of coffee	
282	4 m	wipe, medium shot	chain-gang style, Mrs Bönike, Anni and Kurt hand each other beer bottles	
283	6.6 m	full shot	light shines from the tent onto the ground in front of it; through the tent's entry one sees the table extended into the front room; Fritz enters with a crate full of beer bottles on his shoulder, places it on a stack of other crates next to the tent, brushes the dust off his black suit, heaves a crate of empty bottles onto his shoulder and exits the way he came, with his left hand in his pocket	
284	5.7 m	medium shot; music starts: 'Entry of the Gladiators'	Anni winds up a gramophone in the corner near the clock, sets the needle on the record and turns to the left	

Shot	Length	Editing / Sound	Description	Title / Dialogue
285	2.6 m	see 274	Mrs Bönike hands in a plate with food	
286	6.5 m	see 283		
287	3.5 m	see 282		
288	3 m	close-up	a guest with moustache eating his food	
289	4 m	see 275	Anni is eating while standing, bent over the table	
290	3.2 m	close-up	the man with the dark bow tie pokes at a bone on his plate with his fork; after he has greedily eaten the meat, he puts the bone on the plate	
291	5.8 m	close-up	pieces of meat on bones are placed on the platter and immediately picked up with forks or hands till the platter is empty	
292	4.7 m	medium shot; march music ends	Uncle Otto chews on a large bone he holds in his hands; his wife eats with knife and fork; two empty beer bottles in front of Otto	
293	5.7 m	wipe, medium shot	Uncle Otto has shed his jacket and tie and opened his shirt, nine empty beer bottles in front of him; toasting Mr Bönike to the left, he drinks a pint in one gulp; Mr Bönike sets his smaller glass on the table	
294	3.6 m	medium shot	the girl with the pearl necklace drinks from a beer glass; the young man with tousled hair on her right drinks from a bottle; he bends the girl back and kisses her; the second young man clinks glasses with his partner while looking at his neighbour kissing	
295	8.9 m	medium shot	Fritz once again brings in a crate of beer, puts it down and brushes the dust off his jacket; Anni comes out of the tent	Anni: Can I help you? Fritz [*turns round briefly*]: No need. Anni: Want to come in? Fritz [*cleaning his*

Shot	Length	Editing / Sound	Description	Title / Dialogue
				trousers]: What for?
296	2.1 m	close-up		Anni: Wait a minute [*short pause*], you don't want this whole engagement, right?
297	1.3 m	close-up		Fritz: Of course not!
298	5.4 m	see 296		Anni [*turning away*]: Hm [*pause*]. Why are you doing it then?
299	4 m	see 297	Fritz puts a handkerchief in his pocket and then shoves his hands in his pockets	Fritz: I have no choice.
300	1.8 m	full shot	Fritz bends down, takes a beer and opens it; Anni exits left; in the background the entrance to the tent with the guests inside	
301	1.8 m	close-up song: 'Ein Prosit...'	Fritz drinks from the bottle and looks at Anni; singing from the tent	
302	10.5 m	full shot; pan to right and back	the guests are standing at the table singing and rocking back and forth, especially Otto's wife; some partners have changed places; there are now also children among the guests	
303	1.6 m	extreme close-up; music starts	the gramophone needle is placed on a record	
304	9.6 m	full shot song starts: 'Schöner Gigolo, armer Gigolo'	the guests are sitting again at the table, in the middle of the image is Otto's wife and one of the young men on whom the girl with the pearl necklace is leaning; she is singing along with the gramophone record; Otto's wife and others join in; in the background is the Bönikes' wall-hanging	
305	2.5 m	see 293	Mr Bönike again takes a beer bottle and pours some for Otto	
306	4.6 m	medium shot	the man with the bow tie, with sweaty face, drinks from the bottle; on his right Mr Bönike,	

Shot	Length	Editing / Sound	Description	Title / Dialogue
307	3 m	pan	who gets a bottle from under the table and drinks the singing and drinking guests	
308	1.3 m	long shot music: record continues	Fritz is sitting and smoking a cigarette to the right of the open tent; Kurt comes out	
309	2.3 m	medium shot	Otto's wife has grabbed the head of the man next to her, kisses him, then slaps his face; the second man has put his arm round the girl with the pearl necklace while the other girl lays her head on his shoulder	
310	2 m	see 308	Kurt goes to Fritz	
311	1.6 m	see 308 music ends	everyone is swaying to the music	
312	5.2 m	medium shot	Kurt and Fritz watch a guest who comes out of the tent and walks behind them	Fritz: Nothing to eat, but he's got to have patent leather shoes.
313	1.6 m	full shot	dark camping area; the man walks to a tree	
314	3.4 m	see 312		Fritz: Unbelievable. Kurt: Well, if you're celebrating this kind of engagement, how can you be surprised that people get drunk
315	11 m	full shot pan right	Uncle Otto, completely drunk and with a cigar in his mouth, gets up and totters along the table, pushing over plates and glasses; his wife threatens him, also gets up and follows him; Otto falls variously on the seated guests and the table; his wife pushes him from the side; the young man and the girl with pearl necklace are kissing in the background	
316	25.8 m	full shot	Uncle Otto can barely hold himself up, clinging to the head of one of the guests; he totters, holds himself up on a post and finally falls flat in front of the tent, bringing down a stool	Otto's wife: Otto! Otto! [with authority] Come back right away! Otto's wife: Oh! Kurt's voice: Let'm alone!

Shot	Length	Editing / Sound	Description	Title / Dialogue
		pan right (to include Kurt and Fritz) camera pan to follow Otto	with a tub; Otto tries to stand up with the help of his wife; he curses to himself; she tries to hold him by his suspenders while he tries to move forward, swaying dangerously; he pulls himself free, falls forward against the beer crates and pulls down the dishes from a table nearby; his wife follows him with raised arms, warning and cursing him; he falls in the grass; Kurt watches him while Fritz has been staring blankly the whole time	If he wants to go swimming, it's good for him! Otto's wife: Otto, you're going to be the death of me yet. Otto's wife: Otto, you stay here and be done. [*upset*] Swimming at night with a belly full of beer. Uncle Otto: My body belongs to me.
317	3.4 m	full shot	in front of two tents Anni and Gerda are adjusting a blanket over a fully packed handcart; in the background tottering figures	
318	7.6 m	medium shot	Mr Bönike totters over to Fritz and Kurt, who are still in front of the tent	Mr Bönike: What's up with the beer, Fritz? Fritz: Just whistle and I'll run! [*to Bönike who disappears behind them*] Just whistle! [*sharply*] Whistle!
319	10.6 m	see 317	Bönike enters from the right Gerda and Anni exit, pulling the handcart; Mr Bönike remains standing with his hand on his chin	Mr Bönike: What are you up to? Anni: Get Mother and your things! We're moving away from here. [*Gerda goes to the cart's drawbar*] Mr Bönike: Gerda put a bee in your bonnet?
320	3.5 m	see 318	Kurt looks over Fritz to the tent	
321	6 m	medium shot	Anni, Gerda, Mrs and Mr Bönike are standing in front of the tents around the handcart; Mr and Mrs Bönike exit right with the handcart; Anni and Gerda turn abruptly in the other direction and leave	Mr Bönike: Where can we go? Mrs Bönike: We're not just gypsies, on the road in the middle of the night. You've gone nuts!

Shot	Length	Editing / Sound	Description	Title / Dialogue
322	5.7 m	full shot	from the left Mr Bönike pulls and Mrs Bönike pushes the cart in an arc to the tent; the party guests and Fritz are standing in front of the tent; the Bönikes stop in front of them	
323	10.1 m	medium shot; fade-out	over the cart to Fritz and Kurt, on the right Mrs Bönike, on the left Mr Bönike and two guests; Mr Bönike takes the steering rod again and they exit left with the cart	Mrs Bönike: You've got to be really ashamed. Mr Bönike [*puts his arms on Fritz's shoulders*]: She's gone nuts. Simply ran away. Mrs Bönike: Don't worry, Fritz, we'll stay with you. Fritz [*sarcastically*]: What a joke.
324	4.2 m	fade-in; full shot	Gerda and Anni are standing in a stairwell in front of an apartment door; Anni nods.	Gerda: So, now you're going to live with me, next Sunday you'll come with me to the athletic games and you can forget Fritz.

[*Reel VI*]

				[Title III]: Who Owns the World?
325–340	45.2 m	fade-in; montage; strongly rhythmical music with 'Solidarity Song' motifs; fade-out	cranes, coal piles, silos, dollies, wagons on steel bridges, chimneys spewing smoke, large factories	
341	30.3 m	fade-in; full shot	large clubroom in a wooden building, on the wall in the background hangs a banner; young people and children, some in the uniform of the Fichte athletes,[22] are busy with various jobs to prepare the athletics festival; on the left some others are waiting behind a wooden barrier; in the foreground a young boy	[Banner]: Worker-athletes against the race for records: become a worker-athlete. Distributor: Wedding! Young man's voice: Here! Distributor: Two hundred. [*hands them over*] Distributor: Reinickendorf! Young man's voice: Here!

Shot	Length	Editing / Sound	Description	Title / Dialogue
		pan left travelling shot travelling shot continues right travelling shot continues right travelling shot continues right	distributes printed leaflets, calling out the names of city districts and checking off their names on a list; he goes to the left with the leaflets and hands them out; a group of young people work with an offprint machine; a table where Gerda and another girl are stirring paint; Kurt enters from the right and teases her by holding the mixing stick to her nose; Gerda laughs and Kurt continues to the right, kneels, puts the paint can on a piece of paper and begins to paint on a huge piece of white paper spread on the floor; a group sits at a table and works on banners; in the background a young man puts small flags on a city map hanging on the wall	Distributor: Eighty. [*hands them over*] Distributor: Charlottenburg! Young man's voice: Here! Distributor: One hundred and twenty . . . Friedrichshain! Young man's voice: Here! Distributor: One hundred and fifty . . . Pankow! . . . not here . . . Mitte! Voice of a young man: Here! Distributor: Schöneberg! Voice of a young woman: Here! Distributor: One hundred . . . Tempelhof! Voice of a young man: Here! Distributor: Eighty . . . Wilmersdorf! Voice of a young man: Here! Distributor: Eighty . . . Prenzlauer Berg! Voice of a young man: Here!
342	6.3 m	full shot	Gerda is sitting at a table mixing paint in the foreground; Kurt kneels on the floor behind her and paints large letters	Kurt: Where is Anni today? Gerda: She's coming, she had to go to the printer. Kurt: What's up with her? Gerda: What do you mean? She's still living with me.
343	3.5 m	close-up; dolly	Kurt raises his head	Kurt: That is really inconvenient for her, that she broke up with Fritz right at this time.
344	10.1 m	full shot pan right to medium shot	a long table where young people and children are working; in the background a sign; a young man is pasting, a young woman in a uniform brings a roll of cloth and spreads it out next to him on the table	[Sign]: Sports equipment room Young man [*irritated*]: I didn't even get home last night, I've got to sleep sometime. Tomorrow I'm supposed to compete in the swimming marathon.

Shot	Length	Editing / Sound	Description	Title / Dialogue
				Young woman [*hits the table with her fist, insistently*]: No, you've got to finish the banner. Look, it'll be done pretty soon.
			she exits right; he pushes the cloth aside and turns back to his work	Young man [*shouting at her*]: Yeah, and when am I supposed to sleep?
345	23.5 m	medium shot travelling shot in front of Fritz, pan to Gerda	a door with two posters; Fritz enters and goes to Gerda; in the background a bulletin board with posters;	[Poster left]: Wrestling match [Poster right]: 'Major Sports Meet of the All Workers' Sports Leagues, Sunday, 12 June. Swimming, Rowing, Motorcycle, Bicycle Races Begin at 9 a.m.'
			Gerda cleans off her hands and adjusts her skirt;	Fritz: Hi Gerda, so Anni's living here now? Gerda: Yes, sure. Fritz: I've been looking for her the whole week. Where is she running around till late at night?
			Kurt enters from the right with a can of paint that he places on the table	Kurt: She's not running around. She's with us and works here. Gerda: She was here before, too, before you came along and took her from us.
			Kurt with a look at Gerda that indicates his critical attitude towards Fritz	Fritz: I convinced her that she didn't have the stuff for your athletics. [*pause*] In my view some women don't have what it takes. [*forcefully*] Some do and some don't. Gerda: I think she feels fine here with us.
346	7 m	medium shot	a group of young people	First: I can't come tomorrow, I'm out of money. Second: I have only twenty pfennigs too. Can't you give us something?
			they get some money	Third [*laughing*]: Sure.

Shot	Length	Editing / Sound	Description	Title / Dialogue
347	10.6 m	medium shot pan to poster	Gerda on the left, straightening her blouse, next to her Kurt and Fritz; Kurt pulls Fritz up to the bulletin board where the poster is hanging	Fritz: By the way, I was laid off yesterday. Kurt: That's bad. [*puts on his cap*] Gerda [*pointing to poster*]: Look at that! And if you want to talk to Anni, come on out with us tomorrow. Kurt: The competitions are in the afternoon. There you can hear a few things that won't do you any harm.
348	1.8 m	dissolve, full shot	a street; meeting point for motorcyclists, who line up their bikes	
349	1.9 m	extreme close-up	Kurt in leather clothing starts his motorcycle	
350	2 m	see 348	other racers follow Kurt's example	
351	1.9 m		the motorcyclists drive by a group of uniformed children and young people	
352	2.3 m	full shot	motorcyclists with and without sidecars turn a corner	
353–358	17.2 m	montage; accompanied by the refrain of the 'Solidarity Song' sung and whistled by a chorus	worker-athletes march through the streets singing the 'Solidarity Song'; motorcyclists and bicyclists pass them by; Anni is marching together with a group of women athletes in a forest area; tent residents watch them pass by	[Song]: [1] Forward, without forgetting / Where our strength is now to be! / When starving or when eating / Forward, not forgetting / Our solidarity! [2] Forward, without forgetting / Our street and our field / Forward, without forgetting: / Whose street is the street / Whose world is the world?[23]
359–392	64.7 m	montage; accompanied by 'Athletics Song', sung by Ernst Busch in solo with	the starting signal for the motorcyclists is given at the race course; in the background are banners and on the right there are many bicycles; the motorcycle race; signal for the	[Banner]: Buckow Triangle Race [Banner]: Derop Petroleum [Song]: [1] Coming out of the crowded flats /

Shot	Length	Editing / Sound	Description	Title / Dialogue
		orchestra	start of the women's regatta and swimmers; short takes of the motorcycle, rowing (close-up of Gerda in boat) and swimming competitions; Kurt (#48) is almost always in the lead among the motorcyclists, who are now arriving at the finish; the swimmers in the end spurt; the rowboats finish	The darkened streets of embattled cities / You come together / To struggle together. / And learn to win. / And learn to win. [2] You bought the boats / From the pennies you sacrificed / And you saved the bus fare by starving. / Learn to win! / Learn to win! [3] After the gruelling struggle for the necessities / For a few hours / You come together again / To struggle together. / And learn to win![24]
393	1.6 m	full shot; applause begins	the motorcyclists at the goal; Kurt is the winner and is surrounded by well-wishers, who applaud him	
394	1.1 m	medium shot	Gerda is sitting in a boat and laughing	
395	0.5 m	full shot; see 393		

[Reel VII]

Shot	Length	Editing / Sound	Description	Title / Dialogue
396	2.7 m	medium shot	a flag waving in the breeze	
397	11.7 m	full shot; pan right over the winners and pan left back	spectators stand close together in front of a dais for the winners with a huge banner spanned across it; the winners go up to the tribune on the left and form a line from the right	[Banner]: Solidarity
398	1.1 m	medium shot	Kurt	
399	2.3 m	medium shot; applause ends	Gerda and another woman athlete	a sharp whistle followed by the call 'Hey!'
400–412	43 m	actors whistling	The agit-prop theatre group 'Das rote Sprachrohr'[25] sings and plays 'The Song of the Red Unity Front': the group introduces itself as 'voice of the masses' and, while whistling, moves in a	[Song]: We are the 'red megaphone'. / Megaphone of the masses we are. / We speak what oppresses you. / We speak what oppresses

Shot	Length	Editing / Sound	Description	Title / Dialogue
			choreographed pattern around the stage until they form a half-circle;	you, / We are the 'red megaphone'. / Megaphone of the masses we are.
			the scene of eviction is both spoken in solo voice and sung in chorus using large, clear gestures;	Köslin Street, Wedding district, back building. The landlord throws out an old renter. He brings
			the eviction is so 'rough' that the evicted man is thrown into the audience;	along the furniture mover: 'Go ahead and load up the junk.'
			the entire scene has a strong rhythm, is very disciplined and stylized in its presentation;	'Wait a minute. You must've made a mistake. We've lost our welfare benefits, Mr Landlord.' –
			at the end the actors dance to the music of their song;	'You're half a year behind in rent. God knows, my patience has run out.'
		applause	the spectators, among them Fritz and Anni in the first row, applaud	Patience, patience – that's a crazy thing. The neighbours, proles, are building a circle. The furniture mover asks, he discusses, until even . . . the last one understands.
413– 435	52.9 m	montage mass chorus sings the 'Solidarity Song' (see 353–8)	the theatre group Red Megaphone stands in a line on stage and begins singing the 'Solidarity Song'; the crowd of thousands joins in; the audience and the winners on the dais; the crowd in front of the stage; young athletes, older workers, audience with banners and a flag (see 396)	[Song]: [1] Forward, without forgetting / Where our strength is now to be! / When starving or when eating / Forward, not forgetting / Our solidarity! [2] First we are not all here now / Second it is but one day / When the work of one week's time / Still is heavy in our bones. [3] Forward, without forgetting / Where our strength is now to be! / When starving or when eating / Forward, not forgetting / Our solidarity! [4] First we are not all here now / Second it is but one day / And now those lying in the meadow / Otherwise

Shot	Length	Editing / Sound	Description	Title / Dialogue
				are in the streets. / [5] Forward, without forgetting / Our street and our field. / Forward, without forgetting: / Whose street is the street / Whose world is the world?
436	4.9 m	medium shot mixed voices continue pan left	the demonstrators disperse; the winners leave the dais; the crowd dissolves	
437	11.3 m	full shot	the crowd pushes towards a camp site located in the woods, among them Kurt and Gerda (he in leather, she in a sporty dress); Gerda lays her arm on Kurt's shoulder	
438	2.7 m	medium shot	the theatre group is packing up instruments on the stage	
439	6.4 m	medium shot	Kurt and Gerda are standing next to a man selling newspapers; Kurt is reading a brochure called 'Birth Control'; he buys the magazine 'Factory and Union'; they move on	Kurt: [*returning the brochure*] I have that one already.
440	3 m	full shot	a large group of athletes is sitting in a meadow; others are standing around them; they laugh as a young woman tries to stand on her head	
441	1.7 m	medium shot	women athletes are sitting on the grass and laughing; one of them eats an apple; a second one takes it and eats it	
442	2.5 m	medium shot	swimmers are lying on the grass, two are reading the newspaper	
443	1.7 m	medium shot	many parked bicycles, some leaning against trees	
444	1.6 m	close-up	front wheels of racing bicycles	
445	2.1 m	medium shot	empty rowing boats in the water	
446	1.1 m	medium shot	sterns of three paddle boats	

Shot	Length	Editing / Sound	Description	Title / Dialogue
447	9 m	medium shot; high, oblique angle	three young men are lying on the grass, their heads bent over a book; one reads aloud	Young man: Listen, I'll read it again now: 'A real state,' says Hegel, 'and a real state government emerge only when there are already distinct classes, when wealth and poverty increase greatly and when the situation is such that a large number can no long satisfy needs in the accustomed way.'
448	2.9 m	full shot	in front of a tent Anni and Fritz are lying on the grass, resting on their elbows; they are looking straight ahead; Fritz looks over to Anni; behind them another man is lying in the same posture, reading a newspaper that another one is reading as well over his shoulder; in the background are other worker-athletes standing, lying and talking	
449	15.4 m	medium shot; travelling shot in front of the couple	Gerda and Kurt are walking by the tents; a group of young people march by them; worker-athletes sitting, lying, playing, singing and laughing everywhere	Voice from a tent: Now hold still! Gerda: Fritz always wanted to have his freedom. Kurt: At 13 Marks 20 a week, freedom is worth shit. Gerda: Well, then he can marry Anni. Kurt: I'm sure he'll do it. Gerda: At least she is still earning money.
450	8.3 m	see 448	they look into each other's eyes	Fritz: You may be right.
451	37.8 m	'Solidarity Song'; noises of the returning participants and spectators drown out the song	athletes put their boats in the water and get in; motorcycles with sidecars are driving along a forest road; several groups of bicyclists follow them, some with flags; a tight group of young athletes and workers – some with backpacks – precede the camera down the	[Song – same text as 413–35]

Shot	Length	Editing / Sound	Description	Title / Dialogue
			stairs and through a tunnel into the subway station	
458	7.6 m	medium shot; the noise in the tunnel becomes louder and louder	the crowd coming down the stairs	

[*Reel VIII*]

Shot	Length	Editing / Sound	Description	Title / Dialogue
459	12.5 m	full shot; voices of passengers and sounds of the train begin	the festival participants push their way into the subway car, some seat themselves and others remain standing as it fills up	
460	7.4 m	medium shot; sound of train accelerating	a man with a goatee is reading the newspaper; he shows his unease as the crowd streams in, adjusts his hat and continues reading	Conductor's voice: Attention! Doors closing!
461	3.8 m	medium shot	passengers standing in the middle aisle	
462	4.8 m		Gerda standing on the left, Kurt turned towards her, standing in the aisle	
463	4.9 m	close-up	Fritz and Anni are seated; his arm is round her shoulders and he gently tousles her hair	
464	8.7 m	full shot, high angle through a luggage net above the net	seated and standing passengers	Man with goatee [*casually from the newspaper*]: In Brazil they burned 24 million pounds of coffee. Voice of a man on the left [*surprised, with disbelief*]: What did they do with the coffee? Man with goatee: They burned it, pure and simple. Man with starched collar: 24 million pounds of coffee burned?
465	1.4 m	close-up		Man with starched collar: That is no more

Shot	Length	Editing / Sound	Description	Title / Dialogue
				than demagogy.
466	1.5 m	medium shot	an older man with glasses is sitting next to a woman; above them is a worker in shirt sleeves leaning on the seat back	Older man with glasses: I read that too but I don't believe it.
467	2.6 m	close-up	among the standing passengers is a man with a white hat, a well-trimmed beard and a bow tie	Man with white hat [*with a contemptuous, pedantic tone*]: Anyone with common sense knows that is simply not possible.
468	10.6 m	medium shot	seated and standing passengers	Man with goatee [*reads from the newspaper*]: 'Burned coffee – Madness of the World Market.' See? There you have it: 'In Santos, the world's largest coffee port, there is more coffee in the warehouses than the world . . . um . . . can buy . . . All together 12 to 15 million sacks . . . more than an entire year's production from Brazil, so . . . And because more and more coffee is added . . .'
469	8.1 m	medium shot, high angle	the passengers grouped round the reader	Man with goatee: '. . . the government has the surplus burned.' Man with starched collar: You don't have to read that. We know about that nonsense. Man with goatee: 'We have expensive wheat and unemployed industrial workers while Argentina has expensive industrial goods and unemployed farmers. And it is all called the world market and is a crying shame.
470	2.2 m	medium shot	passengers standing	Worker in shirt sleeves:

Shot	Length	Editing / Sound	Description	Title / Dialogue
				24 million pounds of coffee burned. That is really a crying shame!
471	0.8 m	close-up		Worker in a sweater: They can do that to us!
472	0.7 m	close-up		Man with white hat: [*with raised forefinger*]: Quite right!
473	3.8 m	medium shot; see 448		Older man with glasses: I don't understand a thing. Burned coffee! What's the purpose anyway?
474	4.1 m	close-up	Fritz and Anni	Anni: That is pure malice on the part of those people. Fritz: Malice? They can't be malicious if they don't . . . [*with thumb and forefinger makes a gesture of counting money*] Voice of man with black hair: So you want to defend the guys, huh?
475	1.4 m	medium shot	the head of the man with black hair appears over the separating wall	Man with black hair: You think it's okay that they burn the expensive coffee?
476	4 m	close-up; see 472		Man with the white hat [*shaking his head and with raised finger*]: Permit me, the man didn't say that at all. The man said quite clearly . . . [*turning to the side*] What is it you said again, neighbour?
477	7.3 m	medium shot	two elder women with high hats pulled over their foreheads	Woman in chequered dress [*to the woman across*]: You know, you should never actually boil coffee, I tell you. [*to the woman on the left with a coral necklace*] Coffee should never boil. [*leaning back exhausted*]

Shot	Length	Editing / Sound	Description	Title / Dialogue
				Once it boils, it is ruined. Woman with coral necklace [*to the woman in the chequered dress*]: And don't even think of pouring the coffee into a tin pot because the aroma just disappears.
478	4 m	medium shot		Man with goatee [*pointing to his newspaper*]: It's all in here. Why did they do it? Because they wanted to keep the price of coffee high. Man with starched collar: You see! Man with goatee: 'You see!' We have to pay the high price!
479	8.3 m	medium shot	several standing passengers	Man with starched collar: And why do we pay the high price? Because our hands are tied. International politics! Man with white hat [*behind him*]: Quite right! Man with starched collar [*lecturing the passengers, with his hat in his hand*]: If we had a fleet, then we'd have colonies too. If we had colonies, then we'd have coffee too. And if we had coffee . . . Voice of the man with goatee: Yeah, what then, in your esteemed opinion? . . .
480	2.7 m	medium shot		Man with goatee: . . . Go ahead and say it. Then the prices will go down, huh? Man with starched collar: No, they shouldn't. But then . . .

Shot	Length	Editing / Sound	Description	Title / Dialogue
481	10.1 m	medium shot; reverse	the man with the starched collar in foreground; Kurt is standing behind him with other passengers	Man with starched collar [*bends down to the man with goatee*]: . . . we'll cut the deal! Kurt [*looks over his shoulder to the man with the starched collar*]: I keep hearing 'we'. Who is that: we? You and me? [*looking in the other direction*] And that gentleman there? [*another direction*] And the lady there? [*another direction*] And the funny man there? So, 'we' cut a deal. [*to the man with the starched collar*] Come on, man, you don't really believe that!
482	11.5 m	medium shot	a man with a grey hat, sitting next to a woman in a white blouse, writes figures on a sheet of paper, pencil in hand	Man with grey hat: 24 million pounds. 36 times 24 . . . carry the zero . . . another zero. Then they threw away 86 million? That's supposed to be a deal? Voice of the woman opposite: That's no deal! Man with grey hat: If one pound costs 3 Marks 60 . . . Woman in white blouse: [*excited*]: What, 3.60? Hey, you must be used to a superior brand.
483	8.4 m	medium shot	over Kurt and other passengers to the man with the starched collar	Man with starched collar [*talking in various directions*]: Gentlemen, I say it again: so long as the people can't save their pennies, they'll never get ahead. Man with white hat [*nodding in the background*]: Quite true! Man with starched collar [*nods to him*] Kurt: Yeah, you really

Shot	Length	Editing / Sound	Description	Title / Dialogue
				look like you save your pennies.
484	12.3 m	medium shot; see 482	group sitting around the man writing figures	Man with grey hat [*pencil in hand*]; Okay: one pound costs 3 Marks 60 . . . Woman in white blouse: But why 3.60? For 2.40 you can get very good coffee. Voice of the woman across: I even bought some for 2 Marks. Man with grey hat [*to the woman across*]: Really? Let's say 3 Marks. That's not the point. Woman in white blouse: Now wait a minute! I say 2.50 and he says 3 Marks and there's supposed to be no difference? Man with grey hat [*looks up in protest*]: 24 million times 300 . . .
485	4.5 m	medium shot; see 463		Fritz [*to Anni*]: That's nonsense, what he's figuring there. [*to those speaking on his left, sharply*] They earn nothing on the stuff they throw away but rather on the stuff they keep and sell to us at a high price.
486	5 m	close-up	Gerda and several other passengers	Worker in sweater [*to his right*]: You've always got to have less than is needed. Otherwise there's no deal! Gerda [*next to him*]; You can only make a deal when there are people who need something and don't get it. Worker in sweater [*nods*]
487	5.7 m	medium shot; see 477		Woman with coral necklace: They're on

Shot	Length	Editing / Sound	Description	Title / Dialogue
		(somewhat further to the left)		welfare but they drink coffee by the pound; you can smell it in the stairwell. I don't know nothing, but I always said to my husband: 'William, you know, there's something fishy there.'
488	3.4 m	close-up; high angle	group with Gerda and Kurt	Man with white hat: Coffee is a luxury in any case. The common people never drank coffee before. Kurt [*looking over his shoulder*]: Before the people used to travel in carriages. [*Another passenger laughs*]
489	19.1 m	medium shot; extreme high angle; camera pans several times from one side to another	the aisle with standing passengers	Man with starched collar [*sharply*]: I forbid this political agitation! Kurt [*next to him*]: What do you mean 'agitation'? You're the one who's campaigning! [*turns his back to him*] Man with starched collar: [*turns suddenly to him, agitated*]: Just keep your temper, young man!
			a brief scuffle ensues between Kurt and the man with the starched collar; Kurt pushes him away; Fritz stands up behind the man and taps his finger on his temple to signal 'you're crazy'	Kurt [*turning quickly*]: I'm not your young man! Man with starched collar [*right next to Kurt*]: It's quite obvious that you never served. Kurt: And you? You were probably an NCO, huh? Worker in sweater [*friendly*]: Kurt, belt him one! Worker behind Kurt [*provoking*]: Give the fool an orange and send him to the orphanage! Man with starched collar [*threatening with his hand*]: You!

Shot	Length	Editing / Sound	Description	Title / Dialogue
				Kurt: Close your trap or the sawdust will come out! [*passengers laugh*] Man with starched collar [*close to Kurt*]: I warn you! Your insult costs 40 Marks. Kurt: Oh man, don't ruffle your feathers! Man with starched collar [*yelling*]: Since when do you talk to me like that? They didn't raise us in the same stall! Man with white hat [*slowly*]: Quite right! Man with starched collar [*turns round and shakes the man's hand*]: Worker behind Kurt: Bow-legged and can't hold a gun! Another worker: Stupid fathead! Worker behind Kurt: Other people've got a head but you've got a pimple! [*loud laughter*] Man with starched collar [*turns round in a huff towards the speaker*]
490	6.2 m	medium shot	group around the older man with glasses	Older man with glasses [*rises*]: But gentlemen, I must insist that you quieten down! You are not alone in the train! You keep talking about coffee in Brazil. Now I ask you, gentlemen: what is it to you what happens to the coffee in Brazil?
491	8.4 m	medium shot	group around Kurt and Gerda	Man with white hat: Quite right! What's more, it's Sunday today. Kurt: Okay, if you're not interested in coffee, then I have another question for you: you do eat bread,

Shot	Length	Editing / Sound	Description	Title / Dialogue
				right, neighbour? What do you say to the wheat that they're using in America to fuel the boilers? Gerda: And what about the cotton?
492	17.6 m	medium shot	a very fat, bald passenger is sitting on the left and dozing; a man in a coat is standing next to him	Man in coat [*talking to the fat man while tapping his arm*]: Ya see, we don't even need that much coffee. We Germans are thrifty people. The main thing is to stay free of those foreigners. Ya know, we should be growing our own coffee in Germany. They grow so many grapes along the Rhine, why not some coffee? Ya see? We could even buy wine in France. And then we'd have peace in Europe, ya see? Fat passenger [*phlegmatic, resigned*]: Yea, the two of us, we're not going to change the world either! Kurt: Right! . . .
493– 494	2.2 m	close-up	the head of the fat passenger looking in the direction of the voice; the man in the coat looks to his left over his shoulder	Kurt's voice: . . . You won't change the world.
495	1.6 m	close-up		Kurt: And the lady there . . .
496	0.9 m	close-up	woman with the coral necklace	Kurt's voice: . . . will not change it either. And the man . . .
497	1 m	close-up	dozing man with glasses	Kurt's voice: . . . will not either . . .
498	1 m	close-up		Kurt [*turned towards the left*]: . . . and an unpolitical person like you . . .

Shot	Length	Editing / Sound	Description	Title / Dialogue
499	0.8 m	close-up	the man with the white hat	Kurt's voice: . . . not by a long shot . . .
500	1.7 m	close-up		Kurt [*turning his head straight, contemptuously*]: And this man here . . .
501	4.6 m	extreme close-up, slight low angle	head of the man with the starched collar	Kurt's voice: . . . he too will not change the world. He is satisfied with the way it is now. Man with starched collar [*provoking, stressing each word*]: And who will change it?
502	6.4 m	close-up		Gerda [*agitating*]: Those who are not satisfied!
503	32.8 m	full shot; 'Solidarity Song' in background	subway station tunnel; passengers with backpacks, bicycles and lunch bags precede the camera through the tunnel	[Song]: Chorus: Forward, without forgetting / Where our strength is now to be! / When starving or when eating / Forward, not forgetting / Our solidarity! Solo [Ernst Busch]: If we saw the sun was shining / On the street and on the field / We could never really think that / This was truly our own world. Chorus: Forward, without forgetting / Where our strength is now to be! / When starving or when eating / Forward, not forgetting / Our solidarity! Solo [Ernst Busch]: For we know well it is but one / Drop into the empty bucket / Yet it cannot clean up / Anything at all for us. Chorus: Forward, without forgetting / Our street and our field. / Forward, without forgetting: / Whose street is the street / Whose world is the world?

Shot	Length	Editing / Sound	Description	Title / Dialogue

Cuts made by the producer[26]

Shot	Length	Editing / Sound	Description	Title / Dialogue
[in 60]				Mrs Bönike: Don't hold the emergency decrees right under his nose.
		between shots 121 and122		[reading of the extradition judgments against the plaintiffs Dickmann and Linde]
[in 205]			[when Anni enters]	[Title]: Criminal Code ¶218, Sec. 1.[27] Off-voice: A woman who kills her foetus in the womb or who permits the killing by someone else will be punished with imprisonment.
in reel IV				[Text]: Petty-bourgeois problems still play a big role in the life of Kuhle Wampe. [Text]: Very different problems occupy the mass of worker-athletes on the weekend.
[in 343]				Gerda: We lent her some money and now everything is okay.
[in 412]				[Conclusion to the 'Song of the Red Unity Front'] The neighbours are standing like one man, that's why the masters are yelling . . . no one gets in. The landlord, the bailiff, the police, under pressure they'll release the apartment.
[in 439]				Newspaper man [*calls out names of newspapers*]

Cuts demanded by the censor:

Shot	Length	Editing / Sound	Description	Title / Dialogue
[in 64]	2.9 m			Mr Bönike: Maybe you should take a look at the

257

Shot	Length	Editing / Sound	Description	Title / Dialogue
				emergency decree about the reduction of unemployment payments; 30 Marks less per month.
[in 207]	6.2 m			Anni: Yes, at both addresses. But it won't work. Fritz: Why not? Anni: 90 Marks! Fritz: And the cheaper one?
[228 . . .]	6 m	among the montage shots	shot of car with the inscription 'Fromm's Act'.[28]	
	36.5 m	between shots 347 and 348	shots of nude bathers at the beach	

Translator's Notes

Part I

Texts and Fragments on the Cinema (1919–55)

1. *Die Brillanten der Herzogin* (Vitascope, 1914) opened in Berlin on 30 January 1914.

2. *Prostitution* (1919, directed by Richard Oswald), a 'sex education' film starring Werner Krauss, Conrad Veidt and Reinhold Schünzel and produced with the collaboration of the sexologist Magnus Hirschfeld.

3. Reference to Swedish directors like Victor Sjöström and Mauritz Stiller, whose films were popular in Germany in the early 1920s.

4. Brecht saw Chaplin's *The Face on the Barroom Floor* (1914, German title *Alkohol und Liebe*) in 1921, when Chaplin's films were first imported to Germany; see the diary entry from 29 October 1921: 'the most moving thing I have ever seen in the cinema, and very simple . . . It is pure art' (GBFA 26/256–7). The Swedish actor Lars Hanson was especially admired in Germany for his lead role in the 1924 Mauritz Stiller film *Gösta Berling's Saga*, based on a novel by Selma Lagerlöf.

5. *Die Abenteuer des Prinzen Achmed* is a shadow or silhouette film produced by Lotte Reiniger in over three years of hand-drawn animation together with Walter Ruttmann, Berthold Bartosch, Alexander Kardan and Walter Rürck, based on motifs from *A Thousand and One Nights*. It opened in Berlin and Paris in 1926, and is considered to be the first feature-length animation film. UFA (Universal Film-Aktiengesell-schaft) was the largest German film industry conglomerate in the 1920s and, as a vertical monopoly, owned production studios, a distribution network and a large chain of cinemas.

6. James Joyce's novel *Ulysses* (1914–22) was published in German in 1927 and considered by Brecht at the time to be among the best novels of the year; it became an object of heated debate in the realism discussions in Moscow in 1934.

7. Brecht is referring here to Erwin Piscator's use of film footage in stage productions at the Theater am Nollendorfplatz; see Brecht's comments in an article originally published in the *New York Times* of 24 November 1935, 'The German Drama: pre-

Hitler', in John Willett, ed., *Brecht on Theatre* (London: Methuen, 1964), pp.77-81.

8. The first extensive use of film footage in a German staging was in Erwin Piscator's Berlin production of Alfons Paquet's *Sturmflut* (Storm Tide, opened on 22 February 1926). In a 1927 fragment called 'Der Piscatorsche Versuch' (Piscator's Experiment), Brecht described in more detail the use of projected film images:

The essential aspect of this experiment consists of the following:

The film integrated into the play production anticipates those parts of the plot in which there is no conflict so that spoken dialogue is reduced and becomes absolutely decisive. The audience has an opportunity to watch and judge for itself certain events that constitute the conditions for the protagonists' decision without having to see the events through the responses of the characters upon whom they act. The figures can speak freely because they no longer actually have to inform the audience: the speaking as such draws attention to itself. Moreover, the contrast between the flat, photographic reality and the live word in front of the film can be used with special effects when shifting back and forth from stage to screen to achieve an uncontrollable intensification of verbal expression. The pathos-laden and simultaneously ambiguous word gains credit through the calmly photographed display of a real background. The film makes the bed for the drama.

The speaking figures become immeasurably larger because the surroundings are photographed in their entire breadth. While the surroundings must be diminished or enlarged to fit the unchanging size of the surface, that is, of the projection screen (for example, Mount Everest constantly changes size), the figures always remain the same size . . .

The use of film as pure document of photographed reality, as conscience, still has to be tested by the epic theatre.

(GBFA 21/196–7). See as well 'The German Drama: pre-Hitler', in John Willett, ed., *Brecht on Theatre*, (London: Methuen, 1964), pp. 77–8.

Brecht's own use of film footage remained limited to the 1932 production of *The Mother* in which a documentary sequence of the Russian revolution was planned as a final coda. The two-minute sequence was forbidden by the police, however. Again in his 1951 production of *The Mother* at the Berliner Ensemble, Brecht used a similar sequence of documentary images from the Chinese revolution at the end of the play. Of course, projections of stills and titles were incorporated into Brecht's stage productions as early as 1928 in *The Threepenny Opera*.

9. Probably a reference to Orson Welles's *Citizen Kane*, an RKO production of 1941 in which Welles plays the newspaper tycoon William Randolph Hearst.

10. Brecht is referring to Vsevolod Pudovkin, *Mother* (1926, based on Maxim Gorky's 1906 novel); Grigori Kozintsev and Leonid Trauberg, *The Youth of Maxim* (1935; music by Dmitri Shostakovich); Alexander Zharki and Josef Heifits, *Baltic Deputy* (1937; music by Nicolai Timofiev).

11. Reference to the production by Brecht and Kurt Weill of *The Threepenny Opera* at the Berlin Theater am Schiffbauerdamm (1928).

12. Kurt Weill composed stage music for Brecht's 1931 production of *Man Equals Man* at the Schauspielhaus, Berlin, but it has been lost.

13. The reference is to Caspar Neher's set design for the *Mahagonny* productions at the Neues Theater, Leipzig, in 1930 and at the Berlin Theater am Kurfürstendamm in 1931.

14. Brecht collaborated with these three composers between 1927 and 1932. Kurt Weill composed the music to the *Mahagonny* musical (1927) and opera (1930), *The Threepenny Opera* (1928) and *Man Equals Man* (1931); Paul Hindemith composed music for the first version of *The Baden-Baden Lesson on Consent* (1929); Hanns Eisler composed the music for *The Decision* (1932), the film *Kuhle Wampe* (1932) and *The Mother* (1932).

15. This is a familiar motif in detective novels, which Brecht loved to read. It was also a prominent motif in Theodore Dreiser's novel *An American Tragedy* (1925), which Erwin Piscator staged on Broadway in 1936.

16. Joris Ivens, *Nieuwe Gronden* (New Earth, 1934; music by Hanns Eisler).

17. Wilhelm Dieterle, *Syncopation* (1942; based on the story 'The Band Played On' by Valentin Davers).

18. The features by Dieterle referred to here are: *The Story of Louis Pasteur* (1936), *The Life of Emile Zola* (1937), *Juarez* (1939), *Dr Ehrlich's Magic Bullet* (1940).

19. The features referred to are: Norman Taurog, *Young Tom Edison* (1940); Clarence Brown, *Edison the Man* (1940); Mervyn LeRoy, *Madame Curie* (1943); Werring Rupper, *The Adventures of Mark Twain* (1944); Henry King, *Wilson* (1944).

20. Paul Muni, an American actor of Austrian extraction, played Pasteur, Zola and Juarez; Edward G. Robinson played Dr Ehrlich.
21. Hans Rodenberg was the director-in-chief of the DEFA Film Studio in Babelsberg.
22. Heinrich Kilger was a set designer.
23. The Socialist Unity Party of Germany or SED (Sozialistische Einheitspartei Deutschland) was the name of the East German Communist Party.
24. The reference is to scene one in the *Puntila* play, including Matti's story about his previous employer Pappmann, mentioned later.

Part II
Texts on Radio Broadcasting (1926–1932)

1. Arnolt Bronnen's one-man play *Ostpolzug* (*East Pole Train*) opened at the State Theatre in Berlin on 29 January 1926 (director: Leopold Jessner; actor: Fritz Kortner).
2. Brecht first uses the words apparatus and apparatuses around this time, 1927, to refer both to the physical instrument (the radio) and to the institutions of radio broadcasting. In other contexts he uses apparatus for other institutions such as the established theatre and the opera. See also note 10 of 'The *Threepenny* Lawsuit' in Part IV.
3. Neubabelsberg is a suburb of Potsdam, at the border of south-western Berlin, where large studio lots of the UFA film company (Universal-Film AG) were located.
4. Alfred Braun was the director of the radio play department of the Berlin Broadcasting Studio. He also directed the radio version of Brecht's play *Mann ist Mann* (*Man Equals Man*, 18 March 1927) and of Brecht's adaptation of Shakespeare's *Macbeth* (14 October 1927).
5. Arnolt Bronnen was a regular employee of the Berlin Broadcasting Studio beginning in 1926 and from 1928 to 1933 was the dramaturg for the 'radio play' broadcasts (*Dramatische Funkstunde*) for which he also prepared prose works as broadcast plays.
6. 'Funkstunde Berlin' was the name of the radio play programme under the direction of Alfred Braun at the Berlin Broadcasting Studio.
7. The reference to 'theory' is the italicized text quoted above; it was projected onto a screen behind the participants on the raised platform.

8. The 'Pilgrims' Chorus' refers to Richard Wagner's opera *Tannhäuser* (1845).

9. Reference to Richard Wagner's opera *Die Meistersinger von Nürnberg* (1865).

10. The premiere of Brecht's learning play *Lindberghflug* (later titled *The Ocean Flight* or *Der Ozeanflug*) was on 27 July 1929 at the Baden-Baden Chamber Music Festival. See above, the 'Explanations' about *The Flight of the Lindberghs*.

11. The premiere of Brecht's *Badener Lehrstück vom Einverständnis* was on 28 July 1929 under the simple title *Lehrstück* at the Baden-Baden Chamber Music Festival. Brecht directed, Ernst Hardt (then Manager of Western German Radio Broadcasting in Cologne) was assistant director, Paul Hindemith was the composer and Hermann Scherchen directed the orchestra.

Part III
Screenplays (1930–1932)

1. Reference to Mark Antony's speech over Caesar's body in Shakespeare's *Julius Caesar* (Act III, Scene 2).

2. A reference to Francisco Goya's painting 'St Francis Borgia Attends to a Dying Man' (1788) that possibly inspired the shot.

3. Reference to Francisco Goya's painting 'The Third of May 1808' (1814) in which the execution of rebels is lit by such a lantern.

4. Reference to Honoré Daumier's caricatures of bourgeois men with their fat bellies.

Part IV
The *Threepenny* Material (1930–1932)

1. Georg Wilhelm Pabst was already a well-known director in 1930 when Nero-Film company hired him to direct *The Threepenny Opera*. He had directed successful silent films like *Die Büchse der Pandora* (*Pandora's Box*, 1929) and *Tagebuch einer Verlorenen* (*Diary of a Lost Soul*, 1929) as well as the sound films *Westfront 1918* (1930) and *Skandal um Eva* (*Scandal about Eve*, 1930).

2. Leo Lania was commissioned under contract to work with Brecht, Slatan Dudow and Caspar Neher on the script.

3. The two other scriptwriters – Ladislaus Vajda and Béla Balász – were hired by Nero-Film to complete the screenplay.

4. *Flachsmann als Erzieher* was a comedy based on the play of the

same name by Otto Ernst and directed by Carl Heinz Wolff; it opened on 7 November 1930.

5. German 'bürgerlich' means 'bourgeois' in the sense of middle-class, that is, as distinct from the noble and the peasant or working class. It also means 'civil' or 'civic' in the sense of citizen ('Bürger'). Both meanings echo throughout this text, yet all occurrences are translated as 'bourgeois'. Later in the text Brecht will also use 'kleinbürgerlich' (petty-bourgeois) and 'spiessbürgerlich' (mediocre) to refer not so much to a class designation as to a low-brow or vulgar attitude characteristic of a social stratum striving to become 'bourgeois' but threatened with downward mobility. 'Gross-bürgertum' refers to the wealthy upper class.

6. The contractual term in German is *Grundlage*, which literally means 'foundation' or 'basis', and refers here to the textual basis for the screenplay, hereafter translated as 'basic material'.

7. Berlin theatre critic Alfred Kerr accused Brecht of plagiarism in *The Threepenny Opera* in an article titled 'Brecht's Copy-right' in the *Berliner Tageblatt* (3 May 1929) in which he showed that Brecht used K. L. Ammer's 1907 translations of poems by François Villon without giving due credit. Brecht responded in a statement printed in *Filmkurier* (4 May 1929).

8. The Romanisches Café was a popular meeting place for artists and intellectuals in Berlin's Westend.

9. This is a wordplay on director G. W. Pabst's surname, since 'Papst' – pronounced the same way – in German means 'pope'.

10. Brecht uses the German words 'Apparat' (with its plural form 'Apparate') and 'Apparatur' to refer variously to the entire cinema apparatus (the organization of the film industry or even its institutional and political formation), to mechanical equipment, machines or appliances in general, or specifically to the movie camera or movie projector, depending on context. Contemporaneous German dictionaries confirm the ambiguity in meanings. Throughout Brecht's usage has been translated literally as 'apparatus' and 'apparatuses'.

11. Brecht refers here to two of the largest business holdings in Germany at the time, the Krupp munition works and the Allgemeine Elektrizität-Gesellschaft (AEG) or General Electric Company.

12. *Der wahre Jakob* (Hans Steinhoff, 1931) and *Drei Tage Mittelarrest* (first sound film of Carl Boese, 1930) are both light comedies.

13. Reference to the well-known Berlin theatre critic Alfred Kerr and his counterpart in Frankfurt, Bernhard Diebold.

14. Brecht is referring here to Herbert Ihering's review of the premiere of Carl Zuckmayer's play *Der Hauptmann von Köpenick* at the Deutsches Theater in Berlin (*Berliner Börsen-Courier*, 6 March 1931).

15. A reference to Friedrich Schiller's *Briefe über die ästhetische Erziehung des Menschen* (1793–95).

16. Bruno Kastner (1890-1932), student of Paul Biensfeld, was a stage actor first in Harburg and then in Berlin theatres as well as a film star in the popular cinema.

17. *Battleship Potemkin* (Sergei Eisenstein, 1925).

18. *City Lights* (Charles Chaplin, 1931).

19. *The Road to Life* (Nicolai Ekk, 1931), one of the first Soviet sound films screened in Germany.

20. Brecht is referring here to the social behaviourism of philosopher Otto Neurath, whom he had come to appreciate in his reading of the journal *Erkenntnis* (the house journal of the logical empiricists) in 1930–2 and whom he met in 1932–3.

21. *Love Parade* (Ernst Lubitsch, 1929) was Lubitsch's first sound film, starring Maurice Chevalier and Jeannette MacDonald; Fyodor Dostoevski's 1880 novel *The Brothers Karamasov* was adapted in the Soviet Union under the title *Dmitri Karamasov* (Fyodor Ozep, 1930-1).

22. *Alt-Heidelberg* (Hans Behrendt, 1923), adaptation of Wilhelm Meyer Förster's 1903 play.

23. The first film in Germany to show the birth act was *Das Lied vom Leben* (*The Song of Life*, 1931.)

24. Films based on literary texts by the authors mentioned here generated no questions about copyright: Heinrich Mann's novel *Professor Unrat* (*Der blaue Engel*, Josef von Sternberg, *The Blue Angel*, 1930), Alfred Döblin's novel *Berlin Alexanderplatz* (Piel Jutzi, 1931) and Gerhart Hauptmann's drama *Die Weber* (Frederick Zelnik, *The Weavers*, 1927).

25. Brecht is here quoting in full a 1923 case overturning the decision of the lower courts that had found in the writer's favour concerning the status of a film contract.

26. *Nur eine Tänzerin* (Olof Morel-Molander, 1926), starring Lil Dagover, Lucie Höflich, Hans Albers, Jacob Tiedtke.

27. The reference here is to Wenzel Goldbaum's standard commentary on copyright contract law, *Urheberrecht und Urhebervertragsrecht* (Berlin: Georg Stilke, second edition,

1927). Goldbaum also published a commentary on sound-film copyright issues in the same series called 'Stilkes Rechtsbibliothek' under the title *Tonfilmrecht* (Berlin: Georg Stilke, 1929). Goldbaum was Weill's lawyer.

28. Erich Weigert presided in the lawsuit at the Regional Court I in Berlin and delivered the judgment on 4 November 1930.

Part V
The *Kuhle Wampe* Film (1932)

1. The film's German title *Kuhle Wampe* is the place name of a tent and garden colony in an eastern suburb of Berlin. It has often been incorrectly printed in English as 'Kühle Wampe' with an umlaut. The film was first distributed in the United States under the title *Whither Germany?* In English-language reference books and film histories the subtitle *Wem gehört die Welt?* is variously rendered as 'Who Does the World Belong To?', 'To Whom Does the World Belong?' and 'Who Owns the World?'

2. As a result of the bank crash in 1931 the Prometheus Film company, a subsidiary of the International Workers' Aid (Mezhrabpom) and closely allied to the Communist Party, went bankrupt and collapsed in January 1932, when the filming of *Kuhle Wampe* had almost been completed. Praesens Film then took over the production on the condition that actors, scriptwriters, producers and director would forfeit their fees. The private individual who helped finance the film has been variously identified as an entrepreneur who insisted that his car be used in the film as a condition for his sponsorship (seen as the vehicle which transports the family's furniture to the campsite) or as a sponsor who gave 50,000 Marks on the condition that Brecht write him a song.

3. The scriptwriters were Brecht himself and the novelist Ernst Ottwalt, the director Slatan Dudow, the composer Hanns Eisler, and the Austrian production manager Georg Höllering. The reference to a lawyer could be to Georg Höllering, who wrote all the contracts. Or – if referring to the censorship proceedings – to lawyers Otto Landsberg and Paul Dienstag. Scriptwriter Robert Scharfenberg was intermittently involved in the production as well.

4. The company was Tobis Film.

5. The real tent and garden colony Kuhle Wampe was located on the Müggelsee in an eastern suburb of Berlin.

6. The *Fichte-Wandersparte* or 'Fichte Hikers' called itself 'the

only revolutionary organization of all working-class hikers, weekenders and excursionists'. The majority donated their time to the filming of the athletic competitions (see also note 22).

7. German title 'Wir wollten ein Obdach haben', GBFA 14/126–7. The reference in parenthesis is probably to Article 115 of the 1919 German Constitution: 'The domicile of every German is a sanctuary and inviolable. Exceptions are permissible only in accordance with the law.'

8. See 'Das Frühjahr kommt' in GBFA 14/127–8; in English 'The Spring' in Bertolt Brecht, *Poems 1913–1956*, edited by John Willett and Ralph Manheim with the cooperation of Erich Fried (New York: Methuen, 1979), pp. 183–4.

9. See 'Gesang der Sportler' in GBFA 14/115.

10. See 'Solidaritätslied. Sonntagslied der freien Jugend' in GBFA 14/116–18; in English; 'Solidarity Song' in *Poems*, pp. 185–6.

11. Probably refers to the refrain of the poem 'Wir wollten ein Obdach haben' (see note 7).

12. Brecht's wife, the actress Helene Weigel, sings the song in the film.

13. The reference is to a beach scene with nude bathers on a Sunday morning (church bells chime) at the beginning of the final part. It was cut by the censor.

14. Brecht refers here to the athletic competition and the subsequent discussion in the train.

15. Shooting actually began in August 1931, and the completed film was deposited with the Film Inspection Board in March 1932.

16. The Film Inspection Board prohibited the film on 31 March 1932. Two jury members appealed the decision to the appeals board, which confirmed the prohibition on 9 April. The production company made cuts and re-submitted the film. After additional cuts demanded by the Interior Ministry had been made, the Inspection Board released the film on 25 April 1932.

17. Heinrich Brüning of the Centre Party was Chancellor from 1930 to 1932. The 'emergency decrees' were issued on the suggestion of the governing party, while the Social Democratic Party abstained, and they were signed by President Paul von Hindenburg.

18. This is the correct spelling in the credits, but the name is also spelled Ottwalt in other documents.

19. This poem is an early version of 'The Spring' (see Brecht,

Poems 1913–1956, pp. 183–4).

20. Mata Hari was the stage name of the Dutch erotic dancer Margareta Zelle who lived in Paris. In July 1917 she was tried on suspicion of spying for the Germans, condemned to death and executed in October 1917. Brecht wrote a short sketch for a film about Mata Hari in 1926 that was to star Valeska Gert.

21. *Never Love Again* (1931), starring Lilian Harvey.

22. The Fichte Hikers were organized clubs of young people from the working class who combined political militancy with leisure-time sports actitivities (see also note 6).

23. This song is an early version of the published 'Solidarity Song' (see Brecht, *Poems 1913-1956*, pp.185-86).

24. See Brecht's poem 'Kommend von den vollen Hinterhäusern' (GBFA 14/130–1).

25. 'Das rote Sprachrohr' was a Young Communist group organized by the actor Maxim Vallentin in 1928, a leading agit-prop threatre group that performed on improvised stages short, aggressive sketches about topical issues.

26. Owing to the careful notes preserved by the Interior Ministry, the exact contents of the sequences suggested for cuts by the censor have been reconstructed.

27. This is a reference to the law against abortion in the German criminal code.

28. Brand name for condoms.

Index of Works by Bertolt Brecht

The abbreviation *n* indicates a textual note.

General Index

The abbreviation *n* indicates a textual note.